Egypt and the Gulf:
A Renewed Regional Policy Alliance

The Gulf Research Centre Book Series at Gerlach Press

The GCC in the Global Economy
Ed. by Richard Youngs
ISBN 9783940924018, 2012

Resources Blessed:
Diversification and the Gulf Development Model
Ed. by Giacomo Luciani
ISBN 9783940924025, 2012

GCC Financial Markets: The World's New Money Centers
Ed. by Eckart Woertz
ISBN 9783940924032, 2012

National Employment, Migration and Education in the GCC
Ed. by Steffen Hertog
ISBN 9783940924049, 2012

Asia-Gulf Economic Relations in the 21st Century:
The Local to Global Transformation
Ed. by Tim Niblock with Monica Malik
ISBN 9783940924100, 2013

A New Gulf Security Architecture:
Prospects and Challenges for an Asian Role
Ed. by Ranjit Gupta, Abubaker Bagader,
Talmiz Ahmad and N. Janardhan
ISBN 9783940924360, 2014

Gulf Charities and Islamic Philanthropy
in the 'Age of Terror' and Beyond
Ed. by Robert Lacey and Jonathan Benthall
ISBN 9783940924322, 2014

State-Society Relations in the Arab Gulf States
Ed. by Mazhar Al-Zoby and Birol Baskan
ISBN 9783940924384, 2014

Political Economy of Energy Reform:
The Clean Energy-Fossil Fuel Balance in the Gulf
Ed. by Giacomo Luciani and Rabia Ferroukhi
ISBN 9783940924407, 2014

The Silent Revolution: The Arab Spring and the Gulf States
Ed. by May Seikaly and Khawla Mattar
ISBN 9783940924346, 2014

Security Dynamics of East Asia in the Gulf Region
Ed. by Tim Niblock with Yang Guang
ISBN 9783940924483, 2014

Islamic Finance: Political Economy, Performance and Risk
Ed. by Mehmet Asutay and Abdullah Turkistani
ISBN 9783940924124, 3 vols set, 2015

Employment and Career Motivation in the Arab Gulf
States: The Rentier Mentality Revisited
Ed. by Annika Kropf and Mohamed Ramady
ISBN 9783940924605, 2015

The Changing Energy Landscape in the Gulf:
Strategic Implications
Ed. by Gawdat Bahgat
ISBN 9783940924643, 2015

Sustainable Development Challenges
in the Arab States of the Gulf
Ed. by David Bryde, Yusra Mouzughi and Turki Al Rasheed
ISBN 9783940924629, 2015

The United States and the Gulf:
Shifting Pressures, Strategies and Alignments
Ed. by Steven W. Hook and Tim Niblock
ISBN 9783940924667, 2015

Africa and the Gulf Region:
Blurred Boundaries and Shifting Ties
Ed. by Rogaia Mustafa Abusharaf and Dale F. Eickelman
ISBN 9783940924704, 2015

Rebuilding Yemen: Political, Economic and Social Challenges
Ed. by Noel Brehony and Saud Al-Sarhan
ISBN 9783940924681, 2015

Science and Technology Development in the Gulf States:
Economic Diversification through Regional Collaboration
Ed. by Afreen Siddiqi and Laura Diaz Anadon
ISBN 9783959940023, 2016

Higher Education Investment in the Arab States of the
Gulf: Strategies for Excellence and Diversity
Ed. by Dale Eickelman and Rogaia Mustafa Abusharaf
ISBN 9783959940122, 2016

Iran's Relations with the Arab States of the Gulf:
Common Interests over Historic Rivalry
Ed. by Maaike Warnaar, Luciano Zaccara and Paul Aarts
ISBN 9783959940047, 2016

Egypt and the Gulf: A Renewed Regional Policy Alliance
Ed. by Robert Mason
ISBN 9783959940061, 2016

Intellectual Property Rights:
Development and Enforcement in the Arab States of the Gulf
Ed. by David Price and Alhanoof AlDebasi
ISBN 9783959940108, 2016

The Arab States of the Gulf and BRICS:
New Strategic Partnerships in Geopolitcs and Economics
Ed. by Tim Niblock, Alejandra Galindo and Degang Sun
ISBN 9783959940085, 2016

The Arms Trade, Military Services and the Security Market
in the Gulf States: Trends and Implications
Ed. by David B. Des Roches and Dania Thafer
ISBN 9783959940160, 2016

Gulf Research Centre Cambridge
Knowledge for All

Plymouth University
Charles Seale-Hayne Library
Subject to status this item may be renewed
via your Primo account

http://primo.plymouth.ac.uk
Tel: (01752) 588588

Egypt and the Gulf:
A Renewed Regional Policy Alliance

Edited by Robert Mason

First published 2017
by Gerlach Press
Berlin, Germany
www.gerlach-press.de

Cover Design: www.brandnewdesign.de, Hamburg
Printed and bound in Germany by Hubert & Co, Göttingen
www.hubertundco.de

British Library Cataloguing in Publication Data.
A catalogue record for this book is available from the British Library.

Bibliographic data available from Deutsche Nationalbibliothek
http://d-nb.info/1103244078

ISBN: 978-3-95994-006-1 (hardcover)
ISBN: 978-3-95994-007-8 (ebook)

Contents

Introduction

Robert Mason

Egypt continues to be a cultural and political beacon in the Middle East. It's control of the Suez Canal, cold peace with Israel, concern about neighbouring Gaza, mediation and interest in the Israel-Palestine conflict, and the marginalization of the Muslim Brotherhood are all points of significance. Egypt and what would become the Gulf Cooperation Council (GCC) states of Saudi Arabia, Kuwait, the United Arab Emirates, Qatar, Bahrain and Oman in 1981, have enjoyed relations which go back to the Egypt Eyalet in the Ottoman Empire and the earlier manifestations of Saudi and Wahhabi power in the Arabian peninsula. The relationship has suffered at times, such as during the Egyptian - Saudi proxy war in Yemen in the 1960s and after Egypt signed a peace accord with Israel in 1979. More recently, states such as Egypt and Syria supported the GCC states politically and militarily during the 1991 Gulf War and aimed to set up a deterrence force following it, based on the Damascus Declaration. However, an Arab regional security force did not amount to much until the GCC Peninsula Shield Force (PSF) was strengthened and deployed to Bahrain during protests in Manama in 2011.

The Egyptian military is the largest in the Arab world, and there is a close, and expanding, defence and security relationship between Egypt and the GCC states. For example, Saudi Arabia and the UAE helped finance a Russian arms deal for Egypt worth $2 billion in 2014.[1] Egyptian troops have been involved in defending Saudi Arabia's northern border from a threat posed by Islamic State of Iraq and the Levant (ISIL) in July 2014.[2] Egypt and the UAE both launched airstrikes against Islamist rebels, Libya Dawn, in August 2014, surprising U.S. officials.[3] Furthermore, Egypt was quick to send warships to consolidate the GCC state forces fighting a Houthi insurgency in Yemen in March 2015.[4] This commitment was significantly enhanced by the deployment of 800 Egyptian ground forces in September 2015.[5] Egypt is therefore an important Sunni ally of the GCC states, marked by its inclusion in Saudi Arabia's new Sunni counterterrorism alliance.[6]

In terms of socio-economic linkages, the 1970s and 1980s remains the golden era for Egyptian migrant labour in Arab states (mainly in the GCC). A number of factors have caused a decline in the number of Egyptians found in the Arab Gulf states today: the end of the first Gulf War, the fall in the oil price, a decline in the number of construction workers from Arab states (usually in favour of Asian labour), and various indigenisation processes replacing foreign labour with young nationals who demand more job opportunities.[7] Egypt still maintains a large expatriate workforce in the GCC states, which amounted to some 1.5 million in 2006, mainly located in Saudi Arabia and the UAE.[8] Thus, remittances still represent an important source of revenue for the national economy, far more important than trade for example.[9] The Hajj also attracts hundreds of thousands of Egyptian Muslims to Mecca each year and this helps to maintain a close religious bond.

Since the Arab Spring swept Mohamed Morsi and the Muslim Brotherhood to power in Egypt, thereby establishing a temporary but firm partnership with Qatar, Doha pledged $8 billion to Egypt.[10] However, it was interpreted by many, along with allegations that President Morsi was about to sell off the pyramids or the Suez Canal, as a conspiracy which quickly undermined the new Islamist alliance.[11] Saudi Arabia worked hard since it lost president Mubarak in 2011 to take charge of the counter-revolution against the sweeping changes of the Arab Spring, particularly as the Muslim Brotherhood coming to power in Egypt played into the hands of Iran and its attempts to expand influence. Indeed, Iran attempted a rapprochement with the Morsi government in 2012-13 to try and amalgamate and consolidate the Islamist trend across two of the most populous states in the region. It failed due to the quick removal of president Morsi from power.[12]

The popular 'coup' in 2013 (the extent to which it was legitimate or illegitimate is not within the remit of this volume) also facilitated the demise of the Egypt - Qatar relationship and the Egypt - Turkey relationship due to their respective support for Islamist groups such as the Muslim Brotherhood (which was banned in Egypt in 2014[13]). In contrast, the shift back to a military-backed government served to re-establish and enhance Egypt's relationship with Saudi Arabia, the UAE and Kuwait. These strong bilateral relations underpinned the Egyptian economic conference in Sharm El-Sheikh in March 2015 where the GCC states collectively contributed $12 billion to Egypt's economic development plans, including a new administrative capital to the east of Cairo.[14]

Riyadh alone has invested $4 billion in the Egyptian economy and proposed the expansion of the GCC to include Jordan and Morocco,[15] with the door left open for the inclusion of Egypt at a later date.[16] However, the expansion did not occur mainly due to difficulties in extending what is a geographically contiguous alliance from the Gulf to the far end of the Maghreb and into the Mashreq. Nevertheless, Morocco, Jordan and Egypt remain open to enhancing their consultation and cooperation with the GCC states as increasingly important actors in the Middle East and internationally. The substantial Saudi investment did lead others, such as the UAE and Kuwait, to adopt a similar policy of investing billions into the Egyptian economy in support of a valuable Sunni ally.

This book builds a detailed and nuanced picture of Egypt-GCC state relations based on socio-economic, religious and political connections within an important Sunni axis in the Arab world. These have become increasingly important to Egypt's political economy, international relations and foreign policy calculus, and are likely to remain central in Cairo's decision-making for many years to come. To some extent, this book builds on works about Egypt by notable authors such as Wickham[17], who assesses how the Muslim Brotherhood has evolved over time and how it became a victim of its own success. It considers points raised by authors such as Osman, who covers a range of topics from Islamists to youth.[18] The volume also addresses some of the transitions and unresolved challenges discussed by Korany and El-Mahdi.[19] More broadly, it speaks to a range of literature on Arab and GCC foreign policy making from notable authors such as Niblock[20], Aarts and Nonneman[21], Gause[22], Korany and Dessouki[23], Kamrava[24] and Coates-Ulrichsen[25]. Their consideration of topics such as regional competition and leadership, diplomatic agility, state relations with the Ulema, passive versus active foreign policies, domestic and foreign pressures and constraints, omni-balancing (particularly against marginalised communities and regional threats) and the maintenance of regime stability, are similarly addressed in the following pages.

Structure of the Book

The book is divided into four parts. The **first part** consists of three chapters that look back on the history of Egypt - Gulf relations. Chapter one puts Egypt - GCC state relations in perspective, by delving into the political and socio-religious models of Egypt and Saudi Arabia. Chapter two takes a closer look at the Muslim Brotherhood, especially as a nexus around which some contemporary Egyptian - GCC state relations revolve. Chapter three aids in the conceptualisation of the Egyptian - Saudi rapprochement by considering its merits in preventing the realisation of Hashemite and Saddam Hussein's expansionist policies, as well as providing a valuable bulwark against Iranian regional hegemonic ambitions.

In **part two**, Egypt's contentious relations with Qatar and Turkey are covered. Chapter four assesses the prospects for the Qatar - Saudi - Egyptian triangle and their common emphasis on battling Islamic State and countering Iran. Egypt's relationship with Qatar is shown to be contingent to some extent on continued Saudi support as well as Qatar's relationship with Turkey. Chapter five asks what prospects there can be for an Egyptian - Turkish reconciliation given their polarised policies towards the Muslim Brotherhood and other Islamist groups. Key to the relationship, beyond a range of domestic and international factors, such as EU accession being back on the Turkish agenda, is the role that Saudi Arabia and Kuwait will continue to play in bridging their differences and providing a common platform for constructive interaction.

Part three looks to Egypt's strategic relations. Chapter six focuses on Egypt's relationship with Saudi Arabia and the transitions that have taken place from the King Abdullah to the King Salman era, with an emphasis on shifting Saudi political strategies. Chapter seven looks more broadly to the Egypt - Saudi - UAE strategic relationship with special reference to their common counterterrorism agendas in Libya, Yemen and Syria. It asks whether it is indeed a strategic or tactical relationship considering changes in Saudi outlook following the younger generation of princes coming to power in Riyadh. It also considers the historic competition with Egypt for regional leadership, differing relations with the Muslim Brotherhood and other possible contentions.

In **part four**, we turn to Egypt's role in the regional order. In chapter eight, Egyptian and GCC state security relations are considered after 30 June 2015 and to what extent the institutionalisation of their security relationship can be maintained and perhaps drive broader regional security measures. In chapter nine, Egypt's role as a former regional hegemon, as well as its future power capabilities, are contemplated in line with possible changes in its relations with the Arab Gulf states, Turkey and the wider world. A systematic comparison is made between Egypt's current circumstances after the Arab Spring in 2011 and other critical turning points in its recent history, including: the period from 1906 to the adoption of the 1921 constitution; the Free Officers takeover from 1952; and the presidencies of Sadat and Mubarak. It looks to the likelihood of the Muslim Brotherhood switching to a 'Turkish model' rather than an 'Algerian model' and the fundamentals on which President Sisi is attempting to rebuild the national economy.

The contributors contextualise historical linkages, analyse adversarial postures (especially Egypt's contentious relations with Qatar and Turkey) and study Egypt's strategic relations with Saudi Arabia, Kuwait and the UAE in particular. The book's main argument derives from a complex web of political, socio-economic and military issues in a changing regional and international system. It states that Egyptian regional policy under el-Sisi will generally remain consistent within existing parameters (such as broad counter-terrorism efforts, including against the Muslim Brotherhood). Even though domestic Egyptian circumstances require a broader outlook and orientation, there is strong evidence to support the idea that Cairo wishes to maintain an Arab/GCC-first policy.

Bibliography

Aarts, Paul, and Carolien Roelants, *Saudi Arabia: A Kingdom in Peril,* (London: C. Hurst and Co., 2015)

Aarts, Paul, and Gerd Nonneman, *Saudi Arabia in the Balance: Political Economy, Society, Foreign Affairs,* (New York: New York University Press, 2007)

Coates-Ulrichsen, Kristian. *Qatar and the Arab Spring,* (London: C. Hurst and Co., 2014)

Gause, Greg. *International Relations of the Persian Gulf,* (Cambridge: Cambridge University Press, 2011)

Ghoneim, Ahmed Farouk. 'Labour Migration for Decent Work, Economic Growth and Development in Egypt', International Migration Paper No. 106, (Geneva: International Labour Office, 2010), 6

Kamrava, Mehran. *Qatar: Small State, Big Politics,* (Ithaca: Cornell University Press, 2015)

Kamrava, Mehran. *Beyond the Arab Spring: The Evolving Ruling Bargain in the Middle East,* (Oxford: Oxford University Press, 2014)

Korany, Bahgat, and Rabab El-Mahdi, *Arab Spring in Egypt: Revolution and Beyond,* (Cairo: AUC Press, 2014)

Korany, Bahgat, and Ali E. Dessouki, *The Foreign Policies of Arab States: The Challenge of Globalization,* (Cairo: AUC Press, 2008)

Osman, Tarek. *Egypt on the Brink: From Nasser to the Muslim Brotherhood,* (Yale: Yale University Press, 2013)

Niblock, Tim. *Saudi Arabia: Power Legitimacy and Survival,* (Abingdon: Routledge, 2006)

Nonneman, Gerd. *Analysing Middle East Foreign Policies, and the Relationship with Europe,* (Abingdon: Routledge, 2005)

Wickham, Carrie Rosefsky. *The Muslim Brotherhood: Evolution of an Islamist Movement,* (Princeton: Princeton University Press, 2013)

Notes

1   Egypt Independent, 'KSA, UAE to Finance Russian Arms Deal with Egypt', 7 February 2014, available at http://www.egyptindependent.com/news/ksa-uae-finance-russian-arms-deal-egypt

2   Erika Soloman and Simeon Kerr, 'Saudi Arabia Sends 30,000 Troops to Iraq Border', *Financial Times*, 3 July 2014, available at http://www.ft.com/intl/cms/s/0/3312faba-0286-11e4-aa85-00144feab7de.html#axzz3w5HNRDfz

3   David D. Kirkpatrick and Eric Schmitt, 'Arab Nations Strike Libya, Surprising U.S.', *International New York Times*, 25 August 2015, available at http://www.nytimes.com/2014/08/26/world/africa/egypt-and-united-arab-emirates-said-to-have-secretly-carried-out-libya-airstrikes.html?_r=0

4   Gulf News, 'Egypt Warships Head to Gulf of Aden; Sudan to Take Part in Operation Storm of Resolve', 27 March 2015, available at http://gulfnews.com/news/gulf/yemen/egypt-warships-head-to-gulf-of-aden-sudan-to-take-part-in-operation-storm-of-resolve-1.1479293

5   Reuters, 'Egypt Sends up to 800 Ground Troops to Yemen's War - Egyptian Security Sources', 9 September 2015, available at http://uk.reuters.com/article/uk-yemen-security-idUKKCN0R91I720150909

6   Noah Browing and John Irish, 'Saudi Arabia Announces 34-State Islamic Military Alliance Against Terrorism', *Reuters*, 15 December 2015, available at http://www.reuters.com/article/us-saudi-security-idUSKBN0TX2PG20151215

7   Ahmed Farouk Ghoneim, 'Labour Migration for Decent Work, Economic Growth and Development in Egypt', International Migration Paper No. 106, (Geneva: International Labour Office, 2010), p. 6

8   Andrzej Kapiszewski, Arab Versus Asian Migrant Workers in the GCC Countries', United Nations, 22 May 2006, p. 10, available at http://www.un.org/esa/population/meetings/EGM_Ittmig_Arab/P02_Kapiszewski.pdf

9   See International Organization for Migration, 'Intra-Regional Labour Mobility in the Arab World', available at http://www.egypt.iom.int/doc/iom%20intra%20regional%20labour%20mobility%20in%20arab%20region%20facts%20and%20figures%20(english).pdf

10   Simon Henderson, 'The Emir of Qatar's Oval Office Meeting', The Washington Institute, 22 April 2013, http://www.washingtoninstitute.org/policy-analysis/view/the-emir-of-qatars-oval-office-meeting

11   Mohamad Elmasry, 'Unpacking Anti-Muslim Brotherhood Discourse', *Jadaliyya*, 28 June 2013, http://www.jadaliyya.com/pages/index/12466/unpacking-anti-muslim-brotherhood-discourse

12   For details on why an Egyptian-Iranian rapprochement will be difficult to achieve, see: Robert Mason, 'Why the P5+1 - Iran Deal Won't Change Egyptian - Iranian Relations', *Iran Review*, 21 April 2015, available at http://www.iranreview.org/content/Documents/Why-the-P5-1-Iran-Deal-Won-t-Change-Egyptian-Iranian-Relations.htm

13   BBC News, 'Egypt Court Bans Muslim Brotherhood's Political Wing', 9 August 2014, available at http://www.bbc.com/news/world-middle-east-28722935

14   Heba Saleh, 'Gulf States put their Money on Sisi's Egypt with Pledges Worth $12 Billion', *Financial Times*, 13 March 2015, available at http://www.ft.com/intl/cms/s/0/85c2b3cc-c9a0-11e4-a2d9-00144feab7de.html#axzz3w5HNRDfz

15   Neil MacFarquhar, 'Saudi Arabia Scrambles to Limit Region's Upheaval', *International New York Times*, 27 May 2011, available at http://www.nytimes.com/2011/05/28/world/middleeast/28saudi.html

16   Al Arabiya, 'Egypt Could be the Next GCC Member State, Gulf Sources Say', 29 September 2011, available at http://english.alarabiya.net/articles/2011/09/29/169297.html

17   Carrie Rosefsky Wickham, *The Muslim Brotherhood: Evolution of an Islamist Movement*, (Princeton: Princeton University Press, 2013)

18   Tarek Osman, *Egypt on the Brink: From Nasser to the Muslim Brotherhood*, (Yale: Yale University Press, 2013)

19   Bahgat Korany and Rabab El-Mahdi, *Arab Spring in Egypt: Revolution and Beyond*, (Cairo: AUC Press, 2014)

20 Tim Niblock, *Saudi Arabia: Power Legitimacy and Survival,* (Abingdon: Routledge, 2006)

21 Paul Aarts and Gerd Nonneman, *Saudi Arabia in the Balance: Political Economy, Society, Foreign Affairs,* (New York: New York University Press, 2007); Paul Aarts and Carolien Roelants, *Saudi Arabia: A Kingdom in Peril,* (London: C. Hurst and Co., 2015); Gerd Nonneman, *Analysing Middle East Foreign Policies, and the Relationship with Europe,* (Abingdon: Routledge, 2005)

22 Greg Gause, *International Relations of the Persian Gulf,* (Cambridge: Cambridge University Press, 2011)

23 Bahgat Korany and Ali E. Dessouki, *The Foreign Policies of Arab States: The Challenge of Globalization,* (Cairo: AUC Press, 2008)

24 Mehran Kamrava, *Qatar: Small State, Big Politics,* (Ithaca: Cornell University Press, 2015); Mehran Kamrava, *Beyond the Arab Spring: The Evolving Ruling Bargain in the Middle East,* (Oxford: Oxford University Press, 2014)

25 Kristian Coates-Ulrichsen, *Qatar and the Arab Spring,* (London: C. Hurst and Co., 2014)

1

Brothers in Arms, Strangers in Love: Mapping the Trajectory of Flows Between Two Different Socio-Religious Models in Egypt and Saudi Arabia

Patryca Sasnal

Introduction

Both Saudi Arabia and Egypt are religious Muslim countries and self-made nationalistic entities in the Arab world that aspire to regional leadership – in that they are unique. Saudi Arabia has never really experienced an outright occupation, a fact which adds to its social appeal among Arabs. This is in stark contrast to other Arab countries in the neighbourhood, which are in their majority post-imperial creations. The two countries, however, have formed two different socio-religious models over the past hundred years.[1] They are based on two great currents in Islam: modernism and fundamentalism, which should be seen as figurative ideal religious models that find a more complex realization in the two particular socio-political entities: Egypt and Saudi Arabia.

The Two Socio-Religious Models

Egypt is a secular, revolutionary, modernist republic, where moderate Hanafi and Shaafi jurisprudence prevails, while Saudi Arabia is an Islamic, anti-revolutionary, conservative kingdom with the domination of the socially most oppressive of all established Islamic currents: Hanbali-Wahhabi school. In order to describe the two models in greater detail a differentiation between official and popular Islam needs to be made (Waardenburg 1978; Rodinson 1996; Grandin 1978). Popular Islam consists of both physical religious practices and the much less tangible everyday sources of religious inspiration that drive people in their everyday decisions.[2] Whereas official Islam consists of religious institutions formed by the state and is dependent on it to a lesser or greater degree. Official Islam is usually more controllable than its popular form. If we then consider popular Islam as the socio-religious space that consists of personal comportment, also vis-à-vis other people, religious practices in and outside of the mosque, or even making political decisions, the two Islams are very different in Egypt and Saudi Arabia.

Egypt is a heterogeneous mixture of extremely different social classes – from outspoken atheists and militant secularists, through lower and upper middle class Muslim Brotherhood (MB) or Sisi supporters to ultra-conservative Salafists. Street life is flourishing, public sphere as understood by Habermas (1991) is versatile and extensive. Such societal emanation of Islam has developed as a result of Islamic modernism, an Islam that borrows from other religions and develops with societal changes.

In Saudi Arabia, on the other hand, the public sphere and social space is almost non-existent to the benefit of the private space: there are no public theaters, cinemas, sport facilities or parks, likewise public debate is limited. The society is homogenized, in that in the Kingdom it is officially impossible to profess different religions, social comportment is restricted and supervised. The Saudi societal emanation of Islam has developed as a result of Islamic fundamentalism, an Islam that opposes change.

Official Islams also differ in their content (modernist Hanafi-Shaafi in Egypt and fundamentalist Hanbali-Wahhabi in Saudi Arabia), although the administrative and organizational structure of the Saudi religious model, as will be shown below, was borrowed from Egypt, and – in practice – official Islams have served the same purpose in both countries: legitimizing power, opposing change. Egypt, with its religious institutions that are more than a thousand years old, had been the religious center of the Muslim world for decades. Saudi Arabia, however, ever since it conquered Mecca and Madina in the 1920s from the now Jordanian Hashemites has built its religious appeal on its king being the custodian of the two holy cities[3] and by that token entered into a relationship with the religious Egyptian elite that could potentially be both a rivalry and a partnership.

The Saudi ulama claim to represent the heritage of Muhammad ibn Abd al-Wahhab,[4] who followed Hanbalism, and the Hanbali *fiqh* – the most conservative and resilient to change Islamic jurisprudence established by Ibn Hanbal. Hanbalism was a response to progressive mu'tazilism of caliphe al-Ma'mum. Ibn Hanbal's priority was the cohesion of the community without the slightest traits of inner discord while preventing innovations.[5] It can be achieved through a nonfigurative reading of the Quaran and sunna and the greatest possible temporal and otherwise proximity to the Prophet. The founder of official Saudi religious current - Muhammad ibn abd al-Wahhab - was not a scholar, therefore he could not have continued the literary tradition of Hanbalism but he borrowed from it largely. He enforced collective prayer and legal punishments – he himself stoned a woman for adultery. Accused of heresy, he was forced to seek refuge in an oasis ruled by the Sa'ud family, on the sidelines of all regional alliances. He preached a revival of true religion, going back to the times of the Prophet, rejecting what he called *jahiliyya* (pre-Islamic backwardness), using *jihad* but mostly in its defensive meaning since his community was attacked. Hanbalism-Wahhabism spread with the military conquest finally to Mecca by 1806.

Egyptian Islamic reformism, on the other hand, was not homogenous. It started as a mission to modernize the Muslim community by borrowing from the advancement of the West, shockingly demonstrated by Napoleon's conquest of Egypt in 1798. Such was the vocation of Rifaa at-Tahtawi's writings in early 19th century at the time of Muhammad Ali and it continued until early 20th century in the writings of Muhammad Abduh (died 1905).[6] They advocated reforming Islam, most notably in reviving *ijtihad* – an intellectual effort in interpretation of the text – and borrowing what was best from European political and social systems. Hanbali-Wahhabism was against such innovations.

Early Flows Between Egyptian Reformism and Saudi Hanbali-Wahabism

The Saudi-Egyptian and Wahhabi-Reformist relationship was born in religious conflict. The Egyptian leader Muhammad Ali, who supported and promoted Islamic reformers such as Rifaa at-Tahtawi, conquered Hijaz and Najd, which peaked in the destruction of the Saudi Emirate in 1818. Wahhab's successors then started differentiating between the truly religious and infidels, advocating hostility towards the latter. Still, even the Sauds deported by the Ottomans to Cairo studied at Al-Azhar, among them the most prominent descendants of Ibn al-Wahhab. This way they could acquaint themselves with classic Hanbali texts and relate to other schools of jurisprudence. In the mid-19th century the exiled Wahhabi ulama in different places in Egypt began returning to Najd to form a reborn Saudi Emirate. This is the first flow from Egypt of religious influence of importance.

By the time Saudi Arabia was established the symbiotic relationship between religion and politics had been confirmed, but the creation of Saudi Arabia was a result of religious war. Sauds' conquest of the Arabian Peninsula in 19th century was called by the Wahhabi ulama – a *jihad*. They religiously "purified" the territories captured by the Sa'uds from the bedouins: executed other ulama, put them under house arrest, forced to exile or co-opted them. The Sa'uds and Wahhabis managed to convert the Bedouin tribes to wahhabism and homogenize the terrain they ruled by prohibiting the Bedouins from all peaceful contact with "impious" populations in southern Iraq and Kuwait – only *jihad* on them was allowed.

Abd al-Aziz Al Sa'ud seized Riyadh in 1902 and later created Saudi Arabia in 1932. He married the daughter of the head of the Wahhabi clerics Abd Allah al-Shaykh (and the couple gave birth to the later king Faysal of Saudi Arabia 1964-1975). Thus Saudi Arabia, as the ruling territory of two families, came into being.

Egyptian Rehabilitation of Saudi Wahhabism

In late 19th and early 20th century part of the Egyptian reformism started morphing into an anti-European and anti-Western narrative most prominently in the writings of Muhammad Rashid Rida. This was also the time when Saudi Arabia was being established on the global political map and was trying to shave off the bad image of Wahhabism that the Ottoman empire had disseminated over the decades. Egyptian reformist movement in its more radical current helped in this endeavour. Muhammad Rashid Rida, Muhib ad-Din al–Khatib and Muhammad Hamid al-Fiqi, later the leader of the Salafi Egyptian movement *Ansar as-Sunna al-Muhammadiyya*,[7] promoted king Abdul Aziz's policies that – in their eyes – were a rare instance of an Arab leader not subjugated to European powers. In this respect Rida stood out as the best known at the time. When Ataturk ended the caliphate in 1924 Rida unconditionally supported the Saudi monarchy, which in his opinion consisted of pious Muslims, a statement he often repeated in the widely circulated Egyptian press. The Wahhabi ideology was promoted in Egypt through Ibn Sa'ud's agents, most notably Fawzan ibn Sabiq who distributed religious Wahhabi treatises in Egypt in order to popularize the ideology.[8] In Egypt the time was ripe: new political currents were being born after Sa'ad Zaghloul's revolution of 1919. Egypt was the Arab and Muslim epicenter of thought, therefore the involvement of influential Egyptians in the promulgation of Wahhabism brought significant results. Many landmark Wahhabi texts, such as "The Wahhabi Revolution" of 1936, were written by Saudis who had lived and studied in the heart of the Arab world: Cairo.

Not only did it rehabilitate Wahhabism but also the Saudi king himself was under the influence of the Syro-Egyptian reformism, much more advanced institutionally and intellectually than the local Wahhabis. Such was this influence that the king Abdul Aziz might have tried to dilute Wahhabism in Egyptian reformism.[9] To that effect in 1926 he created the Islamic Institute (*al-Maahad al-Islamiyy*) with Egyptian and Syrian staff who taught religious and non-religious subjects. The Wahhabi ulama were so displeased with this innovation that they prevented students from enrolling at the Institute. This first reformist institution ceased to operate after just one year but it was reestablished in Ta'if in 1945 as Dar at-Tawhid, The House of Unity. Among the 23 professors who taught there until 1957, the majority were Egyptian, some might have been from the Muslim Brotherhood. Yet, the Hanbali-Wahahbi ulama contributed to the school's marginalization by convincing the Saudis not to send their children there.

Overall however, Egyptian reformism helped ameliorate the image of Wahhabism and instructed the Saudi ulama in disciplines they had not yet mastered, namely teaching and publishing. That process created a feedback with repercussions in Egypt. Thanks to the rehabilitation of Wahhabism and putting it in a legitimate context of Islamic history Hanbalism and broader Salafi traditions slowly opened up and were revived in Egypt, although still on a small scale. With the conquest of Mekka and Madina in 1925, Saudi Arabia became the epicenter of the whole Muslim world with its various denominations. Saudi Wahhabism established connections with Hanbali centers elsewhere, also in Egypt where Ansar as-Sunna were formed in 1926.

The climax of this opening up to other traditions came in 1954 when the grand mufti of the Kingdom of Saudi Arabia (KSA) received other muftis including the former Egyptian one Hassanin Muhammad Makhluf tied to the Muslim Brothers. The meeting started a tradition of meetings of grand muftis of the Muslim world and was the beginning of Hanbali-Wahhabism recognizing other traditions, calling for a joint position in countering external challenges.

Peak Flows From Egypt: After 1952

The 1952 Egyptian revolution eventually brought a political cleavage between Egypt and KSA but the cleavage developed slowly. Initially the Sa'uds strongly supported Naser in 1956 against the French, British and Israeli invasion. But the partnership broke off with the 1958 Egyptian accusation that King Sa'ud attempted to assassinate Naser. King's image has been continuously tarnished by presenting him as reactionary. In 1962 a military coup in Yemen, backed by Egypt, established a republican system and shocked the Saudis. The conflict brought Egypt and KSA to a brink of war – Saudi positions were attacked by Egyptian forces from Yemen. The conflict eventually was disastrous for Egypt – tens of thousands of Egyptian soldiers died in Yemen and in 1967 the country lost to Israel in the six-day war. The 1967 defeat marks the beginning of the demise of Arab nationalism to the benefit of Islamism. On that wave and on its oil boom rode Saudi Arabia, which in 1967 opposed Israel vehemently but did not manage to join the war in the days it was being fought. The defeat, however, weakened Egypt so that Saudi Arabia could reassert its role as leader or the Arab world.

The Muslim Brotherhood as a Seeder of Ideas

No other religious organization apart from the Hanbali-Wahhabi establishment has shaped Saudi Arabia as much as the Egyptian Muslim Brotherhood. Since its creation in 1928 it has remained among the most potent emanations of popular Islam in Egypt. When Naser began a crackdown on the MB, thousands of its members found shelter in Saudi Arabia. It constituted the first mass flow of Egyptians to Saudi Arabia. Even if the numbers of people who came to KSA in this capacity is incomparably small in comparison to the influx of labour migration since 1970s, its significance is greater, because the MBs became the Saudi elite, who would later educate not only the Saudis but also the incoming Egyptian workers.

The relationship with the Muslim Brotherhood has proven extremely problematic over the years. It started cordially in 1950s and 1960s when King Faysal decided to give Islamists from around the Arab world safe heaven in the Kingdom. Together with the Hanbali-Wahhabi Egyptian scholars who had already worked there the Muslim Brothers immediately staffed the educational, judicial and religious systems, ostensibly dominating the first one. To them, the Saudi state was the only true Islamic state in the world.[10] They had to renounce interference in political or religious affairs of Saudi Arabia. This oath perhaps might have made them channel their activism in education, after-school activities for the students and the media sector. They became preachers, teachers, doctors, journalists and engineers. Education is of particular importance here because the Muslim Brothers were encouraged to make use of the students' time outside of the class in secondary schools and in universities so that they did not succumb to leftist, secularist ideology. As a result of their activism and thanks to popular acceptance of Islamism in the Kingdom a specific Saudi Islamism emerged in 1970s and 1980s.[11]

Saudi attitude towards the Muslim Brotherhood largely depended on regional geopolitics, rather than just being exemplified in a partnership of the religiously like-minded. In 1950s and 1960s the Sa'uds supported the MB to counterbalance Naser with a popular and modern religious narrative (the endemic Wahhabism was too conservative). They added legitimacy to their pan-Islamic solidarity concept, and supplied skilled workforce to a human resource hungry kingdom. In 1970s Anwar as-Sadat, by way of allying himself with the Saudis but mostly to counterbalance the Nasserists in Egypt, changed his policy vis-à-vis the MB. Released from prisons, the members of the international bureau of the MB convened in 1975 in Mecca to unite and expand their organization.[12] The Saudi rationale changed as well: workforce was still needed but the international context changed and the MB served as a counterweight to Khomeini's influence in the Muslim world after the 1979 revolution. Particularly large amounts of money were then channeled to the activities run by the Brotherhood.[13] Thanks to these funds, the Saudi oil boom, and the millions of people travelling between the two countries, the MB's companies in Egypt thrived. The brotherhood became a free market-dependent organization, which – however – did not lead in the least to its social modernization, due to having been frozen by Saudi conservatism.[14]

But the great Egyptian-Saudi conflict had already started with the prominence of pan-Arabism and the breakout of the "Arab Cold War". Pan-Arabist ideology was dangerous because it was becoming a successful competition for people's hearts and minds by combining social slogans with some elements of religious tradition.[15] It was not inconceivable that the Saudi society might one day want the Egyptian scenario at home. Naser was to have said: "to liberate all Jerusalem, the Arab peoples must first liberate Riyadh."[16] Pan-Arabism not only attracted the people, it was also a potent political tool in giving Egypt immediate regional power status that threatened the young state of Saudi Arabia. Pan-Arabism also reached the Saudi monarchy, where a group of princes led by Talal ibn Abd al-Aziz was so impressed with Gamal Abdel Naser's charisma that in 1962 in Cairo they formed the Free Princes Movement demanding constitutional reform.[17]

Egyptian Model for Saudi Religious Institutions

Egypt used to be a model of religious organization for much of the Arab world. Saudi Arabia also borrowed from it but managed to expand it to new limits and supply it with a new ideology: Hanbali-Wahabism. Politically Egypt was certainly an anti-model but religiously the grand mufti of KSA – Muhammad ibn Ibrahim Al al-Shaykh found it a perfect model to follow. It had the oldest, most prestigious but modern at the same time religious institution: Al-Azhar. He then copied its structure, invited Azharites who espoused Wahabism such as Abd al-Razzaq Afifi to work in KSA and sent Saudi Wahabis to train at al-Azhar. Copying of the structure entailed taking the title of grand mufti (mirrored on the one in Egypt), establishing more than twenty religious studies institutes, including the incubator of Hanbali-Wahabism al-Iman University in Riyadh, and establishing a fatawa issuing house: Dar al-Ifta'. The grand mufti had these institutions under control, along with censorship and publication houses.

As much as the political bilateral conflict continued in 1950s the Sa'uds could not ignore Naser's popularity, particularly his omnipresent firely language, broadcast throughout the Arab world, and some of his decisions. In 1961 Nasser curbed the religious authorities prerogatives in order to keep them in political check. Even though the decision of nationalization of Al-Azhar shocked the Saudis – they feared it would became Nasser's channel - they tried to copy him in their own backyard.

Firstly, to counter Naser they established the Islamic University in Medina, organized in a way that would serve as blueprint for future Islamic organizations: Wahhabis filled the board of directors, while the teachers were Salafists, Egyptian refugees.[18] Secondly, in 1962 King Sa'ud and Prince Faysal did to the Hanbali-Wahhabi establishment what Naser did to Al-Azhar: they fragmented it to end the one-man (the grand mufti's) rule and better control the religious space. But it wasn't until the grand mufti's death in 1969 that Faysal, already the king, managed to turn the one-person grand mufti's office into the newly established multi-people Senior Scholars Body to be able to exert better control over them. This was further facilitated in 1970s with the oil boom, which provided the second source of Saudi ruling class legitimacy, alongside religion. This sharpened the division of labour between the political and religious sphere and pushed the ulama' into the latter solely. But in fact this move opened the Wahhabis to new forms of institution.

Religious institutional structure in Saudi Arabia resembles that in Egypt. Out of all Arab countries Egypt modernized the first and so did its religious institutions. More so, Egyptians were usually the best trained, most modern and professional, so much so that they were often employed by the Saudi royals. In 1911 the blueprint Egyptian Senior Scholars Body was established – today called *Hayy'a Kibar Ulama' al-Azhar* - counting 30 scholars representing all four legal schools of Sunni Islam. Its Saudi counterpart - *Hayy'a Kibar al-Ulama' as-Saudiyya* - was modeled on the Egyptian example when created in 1971. The Saudi committee, however, has much more and much wider prerogatives than the similar body in Egypt, which only oversaw the religious education, rites and ethics. Its name changed over the years, most prominently in 1961 when Naser curbed official Islam's prerogatives and called it Islamic Studies Body (*Majma' al-buhuth al-islamiyya*). When the Saudi body was created one out of three foreigners who became a member was Abd Ar-Razzaq al-Afifi, a dogmatic Hanbali-Wahhabi Egyptian. He arrived in KSA in 1949 and climbed the ranks of its religious establishment until he reached the very top: the Senior Scholars Body.

Only in the beginning of 1950s, when KSA had to establish the educational infrastructure, did the Kingdom start to import religious personnel and send youth to be trained in foreign Islamic institutions. Two prominent Islamic universities in Saudi Arabia were either established by Saudis with doctorates from Al-Azhar (Abd Allah at-Turki established Al-Imam University) or employed Egyptians outright (Muslim Brotherhood professors in Umm Al-Qura university, the oldest one in KSA). Another Egyptian Abd az-Zahir Abu as-Samh was nominated the head of the Committee for the Promotion of Virtue and the Prevention of Vice of Saudi Arabia – the institution responsible for overseeing in practice the comportment of the Saudi society.

From the early days of the Saudi state's existence the ulama', owing to their significant power share, created institutions so vast in scope that a matching infrastructure could not and cannot to this day be found elsewhere in the Muslim world. There are more than 94 000[19] mosques for a population of 30 million people in Saudi Arabia. More than three times as many mosques per capita as there are in Egypt: 80 000 in a country of almost 90 million inhabitants.

Saudization of the Egyptian Model

Since Naser wanted a secular Egypt he needed some level of control over popular religiosity. He managed to achieve it through imposing on Al-Azhar and have the more radical MB members and other radical ulama emigrate to KSA, so that they did not threaten the Nasserist rule at home. Thus, the kingdom became a catalyst for their extreme views.

To counterbalance pan-Arabism and point out its deficiencies in focusing on Arabs solely, the Saudis invented pan-Islamism or Islamic solidarity. In order to boost it the World Islamic League was created in 1962, which aim was to promote Islam in the world. Through the organization the Hanbali-Wahhabi tradition started traveling in the modern times in and outside of the Muslim world. Partly thanks to the rivalry with Egypt Wahabbism grew from a local phenomenon into a global one.[20] The World Islamic League meant to encourage solidarity among Muslims but in reality it just spread Wahabbism outside of its birth nest through building mosques and supplying them with imams, publishing and distributing publications, establishing social centers. Simultaneously the Islamic University of Medina was created. In both of these initiatives (the league and the university) staff was needed as Saudi personnel were lacking. Foreign Muslim instructors were then brought to the country, mostly Egyptians. The flow was encouraged by Naser's reform of Al-Azhar in 1961. The reform divided the institution into smaller parts with duplicated prerogatives in order to weaken it, and ultimately bring under better political control. Many Azharites lost their jobs at the time and, naturally, emigrated to Saudi Arabia to build the new institutions there. These people were also disenfranchised and disillusioned about Nasserism, which pushed them into greater ideological radicalization for which the Hanbali-Wahabi environment was just ripe. Hundreds of Egyptian religious officials found employment in Saudi Arabia.[21] Their presence was also beneficial in fighting pan-Arabism, which they had known first hand and hated.

Wahhabi ulama issued popular anti-Nasserist fatawa, such as the 1961 "Critique of Arab nationalism in the light of Islam and Reality" by Abd al-Aziz ibn Baz who argued that pan-Arabism was essentially a non-Islamic practice, belonging to the times of *jahiliyya*, aimed at fragmenting the Muslim umma. More so he was convinced that Pan-Arabism was a Western conspiracy to destroy Islam[22] like all secularist and nationalist ideologies of Western in origin.

The Reversal: Peak Flows from KSA

The Saudi Support for Egyptian Hanbalism and Salafi Organizations

For a number of reasons there is no transparency in historical financial flows from Saudi Arabia to Egypt: no statistics are published, the connections have a strictly personal, often familiar character and they were established at a time when registering was not common, plus one side of this relationship (KSA) did not even have a state. The extent of personal connections, however, underscores the scope of interconnectedness even if it does not allow for a concrete estimate of the amount of Saudi aid to Egyptian Salafists.

Estimates on Saudi funding of Egyptian religious organizations are usually speculative rather than based on hard data. For example the Egyptian state-controlled media are recorded to have cited unnamed Justice Ministry sources, which had claimed that Saudi Arabia had financed the Salafis with $63 million in 2011 alone.[23] Large financial flows are highly probable since strong ideological and personal connections between Egyptians and Saudis characterize almost all Salafi Egyptian organizations: As-Sunna Al-Muhammadiyya or Ansar as-Sunna, Ad-Da'awa as-Salafiyya and Al-Gam'iyya ash-Shara'iyya. The first one, established in 1926, was led by an Egyptian who made the greatest possible religious career a foreigner can make in Saudi Arabia: Mohamed Hamed El- Fiqi. Other prominent members have worked and lived in Saudi Arabia.[24] Al-Gam'iyya ash-Shara'iyya, the oldest Egyptian Salafi organization set up in 1912, kept strong ties to Ansar as-Sunna and was also influenced by Hanbali-Wahhabi ideology. Finally, Ad-Da'awa as-Salafiyya established in 1970s in Alexandria University and other schools, was also influenced from Saudi Arabia although not by the Hanbali-Wahhabi ulama of the official Saudi Islam but by the re-invented Islamism that had already been established in the Kingdom as a result of the developments in 1950s and 1960s.

There is no coherence in literature on terminology when describing the current that became a specific breed of Saudi version of the Muslim Brotherhood that also incorporated the Wahhabi extreme social conservatism in its ideology: for example for Lacroix it was more specifically the Islamic Awakening or Sahwa,[25] for Mouline it is more broadly Islamism as opposed to Hanbali-Wahhabism.[26] This trend developed out of Egyptian-Saudi social connectedness through the Muslim Brothers. One of the better known shaykhs of the Sahwa was Muhammad Qutb, the brother of MB's Said Qutb, considered the founding father of jihadism. Once he was freed from an Egyptian jail he became professor at the Umm al-Qura University if Mecca since 1971. The name Qutb is perhaps the most famous but the founding father of the Saudi Ikhwan was Manna' al-Qattan. He emigrated to KSA in 1953 and became director for higher studies at the Imam University.[27]

Since the 1960s but particularly in the 1970s with the demise of the pan-Arab project, what can be called "return radicalization" of students, particularly those of al-Gamaa al-Islamiyya, by the Brothers living and working in KSA as well as other Saudi organizations, can be observed.[28]

The Wahhabite Doctrine's only audience outside the Arabian peninsula was in religiously conservative milieus belonging to disparate international groups, including Muslim Brothers (…). All of these have passed through Mecca and returned to their own countries to preach.[29]

The influx of literature from Saudi Arabia that was free of charge played an important role here,[30] as of course did the money. The Egyptian government cracked down on MB's finances making them dependent on petrodollars. Financial flows came directly to Salafi organizations and the MB but also indirectly, through business activity. For example the Egyptian King of Cement, Youssef Nada made his fortune on the Saudi oil boom in 1970s by proving it with cement. Not only was he a businessman but a de facto MB's international ambassador, whom Saudi Arabia regarded as such.[31]

In 1980s a particularly interesting process took place. The Egyptian official Islam was not free from Muslim Brotherhood or Salafi sympathizers – Al-Azhar was known to have had ulama and imams from all currents. So in early 1980s, specifically after Hosni Mubarak became president in 1981 Al-Azhar came closer to popular Islam when it tried to reinvent its political place somewhere between the government and the Islamists (Barraclough 1998). The nationalization of official Islam in 1961 eventually brought fragmentation and the need for the ulama to relate to modern problems and engage in discussions raised by the Islamists. Additionally, the return politicization of official Islam, partially owing to personal and official contacts with ulama in Saudi Arabia, could have been observed. The shaykh of Al-Azhar Abd al-Halim Mahmud in 1976 received a $2 mln contribution from KSA and Kuwait for the expansion of a morphing Al-Azhar.[32]

Saudi support for the Egyptian MB also reached Europe – many Brothers have emigrated there since 1950s and some have been given high posts in the Saudi charitable organizations active in Europe. Murshid Mahdi Akif was both a consultant for the World Assembly of Muslim Youth in Riyadh and the Islamic Center in Munich. Its mosque was opened in 1973 with a generous help from Saudi Arabia.[33] Munich subsequently became the Saudi-sponsored center of Egyptian brotherhood's German activism. Other murshids visited there – Mustafa Mashur, right after he fled Egypt in 1980s.

Immigration as a Carrier of Ideas: Amplified Extremist Ideas Travel Back from KSA to Egypt

Since independence in 1922 Egypt has become more socially conservative – the fact is not well documented scientifically but it is observed in other writings.[34] Most notable is the growing popularity of the veil over the past decades as a symptom of greater conservatism in the social sphere. In early 20th century, like Islamic reformism, the Egyptian feminist movement experienced great popularity and outreach – women ostentatiously took the veil off, as a symbol of backwardness and female subjugation, among them prominent public figures of the day. The movie stars of the time (till 1970s) did not share a trace of the conservatism that is popular in today's cinema.[35] In 1950s when Naser spoke of the MB's idea to oblige women to veil, the whole audience burst into laughter.[36] Popularity of female preachers and greater prospects of marriage are given as reasons for the spread of the veil and social conservatism,[37] since this is expected by the men and the society. The visible growth of conservatism has to do with the growth of the middle class in Egypt since 1970s. With a good degree of certainly the social conservatism of the lower classes has remained constant, as has the liberalism of the elite. Overall, however, owing to the changes of attitudes in the middle class and their numerical growth, social conservatism of the Egyptian society has also increased.

With the emergence of Saudi Arabia not as a backward tribal clan that had a desert to rule but as a lavishly rich and at the same time religious entity with an abundance of oil, its appeal has grown over the decades. Today Egyptians overwhelmingly prefer the Kingdom to Turkey as a model for their own country when it comes to relations between politics and religion,[38] which attests to the increased conservatism described above.

This paper claims that in 1970s and in parallel to the political processes of reducing Egypt's regional role and empowering KSA, the two societies started a slow movement toward one another, diminishing the ideological gap between them and resulting in the radicalization of the Egyptian society, with lesser societal effects on the Saudi society. The conservatism came as a result of the return to Egypt of an ocean of people from immigration to Saudi Arabia.

It wasn't until 1971 that Egyptians started migrating freely.[39] The new constitution authorized permanent and temporary emigration,[40] and more so, the 1973 oil crisis and subsequent rise of oil prices attracted large numbers of immigrant labour. Egyptians were the biggest national group then, beside the Yemenis, working in Saudi Arabia.[41] The flow saw a sharp increase in the influx of Egyptians to KSA in 1990-1994 since Egypt took part in the First Gulf War.[42] Egyptians were particularly welcome in the Kingdom thanks to linguistic, cultural and religious compatibility with the locals, but they were exposed to completely different working conditions than in Egypt. In Saudi Arabia, for example, for decades women had not been allowed to work in male presence, hence they have been confined to home or women-only workplaces. Even with the changes introduced in the past decade the conservative society cannot accept a mixed workplace in general.[43] The current fermale work force participation is at mere 20%.[44]

Neither government provides statistics on the overall number of Egyptians who have spent longer time in KSA since 1970s.[45] A prominent Egyptian writer, however, Alaa al-Aswani, claims that according to his calculations "one in four Egyptians has over the past 40 years gone to Saudi Arabia and back."[46] Egyptian migration to Saudi Arabia certainly needs to be counted in millions. Out of more than 6 million Egyptians abroad one third had used to reside and work in Libya and almost a quarter of this number in Saudi Arabia with some 7.4 % in Kuwait.[47] What has been scientifically counted is that an average spell for an Egyptian in KSA in late 1980s was 3.5 years.[48] Later, in 1990s and 2000s the period a foreign migrant worker continued to spend in the GCC increased even if the overall number of Egyptian immigrants decreased in comparison with Asian workforce. Based on this data it is safe to estimate that at least 10-20 million Egyptians have worked and lived in Saudi Arabia in the past 40 years. Upon return they populated whole districts of Cairo: upper middle class in Nasr City and lower middle class in Faysal. Today Egyptian nationals in Saudi Arabia account for 1 mln (low estimate) to 2 mln people (high estimate).[49] The populations of the whole GCC has grown from 4 mln in 1950 to almost 50 mln today,[50] and the Egyptian one has doubled since 1980s, showcasing the temporal amplification of the process described. Its scale is corroborated by Egyptian Central Bank's data on external revenues: 42% come from Saudi Arabia.

As already proven[51] overseas work experience can play a role in the development process through migrants' higher involvement in the economic and social life of his country, which means that returning migrants are greater social motors than those who have not experienced living and working abroad. Hence, their social impact can be considered commensurately bigger than the non-immigrating origin society even if it is naturally more numerous. The specificity of Egyptian immigration to the Gulf vis-à-vis the West (U.S. and Europe) is such that it is dominated by the middle class (with low skill profile[52]) versus the elite. The middle class immigration soaks in local customs easier: the naturally uneven relationship between the rich employer (master) and the poor employed (servant) drives the latter toward copying the former. The state of migrant affairs in Egypt is often called the "permanence of temporary migration",[53] meaning that migrants travel for work en masse but do not obtain permanent residency status in the receiving country, thus there are bound to inferior legal status. The growing social conservatism in Egypt can be then explained in the changes in attitudes of the middle class, rather than the Egyptian elite, whose specificity (extremely liberal in comportment, educated in expensive international schools in Cairo or in the U.S. or Europe, often having dual citizenship) has not changed significantly. Ahmed Zaghloul Shalata believes an entire generation is coming under the influence of Saudi thought, "hiding thereby our cultural identity in favor of a Bedouin-Saudi-Wahabi one that favours shape over essence, celebrating the religious outlook without caring about behaviour or even the work of the heart."[54]

Egyptians, even if socially liberal upon leaving Egypt, were forced into conservative circles as only such existed in Saudi Arabia, where social life is supervised by Saudi Committee for the Promotion of Virtue and the Prevention of Vice was established particularly to guide people the right path and eradicate unlawful behavior. It encourages people to pray collectively at the right times, prevents mixing of the sexes in public and – to an extent – private, oblige women to dress appropriately (in public that means wearing an abaya, a black robe covering the body completely from the head to the feet), prevent non-Muslims from professing their religion in public, prohibit reproduction and broadcasting of material that is not in line with the Hanbali-Wahhabi dogma, fight alcohol, drugs, prostitution and gambling, fight blasphemous innovations and see to a proper halal meat slaughter. Such behavior has become an unforced everyday reality in Egypt as well. Throughout the past four decades the process of social radicalization multiplied. Not only were the immigrants exposed to social oppression but their children as well. Many of them were educated in KSA by the Muslim Brotherhood. As a result, even though there is no formal obligation to any religious practice in Egypt, as a result of what was described, some segments of the Egyptian society live by the rules formally adopted in KSA.

Spillover in Both Directions – Extremism Beyond Control

Advantageous conditions for the MB to flourish in KSA over the years led to the breeding of thousands of Saudi Islamists who, due to the economic crisis in 1980s, could not be integrated into the state system and felt disenfranchised. They blamed the U.S. and Zionism, not the Saudi state, with which they had collaborated and which was still the closest to the Islamist ideal. Political conditions for it were ripe. The 1979 peace treaty with Israel met with Saudi rage. KSA severed relations with Egypt and stopped all economic aid. The previous year, together with other Arab states the Saudis tried to bribe Egypt not to sign the peace treaty.[55] And the following year, in 1980, Crown Prince Fahd and Saudi ulama called for jihad against Israel for declaring Jerusalem the capital of Israel.[56]

The first rupture between Wahhabism and part of the Islamist movement appeared in 1980s with the war in Afghanistan. The newly born jihadism claimed that it was an individual duty for Muslims to fight the infidels there as mujahidin – Wahhabi position was that it was a general state duty, not a personal obligation. However, the Afghan mujahidin would not have existed had it not been for the Saudi state and the Muslim Brotherhood working together. The Egyptian component of this joint venture included staffing 95% of doctors for the Afghan opposition from the Egyptian Medical Syndicate.[57] Thousands of young Saudis went there to fight – they are said to have been under the influence of radical Egyptian ulama, who emerged in late 1970s in response to local Egyptian politics. At that time again the Saudi establishment thought the MB-inspired movements in KSA as good and beneficial opposition to jihadism that had already used anti-Saudi slogans. Indeed, the Sahwa (Islamic awakening inspired by the MB) did keep firm control over the young Saudis, preventing them from joining the newly formed Al-Qaeda.[58]

The currently still valid vector of Saudi-Egyptian relations should be traced back to 1987 when bilateral relations were reestablished and Egypt welcomed again in the League of Arab States (LAS) (it was suspended in 1979). This decision came as a result of the growing Iranian threat and the Iranian-Iraqi war, in which Iraq was helped by Egypt. The Arabs felt that they needed Egypt in their single, unified camp. The new strength of the Saudi-Egyptian partnership was confirmed in 1990 when Iraq invaded Kuwait. Egypt managed to convince 10 members of the LAS to join the anti-Iraqi coalition and sent 25 000 troops to the Kingdom.

It also brought the greatest rupture to date between the official Islams of Saudi Arabia and Egypt on the one hand and the popular Islams of these countries on the other. A Muslim-Western coalition formed against another Muslim country – it was so controversial to the Arab street that the heaviest religious weapons needed to be emplyed in order to placate the public opinion. After Saddam Hussain's invasion in Kuwait, the Sa'uds agreed to American stationing on Saudi soil, which was reaffirmed as religiously legitimate and necessary in those circumstances by the most important religious figure at the time, both in KSA and Egypt. In August 1990 Abd al-Aziz Ibn Baz, and the Saudi Committee of Grand Ulama issued a fatwa on the issue.[59] In a striking example, however, of the instrumental usage of Islam for the benefit of the political power the same man – Ibn Baz – a couple of decades earlier ruled that Gamal Abdel Nasser cannot call for foreign troops himself.[60]

A similar fatwa was issued by the grand mufti of Egypt – Sayyid Tantawi. In a 72-page booklet he reiterated why it was permissible to allow unbelievers to Saudi Arabia and for Egypt to join the anti-Iraqi coalition.[61] The booklet was released right after the World Islamic League congress in Mecca that debated the Iraqi invasion on Kuwait. Already in 1989 Tantawi emerged as a great Saudi friend when he condemned the demonstrations of Iranian pilgrims during the Mecca hajj, for which he was thanked by King Fahd himself. He then lead an active campaign in the Muslim world on behalf of both Egypt and Saudi Arabia defending the two countries from Islamists' attacks.

The ostentatious cooperation of official Islam with political power, the religious rulings and Saudi governmental policy was a genuine shock for many Islamists in and outside of Saudi Arabia. The Egyptian MB was openly against it. But the Saudi Islamists first wanted to discreetly petition the rulers with an advice that they Islamize the political and public sphere even more. The extent to which the Wahhabi establishment itself was displeased with the decisions of the political government can be demonstrated by the fact that main Wahhabites and even Ibn Baz himself supported that document after he had been reassured that its content would not be made public. But the authors released its contents immediately upon submission to the king in 1991. The move prompted political power to get a stronger grip on official Islam and as much of the popular one as possible. A commission was established specifically to control the preachers and their sermons and a policy of cracking down on Islamists adopted in late 1992. In September 1992 the Committee of Grand Ulama, who have in their majority supported the 1991 Islamist petition now condemned it on the ground that it had been written by ulama of lower rank and contained errors, supplemented soon afterwards with another harsher fatwa that explicitly disavowed membership in sectarian religious and political groups as it could result in fitna. Seven out of seventeen members of the Committee of the Grand Ulama did not sight this fatwa. There were claims that they disagreed with that fatwa and sided with the radicals,[62] such was the internal division within the Saudi conservatives in general.

Hanbali-Wahhabism has always had problems distinguishing itself from jihadism, even though the Hanbali-Wahhabi ulama had gone to great lengths to prove that the ideology of Saudi Arabia is not the same as the jihadi one. But in fact the difference is slight – it mostly revolves around the relation toward the ruler. The rest of the legalist religious scripture is Hanbali, shared by both. Classical Salafism and Hanbali-Wahhabism forbids disobedience or standing against the ruler even if he is not a good Muslim on the grounds that disobedience produces the worst of all possible outcomes: internal Muslim conflict or *fitna*. The form of political government is then secondary in classical Salafism, hence only the jihadis yearn for a caliphate, which in other Salafi circles is not a goal in itself as long as religious duties and the *da'awa* can be performed.[63] Standing up to the ruler requires declaring him infidel (*kafir*). The process of excommunication, its complexity and who can initiate it is then another bone of contention between jihadists and Wahhabis, the latter ones claiming that it requires such a strict procedure that effectively makes it almost impossible.

The problem with the public's understanding of the differences, is that as we have seen, firstly, religion is used as a tool at the hands of the power and, secondly, Islam is so versatile and open to interpretation depending on which texts out of an ocean of scripture a certain decision is based. It is then only natural that official Islam – after all a group of people who symbiotically benefit from the system that legitimizes them – will present the classical Salafi approach to scripture, meaning a ban on opposing the ruler as it safeguards their own position in the system! Entanglement in endless religious debates about which part of scripture overpowers the rest, a war of fatwas on the same topic but with different answers,[64] an obscure process that eventually cannot completely rehabilitate one side and demonize the other since the difference is only in the shade of gray. The similarities are too great. In a continuous but painstaking effort to differentiate between the various, often slight shades of gray in radical Islamism, the Saudi religious establishment found itself caught by its own logic. It was after all part of radical Islamism itself, only a one that wielded power. Flirting with extremism is always dangerous – can seem useful in the short perspective but in the long run breeds more extremism.

Another factor weakening the appeal of a particular center of religious authority over the other is that there is no formal intermediary between a believer and God, a Muslim is not obliged to follow any one's decisions even if these are made by the grand mufti of Egypt or Saudi Arabia. Indeed, authority in Islam *de facto* exists[65] and people greatly respect some ulama and prestigious religious institutions but the authority has been established as a social custom not a dogmatic obligation. In the end, an accepted hadith lets a person decide for herself: *istafti qalbak* (take a fatwa from your heart). Today the biggest fatwas issuing house is not any official institution but the Internet. All shades of religious Muslims can find a convenient fatwa online – even if Islam forbids accepting a fatwa that is suitable for comfort reasons. This, most powerful "fatawa house" added an element of uncontrollability to the religious sphere both in Egypt and Saudi Arabia.

It became even more difficult but at the same time more urgent to distinguish Wahhabis from Islamists after 2001 when it turned out that most of the terrorists who perpetrated the attacks in the U.S. were Saudi: interestingly the leader of Al-Qaeda was Saudi (Usama Ibn Ladin) and the second in command and now the head of it – Egyptian (Ayman az-Zawahiri). Saudi Arabia is the only country where social conservatism is cherished and observed in every day life by the society legitimizing the oppressive part of the ideology shared by Islamists as well, giving them fertile ground to thrive and have a goal to aspire to in countries of their origin.

The aftermath of the attacks speeded up internal Wahhabi modernization. Codification of legal norms based on sharia officially began in 2007 (in Egypt it took place already in 1801!). Among other benefits it served foreign policy in a situation when KSA found itself criticized after 2001 attacks. The school curricula – written by the Muslim Brothers in the past – were supposed to be reexamined and changed.[66] Tightening the grip on official Islam also entailed supervision over the mosque life: making preachers state officials, controlling sermons and publications, granting fatawa issuing prerogatives to the highest ulama only.

Clutching at Straws: Saudization of Egyptian Official Islam

A stronger cooperation with Egyptian ulama and Al-Azhar was established in an effort to promote "moderate Islam" (*wasatiyya*) and a better image of the kingdom. This has lasted for the past 15 years, gaining traction recently with the advanced of ISIS. In February 2015 world congress "Islam and confronting terrorism" was held in Saudi Arabia, gathering grand muftis of the Muslim world and King Salman. The main message broadcast throughout the Arab world was that "Saudi Arabia is with moderate Islam".[67] A similar conference on extremism and anti-terrorism was held in Cairo in December 2014.

There have been many landmark events that have or could have impacted the Saudi-Egyptian relations in the recent 5 years: the fall of Mubarak, the electoral success of Morsi, the deposal of Morsi, the electoral success of Sisi and finally the death of King Abdullah. They were met either with apprehension in Saudi Arabia as long as they shook the internal or regional order, or, with support if they restored the status quo ante. "Fitna, the disorder that gives rise to chaos, was and remains the most feared socioreligious situation of the Arab-Muslim imaginary."[68] The 2011 uprising in Egypt then was watched with utmost apprehension in Riyadh. When Mubarak was being ousted King Abdallah emerged as his most vocal supporter who called the demonstrators "infiltrators":

No Arab and Muslim human being can bear that some infiltrators, in the name of freedom of expression, have infiltrated into the brotherly people of Egypt.[69]

This opinion is part of a longer ideological quagmire that KSA found itself in. Stuck in a mode against reforming ideology it cannot make religiously credible political decisions.

Even if religion in the kingdom is a founding element of the current political system it has also yielded to Egyptian influence over the past century in that official Islam in KSA has become little more than a tool of political power play. The usage of that tool has already been mastered in Egypt: both Morsi and Sisi chose Saudi Arabia as the destination for their first foreign trip, regardless of the Saudi position toward MB or non-MB government in Egypt. The co-optation of the Egyptian official Islam in this endeavor for the past 25 years has become an important factor in attempts to maneuver out of the limbo. Al-Azhar more often than not has been used as a tool of Egyptian-Saudi public diplomacy – like once Rashid Rida, who helped propagate and restore Wahhabi image, today Al-Azhar is defending Saudi Arabia in the eyes of the Muslim public. Only Al-Azhar has the manpower and intellectual ability to do so against other, more extreme ulama. The Saudization of Al-Azhar also manifests itself in the scale of financial flows[70] or in that there are now clerics at Al-Azhar being investigated for attending seminars in Iran.[71] The Grand Shaykh of Al-Azhar – Ahmad at-Tayyib – himself is known to have spoken rather harshly about Iran and did not accept Iranian invitation to visit:

Al-Azhar is not a political authority, and I am no politician; but my visit would be interpreted from a political perspective. So, the political aspect is inevitably present. Interventions in the domestic affairs of Islamic states, such as Yemen, Bahrain, Lebanon and Syria, are endangering their stability, which is both a political and religious issue.[72]

Popular Islam in Egypt has also been exposed to Saudi influence – either *en mass* through *hajj* and *'umra* or, indirectly, by affecting the celebrities of Egyptian popular Islam. For example, the most important televangelist in the 1970s and 1980s in Egypt, Muhammad Matwali ash-Shaarawi, went to KSA in 1950 to teach at the Faculty of Law, at University of Umm Al Qura and again taught for a year in University of King Abdul Aziz in 1981.[73] Amr Khalid, Egyptian televangelist with 16 million followers on Facebook used to work for the Saudi Iqra TV at the time when he became popular on a regional scale.

Conclusion

The paper has argued that the two religious models in Egypt and Saudi Arabia stem from opposing Islamic traditions: that of fundamentalism on the one hand, and modernism on the other. Differences between the two models, however, have clear limits and the two countries have often borrowed from each other's practices within the scope of both official and popular Islams (see chart 1).

Over the past century various stages of the interconnectedness of the two models can be identified (see chart 2). In the first stage until 1960s Egypt remained a model to emulate, because of its historical, political and religious strength. In that period Saudi Arabian model borrowed from it judiciously in three ways: (1) used Egyptian modernism to legitimize Wahhabism and connect it to the millennial tradition of Islamic scripture, (2) reproduced its organizational structure, and (3) used the Muslim Brotherhood as a religiously educated class to staff its education and media institutions, and to build a counterbalance to pan-Arabism. The collateral, unintended effect of it started a feedback process of opening Wahhabism up to other traditions and exposed Egypt to Wahhabism and its influence particularly among Egyptian Salafists.

In the second stage since 1970s, when Saudi Arabia got the upper hand in the relationship with Egypt thanks to its oil wealth and the defeat of Arab nationalism, it started spreading its own model. It came back to Egypt in three ways: (1) through mass Egyptian labour migration that lived and worked in Saudi Arabia, soaking in social conservatism of the Kingdom and bringing it later back to Egypt, (2) strong support for Egyptian popular Islam: Islamism and Salafism both in Egypt and abroad, (3) and later cooptation of the Egyptian official Islam in the service of political interests.

The interaction between the two models, specifically in the second stage of Saudi domination, served as a multiplier of extremism. A simple inference about a one-way radicalization cannot be made, since the trajectory of the traveling of radical religious ideas is neither linear nor one-way and should be considered a complex process that produces feedback and return impact. However, "Egyptization" of Saudi Arabia was stronger in the flow of popular Islam to KSA, while Saudization of Egypt was stronger in the flow of both popular and official Islam to Egypt. It happened so simply because the two forms of Islam merged in the Saudi model between 1950s and 1970s.

The inbuilt problem for Wahhabism in general is perhaps best paraphrased in the following:

Salafiyyin are against Ikhwan because they make people have second thoughts about Islam: about something they should never question.[74]

A religious current that excludes the possibility of change and innovation is bound to stagnate in a fast changing world. So when the MB could have brought the Egyptian socio-religious model closer to the Saudi Arabian one by winning parliamentary and presidential elections of 2012 and taking over the reins, the Saudis felt their own socio-religious model and personal power were threatened by a similar MB emanation in Saudi Arabia.[75] The Salafists, however, did not seem to pose a similar threat to either government. On the contrary, as ideological brothers Salafists in Egypt enjoyed support from Saudi Arabia and from the Egyptian government who reached a formal deal with their biggest organizations: *Al-Gamaiyya ash-Sharaiyya*.[76] The mapping of trajectory of radicalization between Saudi Arabia and Egypt corroborates that harbouring extremism only reinforces it. The two governments seem to be making that same mistake again.

Chart 1: **Sources of Official and Popular Islams in Egypt and Saudi Arabia**

	Official Islam	**Popular Islam**
Egypt	• Al-Azhar establishment • Senior Scholars Body • Dar al-Ifta' and Grand Mufti • Ministry of Religious Endowments	• Muslim Brotherhood • Televangelists • Salafis • Internet
Saudi Arabia	• Hanbali-Wahhabi establishment, including the Grand Mufti • Senior Scholars Body • Ministry of Islamic Affairs	• Muslim Brotherhood / Sahwa • Salafis • Internet

Chart 2: **Mapping the flow of ideas between Egypt and Saudi Arabia**

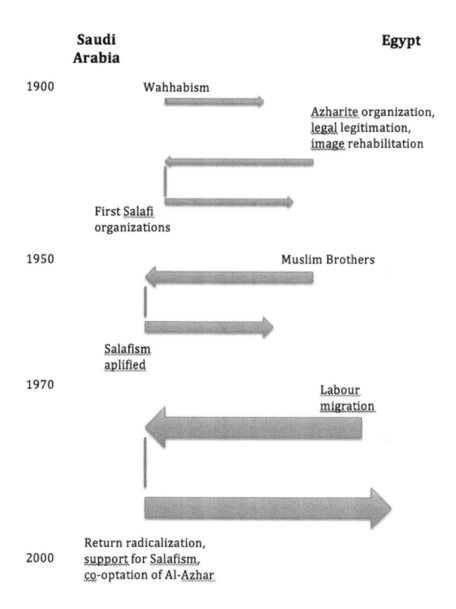

References

Abduh, Muhammad. Al-'Amal al-kamila. Bayrut: Dar Ash-Shuruq, 1993.

Achcar, Gilbert. The People Want: A Radical Exploration of the Arab Uprising. London: Saqi, 2013.

Barraclough, Steven. "Al-Azhar: Between the Government and the Islamists." Middle East Journal 52/2 (1998), 236-249.

Commins, David. "From Wahhabi to Salafi." In Saudi Arabia in Transition. Insights on Social, Political, Economic and Religious Change, edited by Bernard Haykel, Thomas Hegghammer and Stéphane Lacroix, 151-166. Cambridge: Cambridge University Press, 2015.

De Bel-Air, Francoise. "Demography, Migration and Labour Market in Saudi Arabia," European University Institute Explanatory Note 1 (2014).

Eilts, Herman Frederick. "Saudi Arabia's Foreign Policy." In Diplomacy in the Middle East: The International Relations of Regional and Outside Powers edited by L. Carl Brown, 219-244. London, New York: I.B. Tauris, 2004.

Gaffney, Patrick D. "Popular Islam." Annals of the American Academy of Political and Social Science, 524 (1992): 38-51.

Gellner, Ernest. Muslim Society. Cambridge: Cambridge University Press, 1981.

Grandin, Nicole. "Note sur le sacrifice chez les Arabes musulmans." Systèmes de pensée en Afrique noire 3 (1978): 87-114.

Habermas, Jurgen. The Structural Transformation of the Public Sphere. An Inquiry into a Category of Bourgeois Society. Massachussets: MIT Press, 1991.

Humphreys, Stephen S. "Islam and Political Values in Saudi Arabia, Egypt and Syria." Middle East Journal 33/1 (1979): 1-19.

Kapiszewski, Andrzej. Native Arab Popuation and Foreign Workers in the Gulf States. Kraków: Universitas, 1999.

Kepel, Gilles. Jihad. The Trail of Political Islam. London, New York: I.B. Tauris, 2002.

Lacroix, Stéphane. "Understanding Stability and Dissent in the Kingdom. The Double Edged Role of the jama'at in Saudi Politics." In Saudi Arabia in Transition. Insights on Social, Political, Economic and Religious Change, edited by Bernard Haykel, Thomas Hegghammer and Stéphane Lacroix, 167-180. Cambridge: Cambridge University Press, 2015.

McCormick, Barry and Jackline Wahba. "Return Migration and Entrepreneurship in Egypt." University of Southampton, 1-32.

Mouline, Nabil. The Clerics of Islam. Religious authority and political power in Saudi Arabia. New Haven, London: Yale University Press, 2014.

Pargeter Alison. The Muslim Brotherhood. From Opposition to Power. London: Saqi, 2013.

Rodinson, Maxime. Islam and Capitalism. London: Saqi, 2007.

Sasnal, Patrycja. "Pulling the Rope: The Struggle between Official and Popular Islam in Egypt." PISM Policy Papers 104 (2015).

Teitelbaum, Joshua. "Holier Than Thou: Saudi Arabia's Islamic Opposition." WINEP Policy Papers 52 (2000).

Waardenburg, Jacques. "Official and Popular Religion in Islam." Social Compass 25/3-4 (1978): 315-341.

Zahid, Mohammed. The Muslim Brotherhood and Egypt's Succession Crisis: The Politics of Liberalization and Reform in the Middle East. London, New York: I.B. Tauris, 2012.

Zeghal, Malika. "Religion and Politics in Egypt: The Ulema of Al-Azhar, Radical Islam, and the State (1952-94)." International Journal of Middle East Studies 31 (1999): 371-399.

Notes

1   Stephen S. Humphreys, "Islam and Political Values in Saudi Arabia, Egypt and Syria," *Middle East Journal* 33/1 (1979): 3-5.

2   Patrick D. Gaffney, "Popular Islam," *Annals of the American Academy of Political and Social Science* 524 (1992): 38.

3   Saudi Arabia has been paying a special land lease to Jordan ever since.

4   Already in 18th century his successors in Najd referred to themselves in similar terms that Egyptian *salafiyy* organizations use today, i.e. *Ad-Daawa al-islamiyya, At-Tariqa as-salafiyya.*

5   He combined religious activism with, nevertheless, submissiveness to power, did not call for the overthrow of it. Likewise Salafism today. Hanbalism was never as numerous as other schools of jurisprudence: Maliki, Hanafi, Shaafi, because it was never the creed of the ruling power, but it had a great influence on other thinkers. With the rise in prominence of shia dynasties (the Fatimids in particular) the Hanbalis became the bulwark of the "true" Islam and they won eventually over the shia onslaugt. Ibn Taymiyya in Damascus continued and expanded this tradition: fought the shia, ideologically and physically, destroyed popular religious sites, incited jihad. See Nabil Mouline, *The Clerics of Islam. Religious authority and political power in Saudi Arabia* (New Haven, London: Yale University Press, 2014), 36.

6   Mouline has claimed that Abduh was sympathetic to Wahhabism but in 5 volumes of his collected works, together more than 3500 pages, he mentions "Wahabiyya" and Muhammad Ibn Abd al-Wahhab once in the context of the attack of Egyptian Muhammad Ali on the revolting Sauds and Wahhabs in Hijaz in early 19ᵗʰ century. See Muhammad Abduh, *Al-'Amaal al-kaamila*, (Bayruut: Dar Ash-Shuruuq,1993), 1/857.

7   In 1969 the movement was incorporated in al-Gamaiyya ash-Sharaiyya.

8   David Commins, "From Wahhabi to Salafi," in *Saudi Arabia in Transition. Insights on Social, Political, Economic and Religious Change,* ed. Bernard Haykel et al. (Cambridge: Cambridge University Press, 2015), 155.

9   Mouline, 110.

10   Stéphane Lacroix, "Understanding Stability and Dissent in the Kingdom. The Double Edged Role of the jama'at in Saudi Politics," in in *Saudi Arabia in Transition. Insights on Social, Political, Economic and Religious Change,* ed. Bernard Haykel et al. (Cambridge: Cambridge University Press, 2015), 170.

11   Ibid, 168.

12   Mohammed Zahid, *The Muslim Brotherhood and Egypt's Succession Crisis: The Politics of Liberalization and Reform in the Middle East* (London, New York: I.B. Tauris, 2012), 79.

13   Lacroix, 172.

14   Gilbert Achcar, *The People Want: A Radical Exploration of the Arab Uprising* (London: Saqi, 2013), 99.

15   Mouline, 125.

16   Simon Henderson, "After King Abdullah. Succession in Saudi Arabia," *WINEP Policy Focus* 94 (2009): 5, accessed July 6, 2016: http://tinyurl.com/zwr7ae7

17   The movement did not get popular backing.

18   Jakob Skovgaard-Petersen, *Defining Islam for the Egyptian State: Muftis and Fatwas of the Dār Al-Iftā* (Laiden, New York, Köln: Brill, 1997), 189.

19   "94 alf masjid wa-jami' fi manatiq al-mamlaka wa (2.2) milyar riyal makafat al-'aima wal-mu'adhdhinin," *Al-Jazira,* June 26, 2013, accessed July 6, 2016: http://tinyurl.com/hlajc7t

20   Mouline, 131.

21   Ibid, 133.

22   "Naqd al-qawmiyya al-'arabiyya 'ala daw' al-islam wal-waqi'," official website of shaykh Abd al-Aziz Bin Abdallah Bin Baz, accessed July 6, 2016: http://tinyurl.com/jugkamu

23   James M. Dorsey, "Saudi Arabia Embraces Salafism: Countering The Arab Uprising? – Analysis," *Eurasia Review,* January 13, 2012, accessed July 6, 2016: http://tinyurl.com/gw3cc8x

24   Abdel Razek Afify, Sheikh Abdel Razek Hamza, former member of Grand Scholars (Hai'at Kibar al-'Ulama') in Saudi Arabia, Sheikh Mohamed Abdel Wahab Al-Banna teacher in Mecca Haram, Sheikh Abdel Zaher Abul Samah, Imam of the Grand Mosque and director of Dar El-Hadith philanthropic society in Mecca.

25   Lacroix, 170.

26   Mouline, 241.

27   "Al-Qadi ash-shaykh Mana' al-Qattan… al-mudir as-sabiq li-ma'ahad al-'ali lil-quda' fis-Sa'udiyya," official website of the history encyclopaedia of the Muslim Brotherhood, accessed July 6, 2016: http://tinyurl.com/zykdy5p

28   Interview with Nagih Ibrahim, Egyptian Salafist leader, member of Al-Gamaa al-Islamiyya, March 2015, Alexandria.

29 Gilles Kepel, *Jihad. The Trail of Political Islam* (London, New York: I.B. Tauris, 2002), 69.

30 Alison Pargeter, *The Muslim Brotherhood. From Opposition to Power* (London: Saqi, 2013), 39.

31 Ibid, 118.

32 Malika Zeghal, "Religion and Politics in Egypt: The Ulema of Al-Azhar, Radical Islam, and the State (1952-94)," *International Journal of Middle East Studies* 31 (1999): 378.

33 Pargeter, 111 and 163.

34 For examples see: http://tinyurl.com/z7wbs7c, or: http://tinyurl.com/jtag68r

35 Lisa Anderson, "Egypt's cultural shift reflects Islam's pull," *Chicago Tribune*, March 21, 2004, accessed July 6, 2016: http://tinyurl.com/hbehubf

36 "Gamal Abdel Nasser on the Muslim Brotherhood," accessed July 6, 2016: http://tinyurl.com/kx3p3ja

37 "Egypt and the Veil: An Overview," *Asharq al-Awsat*, November 29, 2006, accessed July 6, 2016: http://tinyurl.com/jflwuyt

38 "Egyptians Remain Optimistic, Embrace Democracy and Religion in Political Life," Pew Research Center, May 8, 2012, accessed July 6, 2016: http://tinyurl.com/7yn8vp7

39 Immigration has been encouraged since Sadat became president. More than 5% of Egyptian GDP comes from remittances, although only a little more than 3% of it from Saudi Arabia. It presents the Egyptian government with an argument to continue encouraging immigration as not only remittances are beneficial but also it lessens the pressure on local labour market with a large chunk of hidden unemployment.

40 Art. 52., The Constitution of the Arab Republic of Egypt, 1971, accessed July 6, 2016: http://tinyurl.com/jl64k94

41 On Egyptian immigration in the GCC see Andrzej Kapiszewski, *Native Arab Population and Foreign Workers in the Gulf States* (Kraków: Universitas, 1999), 167-169.

42 Francoise De Bel-Air, "Demography, Migration and Labour Market in Saudi Arabia," European University institute Explanatory Note 1(2014).

43 Louise Redvers, "Keys to The Kingdom: The slow rise of Saudi women," *BBC* April 9, 2015, accessed July 6, 2016: http://preview.tinyurl.com/h4k5p48

44 "Saudi Arabia: Employment Plan 2014," G20, 2015: 5, accessed July 6, 2016: http://tinyurl.com/hyxmhdt

45 In a conversation of May 2015 the International Labour Organization confirmed that such statistics do not exist.

46 Interview with Alaa al-Aswani, March 2015, Cairo. Aswani has also claimed elsewhere that well-paid Egyptian Salafist sheiks work in Saudi religious television channels, Al-Azhar sheikhs teach at Saudi universities and Egyptian businessmen regularly work with the Saudis. See: Alaa al-Awany, "Egyptian Leaders Fail to Defend Migrant Workers in Saudi Arabia," *Al-Monitor*, February 8, 2013, accessed July 6, 2016: http://tinyurl.com/zmw6mlq

47 "Egypt. Migration Profile," Migration Policy Center, European University Institute, 2013, accessed July 6, 2016: http://tinyurl.com/zrh2cpe

48 Figure calculated on a sample of 1526 Egyptian returnees in 1988. See Barry McCormick and Jackline Wahba, "Return Migration and Entrepreneurship in Egypt," University of Southampton, accessed July 6, 2016: http://tinyurl.com/zd2gbk3

49 "Some estimates of the non-nationals by country of citizenship (Saudi Arabia, November 3, 2013)," EUI Gulf Markets and Migration, accessed July 6, 2016: http://tinyurl.com/jdtb6qb

50 GCC: Total population and percentage of nationals and non-nationals in GCC countries (latest national statistics, 2010-2014), EUI Gulf Markets and Migration, accessed July 6, 2016: http://tinyurl.com/nsmtkmu

51 McCormick and Wahba, 5.

52 Ibid, 2.

53 "Migration Facts. Egypt," Migration Policy Center, European University Institute, 2013, accessed July 6, 2016: http://tinyurl.com/hptufuy

54 Mahmoud El-Wardani, "Book review: Roots of the Salafist Movement in Egypt," *Ahram Online*, May 19, 2011, accessed July 6, 2016: http://tinyurl.com/hcxu67b

55 Herman Frederick Eilts, "Saudi Arabia's Foreign Policy", in *Diplomacy in the Middle East: The International Relations of Regional and Outside Powers*, ed. L. Carl Brown (London, New York: I.B.Tauris, 2004) 230.

56 Marguerite Johnson, "Middle East: Jihad for Jerusalem," *Time*, August 25, 1980, accessed July 6, 2016: http://tinyurl.com/ha5tth8

57 Pargeter, 194.

58 In general Sahwa can be considered a buffer zone between the Whhabis and al-Qaeda to this day. Lacroix, 177.

59 "Bayan Hay'at Kibar al-Ulama fi tayid ma ittahadhahu wali al-amr min istiqdam quwwat mu'ahila li rad al-'adwan ala hadhihi al-bilad," *Majalla al-Buhuth al-islamiyya*, part 29, (1410/1411), 249-250, accessed July 6, 2016: http://tinyurl.com/hl5dv6m

60 Mouline, 244.

61 Skovgaard-Petersen, 264.

62 Joshua Teitelbaum, "Holier Than Thou: Saudi Arabia's Islamic Opposition," WINEP Policy Papers, 52 (2000), XIV.

63 Interview with Nagih Ibrahim, Egyptian Salafist leader, March 2015, Alexandria.

64 "War of the Fatwas,", *Guardian*, October 29, 2007, accessed July 6, 2016: http://tinyurl.com/jbjs3v4

65 On the "no cleargy" myth in Sunni Islam see Patrycja Sasnal, *Pulling the Rope: The Struggle between Official and Popular Islam in Egypt*, Policy Paper, PISM, no 2 (104), March 2015: http://tinyurl.com/gwxhhp8

66 "Saudi Arabia's Curriculum of Intolerance," Freedom House, 2006, accessed July 5, 2016: http://tinyurl.com/zfc6o62

67 "Khadim al-haramayn ash-sharifayn: As-Sa'udiyya ma' al-islam al-mu'ttadil... wat-ta'assub wat-tashaddud isa'a lahu," *Ash-Sharq al-Awsat*, February 25, 2015, 4.

68 Mouline, 88.

69 "Egypt protests draw mixed reaction in region," *CNN*, January 29, 2011, accessed July 6, 2016: http://tinyurl.com/zlayny9

70 "Saudi to restore Egypt's 'beacon of moderate Islam'," *AFP*, 2014, accessed July 6, 2016: http://tinyurl.com/zx4hv2b

71 Hoda Badri "Brotherhood and Salafis behind criticism of Iran visit: Ahmed Karima", *Daily News Egypt*, September 24, 2014, accessed July 6, 2016: http://tinyurl.com/hgwcgk2

72 "Al-Masry Al-Youm interviews the Grand Sheikh of Al-Azhar, Ahmed al-Tayyeb (Part I)", *Egypt Independent*, January 24, 2015, accessed July 6, 2016: http://tinyurl.com/jjlaszw

73 In 1963 he was even prevented by Naser from traveling to Saudi Arabia.

74 Interview with Ali Bakr, Al-Ahram Center of Political and Strategic Studies, March 2015, Cairo.

75 2002 – prince Nayef interview for Kuwaiti As-Siyasa: Brotherhood behind all Arab problems: http://tinyurl.com/grdm65q

76 Ismail Rifat, "Ittifaq bayna al-awqaf wal-gama'iyya al-shara'iyya lililtizam biqawanin al-khitaba wa tawfiq awda'iha," *Youm7*, September 17, 2014, accessed July 6, 2016: http://tinyurl.com/hekbhfl

2

The Muslim Brotherhood and the Gulf States: Implications on their Relationship with Egypt

Maged Botros Salib

Introduction

In the Middle East, religion is a pivotal agent for political socialization. Religious beliefs highly influence political beliefs and practices. Additionally, some religions do not recognize any distinctions between religious and public life. As a result, political practices and views are more apt to be shaped by religious values and principles.[1] Religion and politics in the Middle East are the two dimensions that are most influential in formulating state ideology which specifies legitimate domains of the dominant socio-political and economic systems. Religion and politics have been interrelated since the inception of civilization in the Middle East as a substantial source of political legitimacy that stems from religion. This organic link made the rulers keen to seek religious support for their political systems and decisions.

Egypt is the historical Arab leader, and one of the regional powers in the Middle East; its cultural influence is one of its sources of power. Egypt is entrusted as the stronghold of moderate Islam through the "Azhar" institution and university established in 972 AD. Islamic movements thus gain credibility if launched in the land of "Azhar".

Muslim Brotherhood in the Middle East

The Muslim Brotherhood (MB) was founded in Egypt by Hassan al-Banna in 1928 as a religious reform movement which established branches in the 1930s in several Islamic states. The initial capital (500 sterling Pounds) of the MB was donated by the British Embassy in Cairo in March 1928 to its founder Hassan al Banna. The British influence on the MB, Mi6 in particular, was described as: "*...a perceived symbiotic relationship with Egypt's Muslim Brotherhood lent subsistence to the formation and evolution of the first so-called Islamic terrorist group global in its vision and regional in its outreach*".[2] The MB movement is a global organization in 72 countries; the branches operate independently in response to the local conditions in each country. As a religious/political organization with a global orientation, the MB teachings stress that loyalty is to God rather to national states; to the international organization rather than to sovereign states. Like some religious streams, they attribute sovereignty to God alone, not to states.[3] The MB was dissolved twice in 1948 and 2014 over several charges of assassinations and terrorism.[4] Almost all founders of Jihadist terrorist organizations such as Al-Qaida and ISIL were originally members of the MB. It is currently a prohibited organization in several countries, including Egypt, the Russian Federation and most of the Gulf States.

The six Gulf Cooperation Council (GCC) states enjoy traditional political regimes which necessitated political stability as their cornerstone policy. The surge of Arab upheavals, that was known as the "Arab Spring", began in late 2010, was a direct threat to the stability of the Gulf monarchies. As a result, the GCC States adopted a policy to influence the development of Egypt, as the Arab key political player through aid and diplomacy. "Gulf policymakers securitized the menace of the Muslim Brotherhood as a transnational threat that linked internal and external considerations".[5] The security and stability in the Gulf area is directly linked to the stability of Egypt; as a result, there are "organic" and strategic ties between Egypt and its historic Gulf allies. Gulf States, except for Qatar, were on high alert when the MB ruled Egypt and who were getting ready to "stretch" east. The Gulf states are justified in fearing the rise of the MB in Arab countries because the Brotherhood has a structure that goes beyond the borders of one country, and thus, the loyalty of its members is not limited to one nationality. The Gulf states remain aware that they are the second-in-line in the MB strategy who aimed to control the oil-rich region to fund its ambitious expansion strategy.

The local MB organizations represent a substantial security challenge to the Gulf monarchies. These groups hold different stakes in each country's political system and gain various forms of support at different levels from the local population. Accordingly, each Brotherhood organization in each Gulf state should be analyzed according to a well-calibrated approach based on the local political dynamics.[6] The MB has a long and influential history in the Arab Gulf. It was brought to the region during the MB's earliest days, in some cases, through personal contacts with its founder.

The MB is going through the most difficult stage in its political history since the Nasserist period. However, unlike the 1950s and 1960s, the Brotherhood can neither count on political support from, nor find a safe haven in, the conservative monarchies of the Arab Gulf. An intra-GCC disagreement that pitted the pro-MB Qatar against the United Arab Emirates (UAE) and Saudi Arabia has come down decisively in favor of anti-MB forces. Combined with the significant challenges that the MB in the Gulf was already facing from disaffected youth cadres and Salafist competitors, the hostile environment will make it impossible for the MB to maintain their previous level of social and political influence inside the Gulf countries.[7]

In several Gulf countries, the MB sought to use the regional wave of popular mobilization to establish new political constraints on the Gulf ruling families. MB members joined public petitions in the UAE and Saudi Arabia calling for political reforms to include elections for the Federal National Council (FNC) and Shura Council. Their influence had at first grown as Gulf governments found them suitable allies in countering Arab nationalism and in manning rapidly expanding state ministries post-independence. Brotherhood members, organised in informal networks, Islamic charities, and where possible, established societies for social reform. In those states that had political openings and active parliaments, such as Kuwait and Bahrain, the MB formed political societies which competed in elections and came to political prominence in the 1990s. While their experience varies significantly from country to country, it is fair to say that the MB played a substantial role in shaping Gulf societies and had a significant impact on national politics.[8]

While the Gulf's MB groups, with the exception of the UAE, have been spared the massive crackdown witnessed in Egypt, they face an uncertain future. The antagonistic political and legal environment should significantly hamper recruitment and the functioning of their many civil society organizations. Moreover, as the Islamist movement committed to and dependent on political participation, the MB will suffer more than their Salafi competitors from the growing intolerance for activism inspired by political Islam. At the same time, a retreat to a less public position, the secret society model, is less viable in today's globalised era.

The Conflict between the Muslim Brotherhood, Secularism and other Islamist Movements

Most of Gulf political-science scholars suggest that the Brotherhood was part of a wider failure by Islamist groups to adjust to modern times. The MB never accepted the idea of a civil state with equality for all its citizens and instead remained tied to the idea of an Islamist state where minorities were respected but unequal. One of the scholars dismissed the notion that the Brotherhood could gain a political foothold in the Gulf where poverty is minimal and societies are harmonious. He suggested that the Brotherhood's views would not make inroads in these societies particularly because Gulf countries are organised based on tribal and family loyalties rather than along ideological lines.[9]

The alliance between the MB and Turkey after 2011 was a mutual interest of the two important political actors: Turkey wanted to revive its historical regional expansionist ambitions to be the Sunni regional state "Khilafa" while the MB wanted to be the religious mastermind of that state.[10] The Gulf States realised that such a Turkey-MB alliance would jeopardize the existence of the Gulf traditional regimes and acted to remove the potential for that alliance to expand.

Despite this pivotal role, MB influence in the Gulf was not unchallenged. The entry of Salafis into politics in the 1980s introduced new Islamist rivals who competed with and at times surpassed the MB in parliamentary elections, government posts and societal influence. Throughout the 2000s, the MB faced disparagement from a growing Salafi trend accusing them of political opportunism and questioning their commitment to Islamic doctrine. A political observer pointed to the role of al-Azhar University in supporting the military and the protests. He said that Egypt's rejection of the Brotherhood was popular and went far beyond the secularists. Abdulla agreed, stating that Salafi groups also supported the military's position. He said: *"I don't think what's happening in Egypt is over identity, the religious vs. the secular. What's happening is everybody has a problem with the Muslim Brotherhood and their methodology."*[11] Several other political science scholars suggested that the Brotherhood's ideology was already responsible for the development of terrorist groups across the region; moreover, they might respond to their loss of power by encouraging terror, but this was expected to speed the destruction of their movement.

At the same time the MB faced challenges in recruiting the younger generation. In contrast to the more informal Salafi networks, the MB has a hierarchical structure based upon deference to elders and compliance with the decisions of the organization. The MB's lengthy process of admission and advancement has appeared more onerous, as alternatives for public engagement and entertainment, outside of religious societies, increased in the expansion of public spaces; such as, restaurants and cafes, virtually all through social media. The openness and diversity of views found in these spaces and expanding media has increased the disaffection with the secrecy and discipline of MB organization. Some youth also chafed at the unwillingness of the MB to adopt more confrontational methods to achieve political change.

Indicators for the younger generation's frustration with the culture and gradualist policies of the MB can be seen in the emergence of independent blogs by MB youth, independent statements made by MB youth cadres taking positions that diverge from the mainstream MB organization, and in the prominence of ex-MB youth in Gulf opposition organizations and networks that emerged around the time of the Arab uprisings of 2011. Social media has enabled a new kind of organization outside of established Islamist organizations, empowering new, unaffiliated youth movements in the Gulf.[12]

The Muslim Brotherhood in Saudi Arabia

The history of the MB within the Gulf States began in the 1930's through amenable relations between its founder, al-Banna, and the Wahhab in Saudi Arabia who introduced him to the ruling family.[13] Their relationship developed in the mid-1950s when Saudi Arabia provided funding and a safe haven to its members who fled from Egypt after the failed assassination attempt on Nasser. Moreover, Saudi Arabia granted some MB members Saudi citizenship. The deeply-rooted relationships between the two allies was summarised by Sadiq in the following statement: *"The nature of the relationship was a 'give and take relationship' for just as Saudi Arabia allowed the Muslim Brotherhood to operate within its territory through its official and semi-official institutions, the group also crystallised a political religious ideology that it was able to use as a steel arm against the kingdoms and its own political opponents both at home and abroad*".[14] In that period, the Egyptian-Saudi relations witnessed political rivalry over Yemen and personal animosity between Nasser and Faisal.

The MB was considered to have both intellectual and religious resources to counteract the socialist/nationalist current in the Arab region. It later became a means to renew Islamic Sunni thought which meant that the Saudi royal family overlooked its political activities. The group "methodically... took control of Saudi Arabia's intellectual life by publishing books and participating in discussion circles and salons held by princes".[15] The Saudi royal family's relationship with the Brotherhood has thus been a mix of support and co-option along with anxiety and antagonism towards the group's political agenda.

Most Saudi Brotherhood figures have maintained a low profile, avoiding public criticism of the palace or calls for change. Some, however, have confronted the royal family on political issues. In the early 1990s, Brotherhood figures joined the al-Sahwa al-Islamiyah (Islamic Awakening) intifada, a movement that focused on opposing the deployment of foreign troops on Saudi soil to liberate Kuwait from Iraq, and also used protests and petitions to demand various political reforms such as the creation of an independent advisory council. In early 2011, several Brotherhood figures unsuccessfully argued for this organization to support other Saudis calling for far-reaching political reforms. These episodes show the group's (selective) interest in partnering with other factions calling for political change, an interest seemingly tempered by careful calculation on not jeopardizing the Brotherhood's position in the kingdom.[16] The Saudi-MB relationship suffered from a number of blows due to the Muslim Brotherhood's decision to support the Iranian Revolution in 1980, as well as their support for Saddam Hussein's invasion of Kuwait which ultimately threatened Saudi Arabia. These political stands created problematic relations and prompted bitterness in regard to the MB's overall intentions in the Kingdom.[17] The Algerian civil war in the 1990's, based on Islamist attempts to overthrow the regime, was one such nightmare scenario to be avoided by the Gulf monarchies. In addition to state attempts to reduce the chances of the MB becoming a political competitor and challenger, the MB has also faced a more restrictive environment in the Gulf since the events of Sept. 11, 2001.

International scrutiny of Islamist movements and their financing understandably increased in the post-9/11 atmosphere, but that is not all. Gulf ruling families also began to shift their political calculations. The rethink began in Saudi Arabia in the mid-1990s after the Saudi ruling family faced serious challenges in 1979 in the form of the 'Islamic awakening', or *Sahwa*, that openly challenged it; albeit in a limited mobilization. It had became clear that the ruling family resented the MB for the politicization of the religious field. In 2002, the Saudi Interior Minister denounced the Brotherhood, saying it was guilty of "betrayal of pledges and ingratitude" and was "the source of all problems in the Islamic world".[18] After 2001, the Saudi Interior Minister Crown Prince Nayef bin Abdul Aziz al-Saud attributed responsibility to the MB for the emergence of international Islamist terrorism. Saudi Arabia came to view the Brotherhood ideology as a school of thought competing for allegiance among the Gulf populations and thus challenging the religious legitimacy on which the Saudi ruling family's alliance with the Wahhabi reform movement rests.[19] After fourteen years, Prince Nayef's son, Prince Mohamed bin Nayef, inherited his father's key political posts and was chosen by King Salman in April 2015 to be the Crown Price and the Minister of Interior. The new Crown Prince adopted a policy which placed political Islam in the political process to encounter terrorism, which will most likely continue to include the MB. One observer has criticised the Brotherhood's role in education in the kingdom and elsewhere, describing their teachings as being in opposition to the idea of the state.[20] Political successions in both the UAE and Kuwait brought about a new and much less sympathetic leadership, and in the case of Abu Dhabi, outright hostility towards the MB organization.

The relationship between the MB and former allies worsened after the Brotherhood ruled Egypt and called for the expansion of the Arab Spring to all Arab countries, amounting to a direct threat to all the Gulf states. It represented a tipping point, after which Saudi Arabia and Emirates, along with Egypt, proscribed the MB as a terrorist organization in 2014. The Saudi royal decree was wide in its application, including reference that belonging to intellectual or religious groups that are extremist, or categorised as terrorist, at the local, regional or international level, was illustrated by supporting them through financial or moral means, or showing sympathy for their ideas and methods, in whichever way, or inciting others to do any of this or promoting any such actions in word or writing.

It is widely believed that Saudi Arabia urged its allies to curtail the MB activities in their countries. As a result, David Cameron, Britain's Prime Minister, announced on April 1st, 2014 an investigation led by the former British Ambassador to Saudi Arabia, into the Muslim Brotherhood.[21] After more than a year of launching that investigation, the long-awaited investigation report was delayed twice due to political considerations. In early 2015, the Saudi Foreign Minister Prince Saud Al-Faisal smoothed the Saudi position saying, "*Our problem is not with the Muslim Brotherhood per se but with a small fraction of the group and our concern that they will not pledge allegiance to a higher power*".[22] Al-Faisal's press release opens up a debate on whether the Gulf states reviewed their foreign policies of what a renewed relationship between Saudi Arabia and the Muslim Brotherhood would look like and the Kingdom's terms for the group's rehabilitation.

In April 2015, a sudden and major shakeup in the Saudi political system including changes to the line of succession, the Minister of Defence, Minister of Foreign Affairs and the Chief of Staff, stirred fears that the support base for Egypt amongst the monarchs' existing court was eroding. The ousted political elite were replaced by generally pro-American policy officials and relatives.

The future role of the MB in the kingdom depends on several internal, regional and international pressures. Religion plays a pivotal role in Saudi's society. Regionally, the Kingdom is torn between Egypt and the MB's allies. Internationally, the United States exercises a lot of pressures to change the Saudi's policy towards the MB, viewing it as an active political actor with a large support base in a turbulent region. The newly-formulated and relatively aggressive policies towards the MB from the capitals of Saudi Arabia, the UAE and Egypt, are taking shaping at an accelerated pace due to pressures from other regional and international political actors and events.

The Muslim Brotherhood in United Arab Emirates

The local Brotherhood group in the UAE, *al-Islah*, has been the most organised non-state actor in the country for decades, and Emiratis linked to it have been key participants in calls for political reform despite the government outlawing political organizations and discouraging political debate. In March 2011, *al-Islah* presented an exceptional petition demanding comprehensive elections and legislative authority for the advisory Federal National Council. Since then, UAE authorities have detained, tried, and sentenced some of its signatories, albeit for unrelated charges.[23] The UAE - Saudi campaign to delegitimize and diminish, if not destroy the MB, was then brought to bear on regional maverick and GCC member state, Qatar. The strength of the UAE and Saudi Arabia's resolve can be seen in their hardline tactics, including, the withdrawal of ambassadors from Qatar and the threat of economic sanctions. Their demands focused on Qatar ending its support for Egypt's embattled MB, but also significantly, pressed for the cessation of Qatari support for MB dissidents within the Gulf region, in line with a security agreement signed by GCC interior ministers in 2012. According to leaked copies of that unpublished agreement, it commits Gulf states to cooperate with each other to hunt down those who are outside law or the system, or who are wanted by states, whatever their nationality, and to take necessary action against them across borders and through extradition. But the diplomatic crisis between the Gulf monarchies and Qatar is still festering, most visibly in Egypt, where tensions broke out into the open over the military-led ousting the MB president. Such GCC state tensions are raising questions about their ability to muster a coherent response to a storm of crises rocking the Arab region, including conflicts in Yemen, Iraq, Libya and Syria.[24]

New legal frameworks, implemented at both the national and GCC level, place MB members under continuous risk of prosecution. In practice, with the exception of the UAE, there have not been specific campaigns of arrests against the organization. The wide ranging Saudi interpretation of the terrorism law which suggests that not only belonging to the MB is a crime, but also associating with it at home or abroad, or showing any support or sympathy for its cause through any form of media is a crime, has kept MB activities in check so far. Even in those countries without such broad terrorism legislation, the threat of prosecution or extradition via the GCC security agreement remains. This has dampened the once open and extensive campaign in support of the former Morsi government and jailed MB members in Egypt. It has also prevented Gulf MB activists from supporting each other. For example, several Kuwait MB members faced possible extradition after a case, brought by the UAE, accused them of materially supporting the Emirati *al-Islah*. More recently, a former MB member of Kuwait's parliament had a case filed against him by the Kuwait parliament for criticizing Sheikh Mohammed bin Zayed al-Nahyan, the crown prince of Abu Dhabi.[25]

As the second largest country in the Gulf, the Emirates continues to play an active role in confronting the MB's surge in Egypt by prosecuting a large number of Egyptian and Emirati MB figures in 2013 that were considered to be plotting against the state. The Emirati Government strictly prohibits any MB activity and deported a large number of MB members from its territory. One Gulf scholar argued that the Emirates has arrested Brotherhood members specifically because the organization was a political one, and political groups are forbidden by law. Cases against members of the Brotherhood are therefore conducted on a purely legal basis, and not an ideological one. At the same time, there are suggestions that the Brotherhood had begun a vicious campaign against the Emirati government, charging that the Brotherhood supports Iran against the UAE and then also attacked the UAE when it did not back the Brotherhood in Egypt.

In 2013, the UAE witnessed a crackdown on the MB, whereby the government arrested nearly 100 Emirati members of the MB-inspired *al-Islah* organization on the charge of "forming a secret organization plotting to overthrow the regime." This hardline position gained traction across the Gulf as the regional dynamic shifted with the overthrow of the MB-led Mohamed Morsi government in Egypt. MB activists in Saudi Arabia and Kuwait publically criticised their governments' political and financial support for Egypt's new political regime. They were also openly supportive of rebel groups in their deepening civil war in Syria. Both positions most likely contributed to the decision of the Saudi government to adopt a new anti-terrorism law in early 2014 which took the extraordinary step of specifically naming the MB among a list of banned terrorist groups. The UAE followed with its own anti-terror law in November 2014, officially designating the MB, and significantly, its civil society organizations in the West as terrorist organizations. When it comes to countering the Brotherhood, the UAE has been more proactive than other Gulf governments due to the imminent threats posed to its national security.[26]

The Muslim Brotherhood in Bahrain

Bahrain, arguably Saudi Arabia's closest ally, has adopted a cautious policy towards MB activities. Bahrain didn't prohibit the Sunni MB because of the critical tension between the majority Shi'a and minority Sunnis on its territory during the Arab Spring; indeed, MB-dominated political parties have a substantial number of parliamentary seats.[27] Despite the unquestioned loyalty of Bahrain's MB and its key role in standing by the ruling family in Bahrain's ongoing political crisis, the government did undertake electoral re-districting in September 2014, widely perceived to be to the MB's disadvantage. In the November parliamentary elections, the MB won only one seat, while they chose not to run candidates in municipal elections in which they previously had good representation. They also had their ministers in the cabinet resign, and are having their influence curbed in Bahrain's Ministry of Education.[28]

The ruling families in Bahrain and Qatar have each co-opted local Brotherhood organizations, albeit in different ways. Bahrain's *al-Minbar* Islamic Society, the political arm of the local Brotherhood's *al-Islah* Society, is one of the few such organizations permitted to operate in a country where political parties are outlawed. Many believe that Bahrain's Royal Court and the Islamic banking sector bankroll this group. Government support for the Sunni *al-Minbar* society reflects the Sunni royal family's fundamental interest in offsetting the country's Shi'a majority, which is well-represented in parliament. *Al-Minbar* has won parliamentary seats in each of the three elections held since 2002, where it generally supports the monarchy's political and economic agenda, while pursuing its own Islamist social objectives, in conjunction with the Sunni Islamist group, *al-Asalah*. In February, for example, Minbar announced that it would boycott the national dialogue ostensibly intended to address Shi'a political disgruntlement. The group claimed it was protesting the Shi'a opposition's "silence" about acts of violence that erupted during the second anniversary of the country's 2011 uprising.

The MB's troubles have come at the benefit of their Salafi competitors. In Bahrain, Salafi candidates gained on the MB in Bahrain's parliamentary elections of 2014 and now hold 50 percent of the municipal council chairmanships. However, despite supporting government interests, *al-Minbar* does pose certain hazards to Bahrain's rulers. One danger lies in its potential to side with one royal faction over others on issues such as Sunni - Shi'a relations and political reform.[29]

The Muslim Brotherhood in Qatar

Qatar, as a small state with a flourishing oil and gas based economy, seeks to fill a political vacuum in the region, and play a wider regional role. This ambition has led it to take a contradictory stand, supporting the MB over what could be expected to be a more pro-GCC/anti-MB stance from a small state. After the 30 June popular revolution against the MB in Egypt, the Gulf states, except for Qatar, invested in financial and diplomatic leverage to support the choice of the Egyptian people which happened to coincide with their own national interests. Qatar waged a fierce diplomatic, media and funding battle to destabilize the new and popularly supported regime. This led to a severe diplomatic crisis among the six GCC states: "The most visible manifestation of the tensions was the March 2014 decision by Saudi Arabia, the United Arab Emirates and Bahrain to withdraw their ambassadors from Doha in the name of 'security and stability." The decision reflected the deep and continuing anger felt in Riyadh and Abu Dhabi over Qatar's pro-Islamist policies. Qatar was continuing to give a degree of assistance to members of the Muslim Brotherhood that had escaped Egypt.[30]

Saudi Arabia and the United Arab Emirates exercised political pressure on Qatar to expel the exiled Islamists and curb the activities of *Al Jazeera*. The executive cadres of the MB who took refuge in Qatar made the best use of the historical rivalry between the ruling elite of Qatar and the rest of the Gulf ruling regimes. The MB cadres strongly supported the Qatari regime and bitterly criticised the Gulf regimes that endorsed the 30 June revolution in Egypt. Qatar, having struck an alliance with the MB in a play for regional influence, financially supported the group's former government in Egypt, opposed the new Egyptian political system and provided a haven to Islamists in exile after the subsequent crackdown.[31]

In Qatar, the local Brotherhood affiliate dissolved itself more than a decade ago, partly to avoid contentious relations with the country's rulers at the time, when other Gulf governments were arresting Brotherhood supporters. Today, most former members see little reason for anti-government agitation in a country that has become host and home to some of the region's most famous Brotherhood figures. Qatar continues to provide public platforms to these individuals, and its foreign policy since 2011 has been anchored in support for Islamist groups. As a result, there is little evidence of Brotherhood political activism on the ground in Qatar against the government. Yet, younger elements of the original Qatari Brotherhood who did not agree with the decision to dissolve the group may be engaged in underground activity. Although Qatar asked some Brotherhood members to leave Doha because of their political activities, only 10 or fewer have done so according to Brotherhood leaders and Qatari officials. "*We have not asked them to leave in any way, and we have not bothered them in any way,*" the official said.[32]

Relations between Egypt and Qatar turned hostile in 2013 when the Egyptian popular revolution, supported by the military, ousted Mohamed Morsi of the Muslim Brotherhood. Having cultivated the Brotherhood as an ally in regional politics, Qatar sharply criticised the military takeover and provided a haven for Brotherhood leaders in exile. The Gulf monarchies, led by Saudi Arabia and the United Arab Emirates, are major sponsors of Egypt's new military-backed government, and until now, have pressed hard for Qatar to fall in line with them. Saudi Arabia, to mend the dispute and unite all the Sunni Arab states against the influence of Shi'a Iran, brokered a partial conciliation between Egypt and Qatar. As a result of the pressures exercised by King Abdullah of Saudi Arabia, Qatar asked several of the MB leaders to leave and look for an alternate save haven "to avoid causing any embarrassment for the state of Qatar".[33] However, Qatar resumed its bitter criticism of the Egyptian government soon after the death of King Abdulla of Saudi Arabia. Abdul Latif al-Zayani, Secretary General of the GCC, rejected Egyptian accusations of Qatar destabilizing Egypt, and said in a statement: "*These accusations do not help to consolidate Arab solidarity at a time when Arab countries are subjected to major challenges to their security, stability and sovereignty.*"[34] On the same day, the Gulf Cooperation Council issued a press release and denied the secretary general's statement.

The Muslim Brotherhood in Kuwait

Kuwait has similar internal political dynamics to Bahrain, as several members of the opposition in the Kuwaiti parliament, known as "Islamic stream", support the MB. The

Kuwaiti leadership and government face fierce opposition and criticism in the parliament when channeling economic assistance to Egypt after the overthrow of the MB in Egypt. The extent of the political challenge for the MB across the Gulf is seen in Kuwait and Bahrain where the MB openly maintains political societies. Kuwait's Islamic Constitutional Movement (ICM), the political wing of Kuwait's MB, has observed an opposition boycott of the parliament since the emir unilaterally changed the electoral system in 2012. This has been a costly strategy, depriving the movement of the benefits that accrue from legislative presence, both in publicity and being able to access government revenue streams, jobs and contracts. It has also left them without the parliamentary platform to confront policies that will be damaging to their future, such as, the current purge of MB from the Ministry of Awqaf and Islamic Affairs and the constraints placed on MB and Salafi charitable activities. In Kuwait, Salafi loyalists have maintained representation in parliament and enjoy excellent relations with the Kuwait government.

The Kuwaiti Muslim Brotherhood is a superbly organised and extraordinarily wealthy monolith that has, at various times, worked both with and against the ruling family. Its political fortunes increased significantly following the 1990-1991 Iraqi occupation when local Islamist associations and figures organised resistance activities and community services. More recently, the Brotherhood's political wing, the ICM, also known by its Arabic acronym *Hadas*, joined other opposition groups in 2014, in major protests against a government ruling on electoral procedures. Hadas's proven willingness to work with opposition factions, combined with its potential to benefit from the growing strength of more-conservative tribal elements of Kuwaiti society, suggest that the group will pose an increasing challenge to the ruling family's monopolization on power going forward.[35] The threat of political retribution against its numerous charities and civil society organizations has led the Kuwaiti MB to take the momentous decision to separate the political apparatus represented by the ICM from the "Nizam" or mother organization. While this is expected to be an ongoing process, the ICM already has independent decision making authority, and has plans to accept non-MB members in the future.

In Kuwait, the MB has consistently been in the coalition of political societies, protesting initially for the resignation of the prime minister, and later for constitutional amendments to further empower the parliament toward the creation of a full parliamentary monarchy.[36]

The Muslim Brotherhood in Oman

In Oman, Brotherhood influence is limited by the group's Sunni roots. Unlike in most other Gulf States, Sunnis make up a minority (15-20 percent) of the Omani citizenry, this is mostly Ibadi Muslim. Nevertheless, the Brotherhood does operate secretly there, and the government has taken action against it in the past. In 1994, authorities arrested hundreds of individuals presumably linked to the Brotherhood, charging them with subversion. Those tried in court included a former ambassador to the United States, a former air force commander, and two undersecretaries of government ministries, suggesting that key Brotherhood figures permeated high levels of government. Given its limited appeal to most Omanis, the Brotherhood should be viewed as a wider threat to the government but only when collaborating with other groups. The most likely impetus for such collaboration would be the unexpected departure of Sultan Qaboos bin Said, who has been ruling the country for nearly forty-three years. Without a publicly identified successor, his removal could signal a reopening of old political fissures.[37]

The above-mentioned factors led to the conservative stand of the Omani political system towards the Gulf crackdown policy against the MB. Yet it remains an open question whether Gulf political authorities have provided sufficient alternative pathways for engagement with MB's constituencies. State-affiliated Ulama have been losing credibility for decades, and new formations to counter the MB, such as the Emirati-based Muslim Council of Elders, have yet to prove their popular appeal. This leaves the Islamic political field "up for grabs" at exactly the time it faces its most formidable existential threat: the Islamic State.[38]

The Fall of the Muslim Brotherhood

One of the political observers attributed the Egyptian 30 June popular revolution, to a rejection of its policies at the popular level and a failure to adapt to the evolution of the Egyptian society that tried to unilaterally force unpopular changes. One of them stressed that the Brotherhood had governed in an exclusionary fashion after resuming power.[39] The Brotherhood had gained power because Egyptians voted with their hearts and not their minds; they thought the Brotherhood to be pious and good people. At the same time, they criticised American policymakers who trusted the Brotherhood's promises of moderation.[40] The Brotherhood had proven itself to be incompetent at national governance, constantly adopting a narrative of victimization rather than recognizing their own shortcomings. The Brotherhood failed to understand that its position in power depended on popular support and believed elections had granted them total legitimacy. It has been called: "dictatorship of the majority."[41]

The Arab Gulf States played a crucial role in the economic stability of Egypt after the 30 June 2013 revolution against MB rule. The huge economic assistance program was a clear message that most of the GCC states were fully supportive of the Egyptian will to get rid of the MB surge in the Middle East. One political observer described the bitter mental state of the Brotherhood in Saudi Arabia after Morsi's fall as a "shattered dream syndrome" and argued that these teachings made many young people hate their countries and could yet inhibit national development around the region.[42]

References

Abdulla, Abdulkhaleq. "Gulf Perspectives on the Muslim Brotherhood." Paper presented at a meeting for the Brookings Doha Center (BDC), Doha, 9 October 2013.

Al-Sadiq, Mohamed. "Saudi Arabia and the Muslim Brotherhood: a conditional return," *Middle East Monitor*, 18 February 2015.

Boghardt, Lori Plotkin. "The Muslim Brotherhood in the Gulf: Prospects for Agitation," Washington D.C.: The Washington Institute, Policy Watch, paper number 2087, 10 June 2013.

Botros, Maged. "Politics and Religion." paper presented at an annual international conference for Aarhus University, Aarhus, Denmark, 23-25 May 2013.

Coates, Kristian Ulrichsen. Egypt-Gulf Ties and a Changing Balance of regional Security, Houston: Institute for Public Policy, Rice University, 12 January 2015.

Danziger, James. Understanding the Political World. Boston: Pearson, 2013.

Diwan, Kristin Smith. "The future of the Muslim Brotherhood in the Gulf", *The Washington Post*, 16 March 2015.

Heck, Gene W. When Worlds Collide. Lanham: Rowman and Littlefield Publishers, Inc., 2007.

Husain, Mir. Global Islamic Politics. New York: Longman, 2003.

International Religious Freedom Report 2009. U.S. Department of State, October26, 2009.

Kepel, Gilles. The War for Muslim Minds: Islam and the West. Cambridge: Belknap Press, 2006.

Kirkpatrick, David D. "Gulf Leaders Back Qatar in Its Feud with Egypt." *The New York Times*, February 20, 2015.

Kirkpatrick, David D. "Gulf States and Qatar Gloss Over Differences, but Split Still Hampers Them." *The New York Times*, 20 December 2014.

Loveluck, Louisa. "Qatar asks Muslim Brotherhood members to leave country." *The Telegraph*, 13 September 2014.

Shobokshi, Hussein. "Gulf Perspectives on the Muslim Brotherhood." Paper presented at a meeting for the Brookings Doha Center (BDC), Doha, 9 October 2013.

Sultan, Jassim. "Gulf Perspectives on the Muslim Brotherhood." Paper presented at a meeting for the Brookings Doha Center (BDC), Doha, 9 October 2013.

Steinberg, Guido. "Gulf States and the Muslim Brotherhood." Paper presented at a meeting for the German Institute for International and Security Affairs, Berlin, 21 March 2014.

The Economist "The Muslim Brothers and the Gulf. Under the gun." 2 Apr 2014.

The Middle East Media Research Institute, MEMRI. (Washington DC.: May 13, 2015), Clip No. 4926.

Notes

1 James Danziger, Understanding the Political World (Boston: Pearson, 2013), 96.

2 Gene W. Heck, When Worlds Collide (Lanham: Rowman and Littlefield Publishers, Inc., 2007), 103.

3 *Mir Husain, Global Islamic Politics (New York: Longman, 2003), 125-130. The Middle East Media Research Institute, MEMRI. (Washington DC.: May 13, 2015), Clip No. 4926.*

4 Maged Botros, "Politics and Religion" (paper presented at an annual international conference for Aarhus University, Aarhus, Denmark, May 23-25, 2013).

5 Kristian Coates Ulrichsen, Egypt-Gulf Ties and a Changing Balance of regional Security (Houston: Institute for Public Policy, Rice University, January 12, 2015)

6 Lori Plotkin Boghardt, The Muslim Brotherhood in the Gulf: Prospects for Agitation, (Washington D.C.: The Washington Institute, Policy Watch, paper number 2087, June 10, 2013).

7 Kristin Smith Diwan, "The future of the Muslim Brotherhood in the Gulf", *The Washington Post*, March 16, 2015.

8 Ibid.

9 Jassim Sultan, Gulf Perspectives on the Muslim Brotherhood, (Doha: the Brookings Doha Center (BDC), October 9, 2013).

10 Botros, "Politics and Religion."

11 Hussein Shobokshi, Gulf Perspectives on the Muslim Brotherhood, (Doha: the Brookings Doha Center (BDC), October 9, 2013).

12   Diwan, "The future of the Muslim Brotherhood in the Gulf."
13   Guido Steinberg. "Gulf States and the Muslim Brotherhood," (Berlin: German Institute for International and Security Affairs, March 21, 2014).
14   Mohamed Al-Sadiq, "Saudi Arabia and the Muslim Brotherhood: a conditional return", *Middle East Monitor*, February 18, 2015.
15   Gilles Kepel, The War for Muslim Minds: Islam and the West. (Cambridge: Belknap Press, 2006), 173–74.
16   Boghardt, "The Muslim Brotherhood in the Gulf: Prospects for Agitation."
17   Al-Sadiq, "Saudi Arabia and the Muslim Brotherhood: a conditional return."
18   Ibid.
19   Steinberg, "Gulf States and the Muslim Brotherhood."
20   Shobokshi, "Gulf Perspectives on the Muslim Brotherhood."
21   The Economist, "The Muslim Brothers and the Gulf. Under the gun," 2 April 2014.
22   Al-Sadiq, "Saudi Arabia and the Muslim Brotherhood: a conditional return."
23   Boghardt, "The Muslim Brotherhood in the Gulf: Prospects for Agitation."
24   David D. Kirkpatrick, "Gulf States and Qatar Gloss Over Differences, but Split Still Hampers Them", *The New York Times*, Dec. 20, 2014.
25   Diwan, The future of the Muslim Brotherhood in the Gulf.
26   Boghardt, The Muslim Brotherhood in the Gulf: Prospects for Agitation.
27   U.S. Department of State, *International Religious Freedom Report 2009*, (October26, 2009).
28   Diwan, "The future of the Muslim Brotherhood in the Gulf."
29   Boghardt, "The Muslim Brotherhood in the Gulf: Prospects for Agitation."
30   Ulrichsen, "Egypt-Gulf Ties and a Changing Balance of regional Security."
31   Kirkpatrick, "Gulf States and Qatar Gloss Over Differences, but Split Still Hampers Them."
32   Louisa Loveluck, "Qatar asks Muslim Brotherhood members to leave country", *The Telegraph*, September 13, 2014.
33   Ibid.
34   David D. Kirkpatrick, "Gulf Leaders Back Qatar in Its Feud with Egypt", *The New York Times*, February 20, 2015, A10
35   Boghardt, The Muslim Brotherhood in the Gulf: Prospects for Agitation.
36   Diwan, "The future of the Muslim Brotherhood in the Gulf."
37   Boghardt, "The Muslim Brotherhood in the Gulf: Prospects for Agitation."
38   Diwan, "The future of the Muslim Brotherhood in the Gulf."
39   Shobokshi, "Gulf Perspectives on the Muslim Brotherhood."
40   Abdulkhaleq Abdulla, "Gulf Perspectives on the Muslim Brotherhood" (paper presented at a meeting for the Brookings Doha Center (BDC), Doha, October 9, 2013).
41   Ibid.
42   Shobokshi, "Gulf Perspectives on the Muslim Brotherhood."

3

Saudi-Egyptian Relations in Historical Perspective: The Foundations of a Solid Entente

Elie Podeh

Introduction

In April 2012, Saudi Arabia closed its embassy in Cairo in response to Egyptian demonstrations in front of the embassy protesting the detention of an Egyptian lawyer in Saudi Arabia. In June that year, the election of President Muhammad Mursi, a leading member of the Muslim Brotherhood, exacerbated the political and ideological differences between Egypt and the Saudi Wahhabi-led dynasty, and the relations between the two countries deteriorated further as a result. Still, a mere two years later, on September 8, 2014, Saudi Foreign Minister Sa'ud al-Faysal inaugurated in Cairo what is considered to be the largest Saudi embassy in the world, and on the following day, al-Azhar Institute bestowed an honorary posthumous doctorate upon the late Saudi King 'Abdallah. More than a symbolic act, the opening of the new embassy was a true manifestation of the recovered warmth in Egyptian-Saudi relations, triggered by Mursi's removal from power (July 2013) and 'Abd al-Fattah Sisi's election (June 2014). The political and economic rapprochement was buttressed by the two countries' shared interests vis-à-vis several regional crises such as in Syria, Yemen and the Gulf. King Salman, who assumed the throne after the death of King Adballah in January 2015, introduced some important changes in the Saudi regional foreign policy, yet it seems that the Egyptian-Saudi alliance remains strong.

The aim of this article is to place current Saudi-Egyptian relations in historical perspective. It advances two arguments: First, in spite of occasional conflicts and divisions, the Saudi-Egyptian alliance has historically proven itself to be the most solid axis in the Arab political system. And, second, Saudi-Egyptian relations have been affected – mainly from the Saudi side – not only by realist but also ideational considerations.

Saudi-Egyptian Relations: A Historical Note

Saudi Arabia's foreign policy in the Middle East region is mainly driven by security concerns. The ceaseless quest for security, as one writer put it,[1] emanates from the kingdom's geographical vulnerability (its long borders), which hampers its ability to defend its rich oil fields. The kingdom's external security dilemma is compounded by domestic security concerns, specifically the need to safeguard the stability, legitimacy and survival of the Saudi royal elite. At the same time, Saudi Arabia harbors hegemonic aspirations in the Arabian Peninsula, perceived as a Saudi *Lebensraum*. Traditionally, Saudi's role in the Arab and Middle Eastern system focused on preventing the emergence of regional hegemons through the use of balancing and bandwagoning tactics.[2] Occasionally, however, and particularly in the post-oil boom era of the 1970s, Saudi decisions makers entertained notions of Arab leadership to fill regional power vacuums. These aspirations manifested themselves in various mediation attempts in Arab crises in Lebanon, Iraq and Palestine, as well as the launching of two initiatives to resolve the Arab-Israeli conflict (the Fahd Plan, proposed in1981-82, and the 'Abdallah Initiative, proposed in 2002).[3] Yet, Saudi foreign policy cannot be explained only in realist terms. The Saudi elite have always been concerned by ideational or ideological threats as well – be it Arabism or Islam – which pose a challenge to the Saudi legitimacy. According to Lawrence Rubin, states engage in ideational balancing in response to ideological threats, through media technologies, transnational networks, and the manipulation of symbols.[4]

Relations between Egypt and Saudi Arabia since the early twentieth century can be divided into eight stages. The first period, characterized by animosity and rivalry, commenced with the conquest and expulsion of the Hashemites from the Hijaz in 1926 by 'Abd al-'Aziz bin Sa'ud. While the eviction of the Hashemites from the Muslim holy places in Mecca and Medina by the Saudis also served Egyptian regional interests well, as it reduced Hashemite influence over the newly established states of Iraq and Trans-Jordan, Egypt and other Arab Sunni political entities abhorred the idea that the holy sites were under the control of the rival Wahhabi movement, a religious creed that belongs to the radical Hanbali School. Despite the shared political interest, two issues soured the relations between Egypt's King Fu'ad and King Ibn Sa'ud in this period: The first was the fact that both kings attempted to install themselves as Caliph of all Muslims. After this position was abolished by Mustafa Kemal (Ata Turk) in 1924, two rival Islamic conferences were held in Cairo and Mecca in 1926 with the aim of selecting a Caliph, but neither succeeded in achieving the desired aim. The second issue of contention was the Egyptian tradition of a dispatching the *mahmal* who carried the *kiswa* (holy carpet) for the holy *Ka'aba* in Mecca.[5] When the Saudis conquered the Hijaz, the Egyptian *mahmal* was attacked by Wahhabi Bedouin, several of whom were killed by the Egyptian soldiers accompanying the delegation. In retaliation, Ibn Sa'ud refused to allow the *mahmal* to be accompanied by Egyptian soldiers. Fu'ad responded by refusing to recognize Ibn Sa'ud's rule and stopped payments to the *waqfs* of the holy sites.[6]

Despite of these clashes, Egypt and Saudi Arabia signed a Treaty of Friendship in May 1936, in which the former recognized the latter as a free and independent state. The treaty was part of a series of Saudi agreements with other Arab players, including Iraq, which were meant to consolidate recognition of the newly-found Saudi state.[7] This treaty opened the second period, which lasted for almost two decades (1936-1956), which was characterized by growing cooperation between Egypt and Saudi Arabia, which was based on their shared fear of Hashemite dynastic plans: The Saudis were concerned by the Hashemite desire to reconquer their forefather's land in the Hijaz, while the Egyptians were concerned by more general Hashemite aspirations to attain hegemony in the Arab world. A series of Hashemite initiatives for unity (the Greater Syria and Fertile Crescent Plans) triggered by Foreign Minister Anthony Eden's May 1941 speech and promise of British support for an Arab unity scheme, prompted a Saudi-Egyptian alliance to block any potential domination scheme.[8] When the idea of establishing an Arab League crystallized in Arab consultations of 1943-1945, Ibn Sa'ud reluctantly pledged his support only after he became convinced that Egypt intended to support a loose association of independent states rather than a genuine union.[9] Articulating a profound understanding of realpolitik, Ibn Sa'ud told the British that he preferred a balance of power system in the Arab world similar to the one existing in Europe.

The anti-Hashemite bloc in the Arab world (which also included Syria) continued to operate in concert even after King Faruq's monarchy was overthrown in July 1952 by an army coup, and Sa'ud assumed the throne after the death of his father Ibn Sa'ud in November 1953. The establishment in 1955 of the Baghdad Pact, a Western-led defense organization in which Iraq played a pivotal role, sparked a vicious Arab cold war.[10] Though the organization was ostensibly aimed at containing the Soviet and communist menace, both Egypt and Saudi Arabia were concerned that the Baghdad Pact would be used as a lever to achieve Iraqi-Hashemite hegemony in the Arab world that would eventually build and use its military independently to recover the Hijaz and avenge the Hashemite defeat at the hands of Ibn Sa'ud.[11] Led by the charismatic 'Abd al-Nasser, the tripartite coalition of Egypt, Syria and Saudi Arabia, buttressed by bilateral agreements, invested great efforts to prevent other Arab states from joining the defense organization. In their desire to isolate Iraq in the Arab world, Egypt and Saudi Arabia developed a division of labor: While the former employed its diplomatic, media and intelligence apparatuses to this end, the latter used its "gold diplomacy" – that is, disbursing financial incentives to political leaders in target states. The apex of their cooperation was in December 1955, when the two states cooperated in preventing Jordan from joining the Baghdad Pact.[12]

A series of events triggered the third stage, which lasted from 1956 to the June 1967 War. The first buds of a change in the Egyptian-Saudi alliance appeared concurrently with the growing popularity in the Arab world of 'Abd al-Nasser and his pan-Arab ideology, which posed an ideational security dilemma to the Saudi elite, as it threatened the kingdom's very stability and legitimacy. A formal rupture between Egypt and Saudi Arabia followed the nationalization of Suez Canal Company in July 1956 and the Suez War, which — notwithstanding Egypt's military defeat — established 'Abd al-Nasser as the undisputed leader of the Arab world. Pan-Arabism and Nasserism helped to heal the Saudi-Hashemite conflict, which had been a major feature of Arab politics for more than 30 years, leading to the formation of the royalist coalition comprising Iraq, Jordan and Saudi Arabia.[13] King Sa'ud's support of the American Eisenhower Doctrine in early 1957, as well as his renewal of the lease on the US Air Force base at Dhahran, were further indications of Saudi Arabia's new regional orientation.[14]

During this decade, Saudi Arabia remained firmly within the royalist anti-Nasser coalition. The cold war between Egypt and Saudi Arabia, which manifested itself as a union between Egypt and Syria (the United Arab Republic, 1958-1961), deteriorated into a hot war when Egypt sent military forces to Yemen, when newly-crowned Imam Muhammad al-Badr was deposed by a coup d'état in September 1962. From 1964, under King Faysal, the Saudis feared that an Egyptian victory in Yemen would serve as a springboard for Nasserist ambitions in the Arabian Peninsula and control of its oil fields. In many respects, the six-year Yemeni civil war that ended in 1968 was a proxy Saudi-Egyptian war between royalists (who allied with Saudi Arabia) and republicans (allied with Egypt), with as many as 70,000 Egyptian troops deployed in Yemen at the peak of the military confrontation. Despite several military moves and peace conferences, the war sank into a stalemate, until Egypt was compelled to withdraw from Yemen following its own devastating defeat and the loss of Sinai in 1967.[15] An offshoot of the Egyptian-Saudi rivalry over Yemen was Faysal's attempt in 1965-1966 to forge a regional bloc of Jordan, Iran and Turkey, based on Islamic identity, under Saudi leadership with American backing. Thus, Saudi Arabia countered Nasser's pan-Arab ideational threat by heightening Islamic identity. In pursuance of this strategy, the Organization of the Islamic Conference (OIC) was established by the Saudis in 1969.[16]

The fourth period extended from the 1967 War to Anwar al-Sadat's visit to Jerusalem in November 1977. This decade was characterized by Egypt's growing economic and financial dependence on Saudi Arabia (as well as on Libya and other Gulf countries). As a result of Egypt's humiliating defeat, the 1967 Khartoum and 1969 Rabat Arab Summit conferences promised financial support from the rich oil countries to the "confrontation states" with Israel. As the war demolished Nasser's pretensions for Arab hegemony, King Faysal was no longer threatened by Nasserism. Moreover, after Nasser's sudden death in September 1970 and the election of his relatively unknown deputy, Sadat, Saudi Arabia gained direct leverage over Egypt through generous financial aid and by lobbying for American support of Sadat's political claims in the conflict with Israel. The fact that Sadat also distanced himself from the country's Nasserist legacy and the Soviet Union in the early 1970s served Saudi interests. In contrast to his predecessor, Sadat was amenable to opening a new chapter in relations with Faysal, based on equality between their countries and recognition of Riyadh's leading position in the Arabian Peninsula.[17] It was hardly a surprise, therefore, that an Egyptian-Saudi (and Syrian) axis developed in the 1973 War: on 20 October, King Faysal announced an embargo on oil shipments to the US. In light of the fact that Libya and Iraq did not join the embargo, the Saudi démarche was indeed noteworthy.[18] Egypt and Saudi Arabia also cooperated in ending the Lebanese civil war in late 1976. The mini-Arab Summit in Riyadh and the all-Arab Summit in Cairo fashioned a package deal that confirmed Syria's hegemony in Lebanon at the expense of the PLO. Saudi Arabia played the role of arbiter, facilitating reconciliation between Sadat and Asad.[19]

The fifth period commenced with Sadat's visit to Jerusalem in November 1977 and lasted until the end of the following decade. Like other Arab states, the Saudi kingdom was surprised by Sadat's unexpected move and, in light of calls by the radical Arab states led by Iraq and Syria to boycott Egypt, attempted to dissuade Sadat from signing a separate peace with Israel. The Saudis were caught in a dilemma: on the one hand, the tremendous impact of Sadat's initiative and its American backing seemed to offer a genuine opportunity to achieve a breakthrough toward a settlement, as the Saudis desired. On the other hand, Sadat's move shattered the Arab consensus that had developed after the Lebanese imbroglio. Therefore, in this stage of the relationship the Saudis sought to maintain open channels of communication with Egypt and the radical states in hope of bringing them together if Egypt's initiative failed. When Sadat crossed the Rubicon and signed the Camp David Accords in September 1978, Saudi Arabia could no longer support Sadat. That November, the Baghdad Arab Summit drafted a series of resolutions boycotting Egypt. When Egypt and Israel signed a peace treaty on March 26, 1979, the resolutions came into effect and Saudi Arabia joined 16 other Arab states in severing diplomatic relations with Egypt. Furthermore, Saudi Arabia and the Gulf Emirates halted all direct aid to Egypt for civil and military purposes.[20] In practice, however, Saudi Arabia and GCC countries found it difficult to fully implement the Baghdad resolutions, particularly its financial provisions, in light of Egypt's centrality in the Arab world, the impact of the Iranian Shi'i revolution (1979), and the protracted Iran-Iraq War (1980-1988). The fact that Husni Mubarak, who was not personally associated with the peace treaty, became president following Sadat's assassination in October 1981, helped repair the rift between Egypt, Saudi Arabia and other Arab countries, and by 1989, Egypt had been re-admitted to the Arab League and all the Arab states including Saudi Arabia, re-established diplomatic relations with it.[21]

The sixth period opened with the Iraqi conquest of Kuwait in August 1990, which led to an Egyptian-Saudi (and Arab in general) rapprochement. The Arab Summit in Cairo on August 10 was marked by the bold determination of the Arab majority coalition — led by Egypt, Saudi Arabia and Syria — to adopt the resolutions necessary to legitimize Arab and international action against Iraq. Member states condemned the Iraqi attack and agreed to dispatch Arab forces to defend the Gulf States against "any Arab aggression." Consequently, Egypt, Syria and Morocco sent troops to Saudi Arabia. Egypt's participation in the anti-Iraqi coalition was reciprocated by writing off $14 billion of its external debt - $7 billion by the GCC States, and the other 7 billion by the US.[22] Following the Western-led operation "Desert Storm" to liberate Kuwait, a pan-Arab security arrangement was signed by Egypt, Syria and the GCC States on March 6, 1991, which stipulated that Egypt and Syria would provide the nucleus of an Arab peace-making force in the Gulf in return for financial aid. Although the declaration had little operational value, it did give expression to the newly established tripartite Arab coalition.[23] The Kuwaiti episode and the resulting Israeli-Arab peace process solidified Egypt's role as the first among equals in the Arab system, and revived the tripartite coalition of Egypt, Syria and Saudi Arabia.[24]

The renewed Egyptian-Saudi alliance that was sparked by the Kuwaiti episode lasted for two decades until Mubarak's fall in 2011. Mubarak made more than 30 visits to the Saudi kingdom between 1981 and 2007.[25] In contrast to Nasser's Egypt, which claimed leadership in championing Arab revolution and independence from the West, Mubarak's Egypt promoted itself as moderator and stabilizer of the Arab world. The Saudi-Egyptian alliance in this period was based on mutual interests in containing the Iranian threat and the spread of Shi'i fundamentalism. The Iranian revolution posed both a regional and a domestic challenge for Saudi Arabia; also, it was perceived not only as a political threat but also as an ideological threat. Ayatollah Khomeini castigated monarchies in general as un-Islamic, to which the Shi'i minority in Saudi Arabia's oil-rich eastern province of al-Hasa responded with protests and demonstrations. According to Guase, "Riyadh has tended to balance against the potential source of domestic threat and support the more conventionally 'powerful' but not obviously threatening actor in regional disputes."[26] Saudi Arabia was also concerned by the changes in Iraq following the US conquest in April 2003. Until then, under various Sunni leaders, Iraq had constituted an Arab bulwark against the spread of Shi'ism and against Iran's aggrandizement policy in the Gulf and the Arab world, but now it not only threatened to complete a circle of Shi'i countries surrounding Saudi Arabia, but also to open the door to growing Shi'i Iranian involvement in domestic Iraqi affairs. Although Egypt did not have a similar sectarian element that opposed the Iranian regime, Iran's growing influence in the Arab system in general, and in the Gulf area in particular, threatened Egypt's perceived leadership role in regional politics.[27] Thus, a combination of pragmatic and ideological considerations led Saudi Arabia, Egypt, and the Gulf countries — with the exception of Qatar and Oman — to forge an anti-Iranian and anti-Shi'i alliance, whose policy included a mixture of conciliatory and aggressive measures against Iran.[28]

The Israeli war against the Hizballah in the summer of 2006 further highlighted the shared interests of the Sunni Arab countries of Egypt, Jordan, Saudi Arabia, and the GCC, all of which would have been pleased to see the Iranian- and Syrian-backed Shi'i organization receive a serious blow by Israel. Israel's disappointing performance in the war heightened concerns of the formation of a Shi'i Crescent — a term coined by Jordan's King 'Abdallah II in late 2004 — extending from Damascus to Tehran, through Baghdad, where a Shia-dominated government had assumed power and was dictating a sectarian brand of politics reverberating across the region.[29]

Egypt's declining influence in the Arab world was concomitant with its growing economic reliance on Saudi Arabia and the Gulf Sheikhdoms, and in this period of the Egyptian-Saudi relationship, between 1991 and 2011, Saudi exports to and imports from Egypt increased tenfold. Though not considered a major partner of Saudi Arabia in terms of overall trade, Egypt is Saudi Arabia's third or fourth foremost Arab trading partner, after Bahrain, the Emirates and Jordan.[30] In 2008, Egypt's volume of trade with Saudi

Arabia accounted for more than a third of its total commerce with the Arab world. More importantly, in this period Saudi Arabia became the single largest investor in Egypt: By 2009, approximately 2,500 Saudi companies had invested almost $11 billion, which helped to restrain Egyptian unemployment levels. In 2009, Egypt also earned some $9.5 billion in expatriate remittances from its approximately one million Egyptian workers living in the kingdom.[31]

As Egypt's role in the Arab world declined as a result of domestic problems, Saudi Arabia under 'Abdallah (first as Crown Prince and since 2005 as King) found itself assuming a major Arab role in the Israeli-Arab peace process (the Saudi Peace Initiative was proposed in February 2002 and later remodeled as the Arab Peace Initiative in March 2002) and in Palestinian politics (the Mecca Agreement was signed between Fatah and Hamas in February 2007). The Saudi dynasty worked diligently to rehabilitate its reputation following the involvement of 15 Saudi citizens in the 9/11 attacks, and turned Saudi Arabia into the most important US Arab ally, challenging Egypt's status in this role. Despite this rivalry, Mubarak's Egypt and 'Abdallah's Saudi Arabia shared mutual interests in preventing Iran from acquiring nuclear capability, reducing Shi'i influence in key Arab countries, and making progress in the Israeli-Palestinian arena.[32]

Egyptian-Saudi Relations Following the Arab Spring

The seventh period in Egyptian-Saudi relations began with the Egyptian Revolution of January 25, 2011 and Mubarak's downfall. This period should be divided into two distinct phases: the first lasted until Muhammad Mursi, the first democratically elected president representing the Muslim Brotherhood (Freedom and Justice Party), was overthrown in June 2013; and the second has extended from 'Abd al-Fattah al-Sisi's rise to power as leader and president of the republic, to the present. The 2011 Revolution in Egypt, occurring two weeks after the ousting of the Tunisian president, was received with unease and apprehension in Saudi Arabia and the Gulf. Understandably, the Saudi elite feared a similar wave of protests in the kingdom that would threaten the stability and very survival of the al-Sa'ud dynasty. No wonder that King 'Abdallah's immediate response was to support Mubarak's regime, stating that "no Arab and Muslim person can allow some infiltrators among the Egyptian people to disrupt Egypt's security and stability in the name of freedom of expression."[33] At the same time, the King urged the US administration to stop pressing Mubarak to submit his resignation in response to popular demand. Mubarak's regime was also supported by the GCC countries, excluding Qatar. Spread of popular demonstrations to neighboring Syria, Libya and Yemen after Mubarak's fall reinforced the view of the Saudi elite that the Arab Spring was a contagious element that could cause a domino effect and undermine the kingdom's stability.[34]

Saudi and Gulf support of Mubarak triggered hostility on the streets of Cairo during the 18 days of the revolution. Rumors that Saudi Arabia was offering asylum to Mubarak further incited the masses, and the Saudi ambassador was temporarily recalled in April 2012, following attacks on the embassy in protest of mistreatment of Egyptian pilgrims in Saudi Arabia and the jailing of an Egyptian lawyer. In May, however, the visit of a large parliamentary delegation to Saudi Arabia managed to defuse the crisis and bring the ambassador back to Cairo in May. Despite several "disconcerting" statements by Egyptian officials, including the new foreign minister, Nabil al-'Arabi, calling for a more neutral Egyptian policy in the region, al-'Arabi and Prime Minister Essam Sharaf visited Saudi Arabia, Kuwait and Qatar, where they reconfirmed Egypt's continued commitment to Gulf security vis-à-vis Iran and received assurances of financial aid.[35]

The election of Mursi, the representative of the Muslim Brotherhood, to presidency in June 2012 threatened to cause a new rupture in Egyptian-Saudi relations. Although the kingdom had given support, including political asylum, to Muslim Brotherhood activists during the Nasserite period, the relations between the Brotherhood and the Saudi kingdom had been strained by the organization's opposition to the Western-led liberation of Kuwait in 1991. Furthermore, throughout the 1990s, a Brotherhood-inspired opposition movement in Saudi Arabia, known as *al-Sahwa al-Islamiyya* ("the Islamic Awakening"), had challenged the kingdom by calling for Islamic reforms. The Saudis also placed the blame for the involvement of 15 Saudi citizens in the 9/11 attacks on the doctrinal activism advocated by the Brotherhood and particularly their important ideologue Sayed Qutb. Minister of Interior Na'if bin 'Abd al-'Aziz, somewhat unjustifiably, laid the blame for all the problems of Saudi Arabia and the Arab world on the shoulders of the Muslim Brotherhood. As a result, the victory of the Islamic *al-Nahda* Party in Tunisia and the Brotherhood's rise to power in Egypt were considered major challenges to the ideological and political orientation of the Wahhabi-led Saudi regime. The fact that these Brotherhood-backed parties came to power through the ballot box suggested that Islam and democracy are not incompatible.[36] These outcomes of the Arab Spring threatened to undermine the Saudi monopoly on Islamic politics, as manifested in its control of the OIC and its responsibility for the Islamic holy shrines in Mecca and Medina.

The fragility of the Saudi-Egyptian relationship was not lost on newly-elected Mursi: During his brief one-year term in office, he visited Saudi Arabia no less than three times – the first, only 11 days after he was sworn in as president in June 2012. He next visited the country in late August to attend the OIC Summit in Mecca; and finally, he attended the Arab Summit for Economic and Social Development in Saudi Arabia in January 2013.[37] In an attempt to allay Saudi suspicions, Mursi made all the "correct" expected statements, such as that Egypt had no intention to "export the revolution"— a phrase reminiscent of the Iranian Revolution ideology — and that the security of the Gulf was Egypt's "red line." Still, other activities attested to a more even-handed Egyptian policy in regional, and perhaps international, affairs. Mursi visited Tehran on the occasion of the Non-Aligned Movement Summit in August — the first visit by an Egyptian president since the 1979 revolution; Iranian President Ahmadinejad made a return visit to Cairo in February 2013. Moreover, while attending the OIC Summit in Mecca in August, Mursi invited Iran to join a quartet with Egypt, Turkey and Saudi Arabia to explore resolutions of the civil war in Syria. The Saudis, suspicious of Mursi's possible drift toward Iran,[38] were reluctant to participate in this initiative, thereby sealing its fate. Although Saudi Arabia and certain Gulf States had pledged financial aid to Egypt, in practice they dragged their feet in transferring the funds. In contrast, Qatar's aid package to Egypt reached $8 billion during Mursi's term in office, in addition to a five-year $18 billion investment package.[39]

Mursi's ouster by the army following mass demonstrations on June 30, 2013 was received with joy and relief by Saudi Arabia and the Gulf countries. King 'Abdallah was quick to congratulate army chief Sisi (then Minister of Defense) and the new interim president, 'Adli Mansur. Barely one week later, Saudi Arabia, the UAE, and Kuwait announced a total of $12 billion in budgetary aid, central bank support and oil products to alleviate Egypt's financial burden following the economic hardships of the Arab Spring. The quick Gulf response, in comparison to the slow aid transfers during the Mursi era, reflected the enthusiasm in which the counter-revolution was received in the Gulf, with the exception of Qatar.[40] Gulf funds allowed Egypt to suspend its unsuccessful and much-delayed negotiations with the IMF over a loan, and to repay its $2 billion loan received from Qatar. The funds also sent a clear message to the Obama Administration, which considered the new Egyptian order to be illegitimate, since it came to power through a military coup.[41] The fact that the Egyptian government declared the Muslim Brotherhood a terrorist organization in late December 2013 was received with satisfaction by the Saudi Arabia and most Gulf Sheikhdoms. In February 2014, Egyptian Prime Minister Hazem al-Beblawi met Crown Prince Salman in Riyadh with the aim of revitalizing economic aid packages provided by the kingdom to support the Egyptian economy. At a press conference during his visit, Beblawi described the relationship between the two countries as a "balancing force" for the Arab region.[42]

Upon 'Abd al-Fattah Sisi's election as president in early June 2014, Egyptian-Saudi relations warmed up instantly. On his way home from Morocco, the 90-year-old Saudi monarch 'Abdallah stopped in Cairo to meet Sisi, reportedly to demonstrate his strong support through a symbolic but brief visit,[43] and in August, Sisi made first foreign visit to Saudi Arabia. According to Saudi Foreign Minister Sa'ud al-Faysal's vague description, Sisi's talks with King 'Abdallah concerned "foreign wars, the intervention of foreign powers, inside seditions, and differences between the Arab states." The two states were also engaged in symbolic politics, as the Saudi king awarded Sisi the Abd al-'Aziz Medal, an honor previously bestowed to distinguished statesmen such as US presidents George W. Bush and Barack Obama.[44] The Saudi gesture was made in response to the honorary doctorate granted to King 'Abdallah by al-Azhar University in July 2014, the first award granted by the institute in over two decades, in appreciation of his support for Egypt and the Islamic religion.[45] Shortly after these symbolic exchanges, the Saudi Foreign Minister inaugurated his country's largest embassy in Cairo in September, which, according to his statement, would help boost cooperation between the two Arab heavyweights.[46] The diplomatic tit-for-tat continued with an exclusive interview granted by Sisi to a Saudi paper, in which he praised Saudi Arabia for its support to Egypt following the pressure against the Muslim Brotherhood, describing King 'Abdallah as "the wise man of the Arabs," whose demand to end Mursi's rule was a well-calculated move based on an evaluation of regional developments following the Arab Spring. Sisi also expressed his gratitude to the King for his call for an international conference to extend economic support to Egypt. Eventually, over 2,000 delegates from 112 countries, including leading US, European and Arab officials attended the impressive conference in Sharm al-Sheikh on March 13-15, 2015.[47]

In late December 2014, Saudi Arabia mediated the Egyptian-Qatari rapprochement, after the two countries' intelligence chiefs met in Cairo to discuss "possible reconciliation" to end the rift that had been triggered by Doha's support for the Muslim Brotherhood after the Egyptian Revolution, including shelter given to several Brotherhood members who fled Egypt after their organization was outlawed in late 2013. One of the results of the reconciliation was the closure of the Doha-based al-Jazeera *Mubasher Misr* news channel, which had been devoted to covering news from Egypt but was known for its favorable coverage of the Muslim Brotherhood. In return, Egypt promised to release three al-Jazeera journalists who were jailed in Egypt. Saudi Arabia's role in the reconciliation, which was motivated by its desire to establish a Sunni Arab bloc against the growing Iranian threat, reflected Saudi Arabia's growing role in Arab politics.[48] Though Egypt-Qatar relations cooled off in February 2015 when Egypt accused Qatar of supporting terrorism, Sisi's meeting with the Qatari Emir Sheikh Tamim bin Hamad al-Thani on the eve of the Arab Summit in Sharm al-Sheikh in late March helped smooth the two countries' differences.[49]

Upon King 'Abdallah's death on January 23, 2015, Egypt suspended its January 25 national celebrations and announced a seven-day nationwide state of mourning. A presidential statement declared that "the Egyptian people will not forget the historical positions of King Abdullah…towards Egypt and its people."[50] As Sisi himself was unable to attend the funeral (he was attending the Davos Economic summit), the prime minister was sent instead. Sisi, however, was quick to pay an official visit to meet the newly-crowned King Salman on March 1. In his interview with the Saudi-owned satellite TV *al-'Arabiyya*, Sisi described the two countries' "long history of stability, solidarity and understanding," and commended the kingdom's supportive position during the 1973 War, the oil embargo, and the popular uprising against Mursi. He also reiterated the oft-repeated maxim that "stability of the Gulf is stability for Egypt" and his new initiative to form a joint Arab force with Saudi Arabia, the UAE and Jordan against Islamic militancy, to ensure the region's stability.[51] Beyond the warm rhetoric, the aim of Sisi's visit was to explore whether the new king was as responsive as his predecessor to the new Egyptian regime and whether the two countries continued to share mutual interests as they faced the myriad challenges in the region.

Salman's crowning seemed to herald a new period in Saudi-Egyptian relations. Khalid al-Dakhil, an important Saudi columnist in the London-based Saudi-owned *al-Hayat*, was the first to allude to the change, following the visit of Turkish President Recep Tayyip Erdoğan to Riyadh, which was concurrent to Sisi's visit: while confirming that King Salman's support for Egypt was firm, Dakhil expressed criticism of "some people in Egypt [who] would like Saudi support to take the form of gifts or an open royal grant or blank check. They don't, for instance, want Saudi Arabia to become closer to Turkey because of the latter's sympathy toward the Brotherhood…The more rational political vision is that the relations between Saudi Arabia and Egypt would not be subject to the position of the Brotherhood or the position toward Turkey. If Egypt's stability is a strategic interest for Saudi Arabia, and it is indeed so, it is the duty of Saudi Arabia to treat the issue of the Brotherhood as a fundamentally internal Egyptian problem." In Dakhil's view, the Saudi-Egyptian-Turkish troika is strategically required to serve the regional balance of power.[52]

Thus, despite of the strategic need and desire for cooperation between Egypt and Saudi Arabia, the two countries have developed different – sometimes contradictory – interests in several regional crises since Salman's crowning. For one, Saudi hostility toward the Muslim Brotherhood was now not as sharp as before as a result of its aspirations to forge a Sunni bloc, comprising also Turkey and Qatar, against Shi'i Iran; for Egypt, a rapprochement with the Muslim Brotherhood was anathema. Second, while Saudi Arabia, Turkey and Qatar sought to remove Syrian President Bashar al-Asad – a move that would also undermine the interests of Iran and Hizballah – Egypt preferred a political solution to reconcile the various opposition factions and the Asad regime. Third, Egypt's geographical proximity to Libya led it to lobby for international military action under a UN umbrella, to strengthen the legitimate government in Tobruk against the militant Islamic rebels. Unsurprisingly, Saudi Arabia was not overly concerned by developments in the remote Libyan territory.[53] Fourth, the opposite occurred on the Yemeni front, as the Saudis became highly apprehensive of the spreading civil war, which led President 'Abed al-Rabo Mansur Hadi to resign on January 22, 2015. Hadi fled to Riyadh on March 25 after the Houthis, a Shi'i Iranian-backed rebel group, seized control of the capital of Sanaa. This development soon developed into a regional hot war. In contrast to Saudi concern and involvement, Egypt's main concern was to ensure the safe passage of ships in the Bab al-Mandab straits rather than to become involved with Yemen's internal conflict.

Indeed, backed by tacit US support, the Saudis were quick to form an Arab coalition force to intervene in Yemen, comprising jet fighters from the UAE, Kuwait, Bahrain, Qatar, Jordan, Morocco and Sudan and four battleships from Egypt.[54] In an operation called Decisive Storm designed to cut the Houthi militias' line of support from Iran, the Saudi-led Arab force's main strategy was to bomb Houthi bases and forces, while imposing an aerial and sea blockade on Yemen. In contrast to Egypt's deployment of more than 30,000 troops in Operation Desert Storm in 1991, its limited participation in the recent operation in Yemen represented more of a moral gesture than significant military support stemming from a sense of obligation to defend the Sunni Arab coalition. While Egypt would not "abandon" the Gulf's security, particularly in light of Saudi financial and energy support,[55]

Egypt was unwilling to send troops against a remote Iranian-Shi'i threat while it was facing domestic turmoil.[56]

The Saudis' new aggressive regional policy was a product of the realization that only a counter-offensive in what was considered a natural Saudi sphere of influence would thwart the political and ideological threat posed by Iran and its proxies. In response to undisguised Iranian boasts of its control of four Arab capitals (Damascus, Baghdad, Beirut and now Sanaa), a Saudi advisor to the royal court, Nawaf Obaid, stated, "Saudi Arabia cannot allow Iran under any scenario to use its 'near status' as a nuclear power to expand its influence and prestige around the region."[57] In Saudi and Gulf eyes, Iran was exploiting emerging Sunni extremism — manifested in the activities and successes of al-Qa'ida, ISIS, *Jabhat al-Nusra* and others — as a pretext for normalizing its relations with the US, with the ultimate aim of achieving regional dominance. For Saudi Arabia, the emergence of an Iran-dominated Yemen that controls Aden, the Strait of Bab al-Mandab, and the Island of Socotra created a theater of Saudi-Iranian competition for regional leadership, as control over Yemen is vital for the kingdom's stability and hegemony in the Arabian Gulf.[58] In light of what was perceived US appeasement toward Iran, reflected in the US-Iranian nuclear negotiations (which culminated in an agreement in July 2015), Saudi Arabia and the GCC felt obliged to take a firm and decisive action in Yemen. However, the Sunni composition of the Arab force suggests that sectarian considerations had also been relevant in the decision to intervene in the conflict between Sunnis and Shi'is in Yemen.[59]

The Saudi-led coalition in Yemen commenced its military operations only days before the annual Arab Summit in Sharm al-Sheikh on March 28. In many ways, the decision to intervene eclipsed the summit itself and possibly embarrassed the Egyptians as it presented the operation to the Arab League as a fait accompli.[60] The final summit communiqué expressed full support for the operation, and the main resolution, which harks back to Sisi's notion of establishing an Arab force, called for the formation of a unified military force to address regional security challenges without referring directly to the Yemeni episode.[61] The resolution was meant to demonstrate that Egypt had not abandoned its perceived leadership role in the Arab system, particularly in view of the Saudi initiative in Yemen.[62] It soon became clear that the process of forming an Arab army – a step that could potentially change the regional balance of power – would be neither easy nor smooth: there are also indications that Saudi Arabia had a hand in thwarting this initiative because of Egypt's limited involvement in the Arab expedition.[63]

In spite of journalistic reports of Saudi-Egyptian disagreements on key regional issues,[64] other signs attested to the solid nature of their relations. First, in early April 2015, Saudi Arabia opened three border crossings in order to allow 7,000 Egyptian expatriates working in Yemen to flee the country.[65] Second, on April 15, Sisi met with Saudi Defense Minister Mohammad Bin Salman in Cairo to discuss the latest Saudi-led Arab airstrikes on Houthi rebels in Yemen. Sisi was quoted to the effect that the "security of the Gulf is a red line for Egypt and an integral part of its national security." At this meeting, Egypt agreed to take part in a major strategic maneuver with Saudi Arabia and other Gulf countries on Saudi territory.[66] Third, on May 3, Sisi made an unscheduled visit to Saudi Arabia, the third visit in the year since his election. The visit took place immediately after King Salman's nomination of a new Crown Prince, Interior Minister Mohammed bin Nayef, and the replacement of the perennial Foreign Minister, Sa'ud al-Faysal, with 'Adel Jubair, Saudi ambassador to Washington. It was speculated that the aim of the visit was to establish direct communications with Saudi Arabia's new generation of leaders and to discuss urgent regional issues on which the two countries do not necessarily share the same policy.[67] Fourth, several days later, King Salman pardoned 76 Egyptian prisoners who had been detained in Saudi Arabia.[68] The new Saudi Foreign Minister Jubair met his Egyptian counterpart, Samih Shukri, and Sisi in Cairo on May 31;[69] and finally, in late July 2015, Deputy Crown Prince and Minister of Defense, Muhammed bin Salman, arrived in Cairo to attend the graduation ceremony of officers from the military academy.[70]

Perhaps the most significant indication of the solid Egyptian-Saudi relations is the flow of financial aid. In the two years since Mursi's ouster in June 2013, Saudi Arabia, the UAE, and Kuwait have given Egypt considerable aid, with estimates ranging from the more conservative figure of USD 29 billion to the more extreme estimate of USD 35 billion. The aid was granted in various forms including oil shipments, cash deposits in Egypt's central bank, and investments.[71]

Conclusion

Since the early twentieth century, Egypt and Saudi Arabia, two key players in the Arab system, have occasionally vied over hegemony, but for the most part cooperated against mutual enemies and in pursuit of shared regional interests. On only three occasions did ideological and political differences divide them: First, during the Nasserite period, when secular pan-Arab ideology threatened to sweep through the Arab world, as Egyptian military forces breached the Saudi sphere of influence in Yemen; Second, when Sadat signed a separate peace treaty with Israel, and third, when Egypt democratically elected a president who belonged to the Muslim Brotherhood, an ideological rival organization. Despite these events, the Egyptian-Saudi alliance has proven itself to be the most solid and enduring political axis in the Arab system, consistently striving to achieve regional stability and equilibrium. This alliance (which was occasionally extended to include Syria) consistently sought to thwart Hashemite ambitions during the 1944-45 negotiations on the establishment of the Arab League, the invasion of Palestine in 1948, and the formation of the Baghdad Pact in 1955. This coalition (again, together with Syria) also waged war against Israel in 1973 and put an end to the Lebanese civil war in 1976. Egypt and Saudi Arabia cooperated to liberate Kuwait from Iraqi occupation in 1991. The formation of the GCC in 1981 under Saudi leadership extended the tripartite coalition further, but Syria's growing reliance on Iran led to its defection and replacement by Jordan.

During the Mubarak era (1981-2011), Egyptian-Saudi relations reflected solid collaboration on political, economic and energy issues. Yet, the winds of change blowing from Cairo in 2011 that led to the toppling of Mubarak threatened to cause a ripple effect in the monarchies.[72] Not only was the Mursi regime democratically elected, it also offered a competitive Islamic model that threatened to undermine the religious foundations of the Wahhabi-led Saudi state. No wonder that this unexpected turn of events in Egypt triggered an unexpected change in the Saudi behavior toward Egypt. The freeze in the relations was, however, quickly reversed with the counter-revolution which brought the army back to power and ousted the Muslim Brotherhood. Initially, relations between Egypt – under Sisi – and Saudi Arabia – under 'Abdallah – returned to the warmth that characterized the Mubarak era. This quick rapprochement stemmed from their mutual interest to contain Iran's hegemonic ambitions in the Middle East (which it sought to realize through Shi'i proxies in Iraq, Syria and Yemen) and to eliminate the terrorist threats of al-Qa'ida, ISIS and its Caliphate State, Jabhat al-Nusra and other Sunni jihadi groups.

Upon Salman's crowning it seemed initially that Saudi foreign policy was undergoing a certain change, leading to a widening gap between the two countries, particularly with regard to their positions on the Muslim Brotherhood, Syria, Yemen and Libya. Yet, Salman's recent five-day visit to Egypt (7-11 April 2016) is a testament to the strong relationship – one might even say the alliance – between the two countries. According to Egyptian media, no fewer than 36 agreements worth $25 billion were signed during the visit, including establishing a Saudi investment fund worth $16 billion, the creation of a free-trade zone in Sinai and building a bridge connecting Africa and Asia. On that occasion, Egypt returned to the Saudis the islands of Tiran and Sanafir, located at the entrance of the Gulf of Eilat, which were leased since 1950.[73] Thus, from a historical perspective it can be concluded that the Egyptian-Saudi alignment in the Post-Arab Spring era is a common feature of Arab politics. Although realist considerations are at the core of these relations, ideological balancing is playing a role as well.

References

Barnett N. Michael. "Regional Security after the Gulf War," *Political Science Quarterly*, Vol. 111 (1996-97).

Bayat Asef and Bahman Baktiri. "Revolutionary Iran and Egypt: Exploring Inspirations and Anxieties," in Nikki R. Keddie and Rudi Matthee (eds.), *Iran and the Surrounding World: Interactions in Culture and Cultural Politics* (Seattle: University of Washington Press, 2002).

Bradley, John. *Saudi Arabia Exposed: Inside a Kingdom in Crisis* (London: Palgrave/Macmillan, 2005).

Cantori, Louis. "Unipolarity and Egyptian Hegemony in the Middle East," in Robert O. Freedman (ed.), *The Middle East after Iraq's Invasion of Kuwait* (Gainesville: University of Florida Press, 1993).

Felci, Vittorio. "Saudi-Iranian Competition in Yemen," in Anna Maria Medici (eds.), *After the Yemeni Spring: A Survey on the Transition* (Milano: Mimesis, 2012).

Ferris. Jesse. *Nasser's Gamble: How Intervention in Yemen Caused the Six-Day War and the Decline of Egyptian Power* (Princeton: Princeton University Press, 2013).

Guase, F. Gregory. *The International Relations of the Persian Gulf* (Cambridge: Cambridge University Press, 2010).

Guase, F. Gregory. "The Foreign Policy of Saudi Arabia," in Raymond Hinnebusch and Anoushiravan Ehteshami (eds.), *The Foreign Policies of Middle East States* (Boulder: Lynne Rienner Publishers, 2002).

Maddy-Weitzman, Bruce. *The Crystallization of the Arab State System, 1945-1954* (Syracuse: Syracuse University Press, 1993).

Nonneman, Gerd. "Determinants and Patterns of Saudi Foreign Policy: 'Onmi-Balancing' and 'Relative Autonomy' in Multiple Environments," in Paul Aarts and Gerd Nonneman, *Saudi Arabia in the Balance: Political Economy, Society, Foreign Affairs* (New York: New York University Press, 2005).

Podeh, Elie. *The Quest for Hegemony in the Arab World: The Struggle over the Baghdad Pact* (Leiden: E. J. Brill, 1995).

Podeh, Elie. "Ending an Age-Old Rivalry: The Rapprochement between the Hashemites and the Saudis, 1956-1958," in Asher Susser and Aryeh Shmuelevitz (eds.), *The Hashemites in the Modern Arab World: Essays in Honor of the Late Professor Uriel Dann* (London: Frank Cass, 1995).

Podeh, Elie. "The Emergence of the Arab State System Reconsidered," *Diplomacy and Statecraft*, Vol. 9 (November 1998).

Podeh, Elie. "Iraq and the Arab System since the 2003 War: A Persistent Marginality," in Amnon Cohen and Noga Efrati (eds.), *Post-Saddam Iraq: New Realities, Old Identities, Challenging Patterns* (Brighton: Sussex Academic Press, 2011).

Podeh, Elie. *From Fahd to 'Abdallah: The Origins of the Saudi Peace Initiatives and Their Impact on the Arab System and Israel*, Gitelson Peace Publication 24 (Jerusalem: The Harry S. Truman Institute for the Advancement of Peace, 2003).

Podeh, Elie. "Israel and the Arab Peace Initiative, 2002-2014," *Middle East Journal*, Vol. 68 (2014).

Podeh Elie and Onn Winckler, *The Boycott That Never Was: Egypt and the Arab System, 1979-1989*, Durham Middle East Papers, No. 72 (December 2002).

Porath, Yehoshua. *In Search of Arab Unity, 1930-1945* (London: Frank Cass, 1986).

Rubin, Lawrence. *Islam in the Balance: Ideational Threats in Arab Politics* (Stanford: Stanford University Press, 2014).

Safran, Nadav. *Saudi Arabia – The Ceaseless Quest for Security* (Ithaca: Cornell University Press, 1988).

Sela, Avraham. *Decline of the Arab-Israeli Conflict: The Quest for Regional Order* (Albany: State University of New York Press, 1998).

Notes

1   Nadav Safran, *Saudi Arabia – The Ceaseless Quest for Security* (Ithaca: Cornell University Press, 1988).

2   See F. Gregory Gause III, "The Foreign Policy of Saudi Arabia," in Raymond Hinnebusch and Anoushiravan Ehteshami (eds.), *The Foreign Policies of Middle East States* (Boulder: Lynne Rienner Publishers, 2002), pp. 196-199; Gerd Nonneman, "Determinants and Patterns of Saudi Foreign Policy: 'Onmi-Balancing' and 'Relative Autonomy' in Multiple Environments," in Paul Aarts and Gerd Nonneman, *Saudi Arabia in the Balance: Political Economy, Society, Foreign Affairs* (New York: New York University Press, 2005), pp. 329-333.

3   Elie Podeh, *From Fahd to 'Abdallah: The Origins of the Saudi Peace Initiatives and Their Impact on the Arab System and Israel*, Gitelson Peace Publication 24 (Jerusalem: The Harry S. Truman Institute for the Advancement of Peace, 2003); "Israel and the Arab Peace Initiative, 2002-2014," *Middle East Journal*, Vol. 68 (2014), pp. 584-603.

4   Lawrence Rubin, *Islam in the Balance: Ideational Threats in Arab Politics* (Stanford: Stanford University Press, 2014), pp. 21-28.

5   This tradition had started in the thirteenth century. The current dispute began in August 1924, when the Egyptian commander of the pilgrimage discovered that the name of King Fu'ad had been removed from the *kiswa* by King Husain. This incident caused friction between the two kings.

6   Elie Podeh, "The Emergence of the Arab State System Reconsidered," *Diplomacy and Statecraft*, Vol. 9 (November 1998), pp. 52-53.

7   Ibid., p. 55; Yehoshua Porath, *In Search of Arab Unity, 1930-1945* (London: Frank Cass, 1986), pp. 182-184.

8   Ibid., pp. 22-39, 262, 306-307.

9   Ibid., p. 261; Bruce Maddy-Weitzman, *The Crystallization of the Arab State System, 1945-1954* (Syracuse: Syracuse University Press, 1993), pp. 15-19.

10   The Baghdad Pact consisted of Britain, Turkey, Iran, Pakistan and Iraq, while the US supported the organization behind the scenes. On this episode, see Elie Podeh, *The Quest for Hegemony in the Arab World: The Struggle over the Baghdad Pact* (Leiden: E. J. Brill, 1995).

11   Safran, *Saudi Arabia*, p. 78.

12   Elie Podeh, "Ending an Age-Old Rivalry: The Rapprochement between the Hashemites and the Saudis, 1956-1958," in Asher Susser and Aryeh Shmuelevitz (eds.), *The Hashemites in the Modern Arab World: Essays in Honor of the Late Professor Uriel Dann* (London: Frank Cass, 1995), p. 89.

13   For more details, see Podeh, "Ending an Age-Old Rivalry," pp. 93-103. It should be noted that during the Suez War, Saudi Arabia sided with Nasser, breaking off relations with Britain and France and declaring an embargo on oil shipments to them. See Safran, *Saudi Arabia*, pp. 79-80.

14   The Eisenhower Doctrine was prompted by the fear of a Soviet move to fill the vacuum created by the Suez War and receding British and French influence. Formally, it proclaimed US determination to use force to support any Middle East country seeking assistance against open aggression by any country under the control of "international communism." See ibid., pp. 82-83.

15   See Jesse Ferris, *Nasser's Gamble: How Intervention in Yemen Caused the Six-Day War and the Decline of Egyptian Power* (Princeton: Princeton University Press, 2013); Safran, *Saudi Arabia*, pp. 92-103; 119-122; 127-133.

16   Avraham Sela, *The Decline of the Arab-Israeli Conflict: Middle East Politics and the Quest for Regional Order* (Albany: State University of New York Press, 1998), p. 86.

17   Ibid., p. 142-143.

18   Ibid., pp. 146-147; Safran, *Saudi Arabia*, pp. 152-160.

19   Sela, *The Decline of the Arab-Israeli Conflict*, pp. 185-187.

20   Ibid., pp. 194-211; Safran, *Saudi Arabia*, pp. 256-264.

21   See, in this connection, Elie Podeh and Onn Winckler, *The Boycott That Never Was: Egypt and the Arab System, 1979-1989*, Durham Middle East Papers, No. 72 (December 2002).

22   Sela, *Decline of the Arab-Israeli Conflict*, pp. 328-330.

23   Ibid., p. 332; Michael N. Barnett, "Regional Security after the Gulf War," *Political Science Quarterly*, Vol. 111 (1996-97), p. 602.

24   Louis Cantori, "Unipolarity and Egyptian Hegemony in the Middle East," in Robert O. Freedman (ed.), *The Middle East after Iraq's Invasion of Kuwait* (Gainesville: University of Florida Press, 1993), p. 351.

25   http://tinyurl.com/zp9ykmk (accessed 6 July 2016)

26   Gause, "The Foreign Policy of Saudi Arabia," p. 197.

27   Egypt severed its diplomatic relations with Iran after the 1979 Revolution, and has not reinstated them. On the history of their bilateral relations, see Asef Bayat and Bahman Baktiri, "Revolutionary Iran and Egypt: Exploring Inspirations and Anxieties," in Nikki R. Keddie and Rudi Matthee (eds.), *Iran and the Surrounding World: Interactions in Culture and Cultural Politics* (Seattle: University of Washington Press, 2002), pp. 305-326.

28   See Elie Podeh, "Iraq and the Arab System since the 2003 War: A Persistent Marginality," in Amnon Cohen and Noga Efrati (eds.), *Post-Saddam Iraq: New Realities, Old Identities, Challenging Patterns* (Brighton: Sussex Academic Press, 2011), pp. 276-279. As described above, Guase rejected the sectarian argument, focusing only on the Saudi concern with the balance of power in the Gulf. See his *The International Relations of the Persian Gulf* (Cambridge: Cambridge University Press, 2010), pp. 180-181.

29   Ian Black, "Fear of a Shia Full Moon," *The Guardian*, 26 January 2007.

30   In terms of export, ranked between 16 and 45; in terms of import, ranked between 15 and 30; the percentage of Saudi export to Egypt out of the total trade did not exceed 1.6%, while the import did not exceed 1.5%). See: http://tinyurl.com/zcljnbb (accessed 6 July 2016)

31   Schenker and Henderson, "Paradoxes of Egyptian-Saudi Relations". See also: http://tinyurl.com/ hr29wtv (accessed 6 July 2016)

32   David Schenker and Simon Henderson, "Paradoxes of Egyptian-Saudi Relations," Policy Analysis, The Washington Institute (December 2009); see: http://tinyurl.com/zj287m7

33   Quoted in Mahmoud Mostafa, "25 January Celebrations 'delayed' to Mourn Saudi King," *Daily News*, 25 January 2015; Adel al-Toraifi, "Saudi Arabia and Egypt: Interests at the time of 'revolution'," *al-Sharq al-Awsat*, 2 May 2012.

34   Madawi al-Rashid, "Yes, It Could Happen Here: Why Saudi Arabia Is Ripe for Revolution," *Foreign Policy*, 28 February 2011.

35   Yasmine Farouk, "More than Money: Post-Mubarak Egypt, Saudi Arabia and the Gulf," Gulf Research Center Paper (April 2014), pp. 7-8.

36   Hicham Mourad, "The Muslim Brotherhood and Saudi Arabia," *Ahram Online*, 15 May 2013. See: http://tinyurl.com/zev2q6z (accessed 6 July 2016); Madawi al-Rashid, "Saudi Arabia Pleased with Morsi's Fall," *al-Monitor*, 4 July 2013; Stephane Lacroix, "Saudi Islamists and the Potential for Protest," *Foreign Policy*, 2 June 2011.

37   Yasmine Farouk, "More than Money," p. 9.

38   Guido Steinberg, "Leading the Counter-Revolution," SWP Research Paper (June 2014), p. 18.

39   Farouk, "More than Money," pp. 11-13.

40   Steinberg, "Leading the Counter-Revolution," p. 18; Ibid; Farouk, "More Than Money," pp. 9-11; David Hearst, "Why Saudi Arabia is taking a risk by backing the Egyptian coup," *The Guardian*, 20 August 2013; Robert Baer, "Why Saudi Arabia is helping crush the Muslim Brotherhood," *New Republic*, 26 August 2013.

41   Farouk, "More than Money," pp. 12-13; "Arab Aid Starts Flowing after Morsi's Departure," *Mada Masr*, 9 July 2013; Sultan al-Qassemi, "The Gulf and Egypt: Long Transitions and Marshall Plans," *ibid.*, 20 January 2014.

42   "Saudi Aid Expected to Flow after Elections," *Mada Masr*, 5 February 2014.

43   Apparently, the king did not leave his plane, which was on the ground at Cairo airport for just over an hour. Sisi and his delegation were on board for just over 30 minutes. See: http://tinyurl.com/hcl5z64 (accessed 6 July 2016)

44   "Sisi Concludes First Official Visit to Saudi Arabia," *Mada Masr*, 11 August 2014.

45   Due to the King's medical situation, the president of the university was commissioned to award the doctorate to the king in person. See Abdul Sattar Hatita, "Saudi King Receives Honorary Doctorate from al-Azhar University," *al-Sharq al-Awsat*, 17 July 2014.

46   "Saudi Arabia Opens Largest Embassy in Egypt," 8 September 2014. See: http://tinyurl.com/j36fchb (accessed 6 July 2016). As will be recalled, the embassy was damaged during a mob attack in April 2012.

47   In an interview with *Okaz*, see "Sisi Applauds Saudi Arabia for its Support of Egypt Post-June 30," *Mada Masr*, 28 October 2014. On the summit, see "Egypt Investment Summit Kicks Off in Sharm el-Sheikh," *al-Sharq al-Awsat*, 13 March 2015.

48   "Qatar, Egypt intelligence chiefs discuss 'reconciliation' in Cairo," 24 December 2014: http://tinyurl. com/jaxuqs2 (accessed 6 July 2016); Zvi Barel, "Egypt and Qatar Reconcile, and Saudi Arabia Becomes the Most Important Political Element in the Middle East," *Haaretz*, 22 December 2014.

49   Pesha Magid, "With Eye to Iran, Saudi Brings Egypt, Qatar Back Together," *al-Monitor*, 30 March 2015.

50   "Egypt's al-Sisi Mourns King 'Abdullah," *Daily News*, 23 January 2015.

51   "Sisi Talks on Relations with Saudi Arabia," 28 February 2015. See: http://tinyurl.com/gmnhasv (accessed 6 July 2016)

52   Khalid al-Dakhil, *al-Hayat*, 1 March 2015. See an English version: http://tinyurl.com/qzyla73 (accessed 6 July 2016)

53   The Egyptian militant position came after the beheading of 21 Egyptian Copts in Libya by the ISIS rebels in mid-February 2015. In retaliation, ISIS camps and weapons stocks in Libya were bombed by Egyptian airplanes. Dina Ezzat, "Egypt Sees the Dawn of the New Colors of Saudi Foreign Policy?" *Ahram Online*, 20 February 2015.

54 Saudi Arabia provided 100 out of the 185 aircraft involved; the UAE contributed 30; Kuwait and Bahrain 15 each; Qatar 10; Jordan and Morocco six each; and Sudan three. See Ahmed Eleiba, "Storm of Resolve," *al-Ahram Weekly*, 2 April 2015.

55 Amira Howeidy and Dina Ezzat, "Dragged to War in Yemen?" *al-Ahram Weekly*, 8 April 2015. In December 2013, it was agreed to link the electric power grids of both countries, producing a total of three thousand megawatts to ease the strain on hours of peak consumption in Egypt. The project is estimated to cost around $1.6 billion, Egypt providing $600 million of the total. See "Electricity Exchange between Egypt and Saudi Arabia," *Mada Masr*, 12 December 2013.

56 Ibid; Mostafa Mohie, "Why is Egypt Participating in Operation Decisive Storm?" Omar Said, "From Desert Storm to Decisive Storm," *Mada Masr*, 30 March 2015. For the opposite view, see Ahmed Eleiba, "Securing Interests," *al-Ahram Weekly*, 2 April 2015. On the comparison to the 1960s, see Jesse Ferris, "Nasser's Ghost Hovers over Yemen," *New York Times*, 1 April 2015.

57 Nawaf Obaid, "A New Generation of Saudi Leaders – and a New Foreign Policy," *Washington Post*, 26 March 2015. See also in this connection: Zvi Barel, *Haaretz*, 27 March 2015; Ian Black, "Iran's Advances Create Alarm in Saudi Arabia and the Gulf," *The Guardian*, 13 March 2015; Anthony H. Cordesman: http://tinyurl.com/zzkjvw9 - 26 March 2015 (accessed 6 July 2016). On Yemen as part of traditional Saudi *lebensraum*, see Gause, "The Foreign Policy of Saudi Arabia," p. 193.

58 Vittorio Felci, "Saudi-Iranian Competition in Yemen," in Anna Maria Medici (eds.), *After the Yemeni Spring: A Survey on the Transition* (Milano: Mimesis, 2012), pp. 150-151.

59 Eyad Abu Shakra, "Saving Yemen," al-Sharq al-Awsat, 1 April 2015. The extent to which this paper came to represent Saudi policy was reflected in Salman Aldosary, "King Salman's Decisive Offer," 29 March 2015; Dina Ezzat, "Politics by Proxy," *al-Ahram Weekly*, 2 April 2015.

60 This interpretation was suggested by Hussein Haridy, former assistant to the Egyptian foreign minister, "Uniting to Combat Islamic State," *al-Ahram Weekly*, 3 June 2015.

61 For the Summit's resolution, see: http://tinyurl.com/hab2dbj - 29 March 2015 (accessed 6 July 2016).

62 See Ahmed Sayed al-Naggar, "Vision and Challenges: The President's Speech and Arab Summit Communique," *Ahram Online*, 2 April 2015; Ahmed Eleiba, "Pondering a Joint Arab Force," *al-Ahram Weekly*, 2 April 2015. Jessica Noll and Stephan Roll, "From Yemen War to Joint Army," SWP Comments 31 (May 2015). See: http://tinyurl.com/jyc9ehb

63 Michael Broning, "The All-Arab Army? Why the Arab League's New Force Spells Trouble," *Foreign Affairs*, 7 April 2015; see also *al-Quds al-Arabi*, 2 September 2015.

64 Medhat al-Zahed, "Cairo-Riyadh Divergence," al-Ahram Weekly, 3 June 2015; Samir Altaqi and Esam Aziz, "Saudi-Egyptian Relations: A Widening Gap?" *Middle East Briefing*, 5 April 2015.

65 *Aharm Online*, 2 April 2015.

66 *Ahram Online*, 15 April 2015.

67 Omar Said, "Why Did Sisi Visit Saudi Arabia?" *Mada Masr*, 3 May 2015; Medhat al-Zahed, "Cairo-Riyadh Divergence," *al-Ahram Weekly*, 3 June 2015; Samir Altaqi and Esam Aziz, "Saudi-Egyptian Relations: A Widening Gap?" *Middle East Briefing*, 5 April 2015.

68 *Ahram Online*, 8 May 2015.

69 Hussein Haridy, "Uniting to Combat Islamic State," *al-Ahram Weekly*, 3 June 2015. The fact that the source is a former assistant to the Egyptian foreign minister lent credence to this information.

70 Khaled Dawoud, "New Warmth between Cairo and Riyadh," *al-Ahram Weekly*, No. 1257, 6 August 2015.

71 For various sources, see Stephan Roll, "Built on Sand: Egypt's Questionable Strategy for Growth and Development," *SWP Comments 15* (March 2015); http://tinyurl.com/hpon4tp; http://tinyurl.com/gvj4fty; http://tinyurl.com/jx3o25u (all accessed on 6 July 2016).

72 John Bradley, a British journalist who predicted the revolution in Egypt, envisioned a similar occurrence in Saudi Arabia, see *Saudi Arabia Exposed: Inside a Kingdom in Crisis* (London: Palgrave/Macmillan, 2005).

73 Elie Podeh, "Saudi Arabia: Lynchpin of the Moderate Axis in the Middle East, *Jerusalem Post*, 14 April 2016.

4

The Qatari-Saudi-Egyptian Triangle
After the Arab Spring

Suhaim Al-Thani

Introduction

This chapter will argue that the relations between Qatar, Saudi Arabia and Egypt have been largely defined by their respective stances on the Arab Spring. Saudi Arabia viewed the prospect for change as a security threat and the Muslim Brotherhood as a hostile organization. Qatar, on the other hand, viewed the sweeping change as an opportunity. It believed that it could work with the emerging governments and did not see the Muslim Brotherhood as a greater threat than any other political party participating in Egypt's political process and elections. The differing stances of Qatar and Saudi Arabia regarding Egypt, brought discord into the normally harmonious GCC relations. Tension escalated to the extent that Saudi Arabia, the UAE and Bahrain, after withdrawing their ambassadors to Qatar, threatened to expel Qatar from the GCC if it did not normalize relations with Egypt and deport the members of the Muslim Brotherhood that resided in Qatar. The Qatari leadership was able to reach a compromise agreement with Saudi Arabia that did not entail the normalization of relations with Egypt. The chapter will put forward the theory that the post- Arab Spring period is divided into three phases which each concern Qatar, Saudi Arabia and Egypt. The first phase is the one in which Qatar has the political momentum. In the second phase Saudi Arabia re-captures its political assertiveness and gains momentum in the region. In the third phase, which began with the accession of King Salman, there is an emerging Saudi Arabian-Qatari partnership being constructed in which Egypt is being drawn in as well.

The first two phases created a volte-face in relations between the three countries. Building on Steinberg 2014's Twin track policy[1], this chapter puts forward the idea that there are two pillars[2] of Saudi policy towards the Arab Spring: balancing Iran and preventing domestic unrest. With the accession of King Salman, the pillar of balancing Iran grew in importance vis-à-vis the domestic pillar and Saudi foreign policy underwent dramatic changes in response. The Kingdom revisited its policies towards Hamas and reversed its policy towards Turkey. This policy shift had a significant affect on Saudi relations with Egypt. Saudi Arabia and Qatar both now view Turkey as being part of a possible alliance to counter the two greatest threats facing the region, Iranian expansion and ISIL. Egypt on the other hand, does not seem to share the same outlook towards Turkey. Yet, Cairo's poor economic conditions and its reliance on investments from the Gulf has driven it to join the newly formed alliance against the Houthis in Yemen, alongside Turkey.

The war in Yemen and the diplomatic escalation with Iran following the execution of Nimr Al Nimr further the importance of balancing Iran and the severe fall in oil prices limits the Saudi Arabian ability to continue funding Egypt at a high level. The chapter will analyse the relationship from the beginning of the Arab Spring and explore future possibilities for increased cooperation between Qatar, Saudi Arabia and Egypt, and the factors that could be detrimental to the trilateral relations. The chapter will put forward the argument that following the ascendance of King Salman to the throne, the future of Saudi Arabia's relations with Egypt will depend on how far it can sustain an ailing Egyptian economy and how useful Egypt can be for the new Saudi alliance. The future of Qatari - Egyptian relations will depend on whether a compromise can be reached over issues of difference and how that will affect Turkish - Egyptian relations as well given Qatar's strategic and historic ties to Turkey. The trend, however, seems to be towards reconciliation, especially following the meeting between the Emir Tamim and President Sisi at Sharm el-Sheikh and consensus the building efforts of King Salman.

The Three Main Phases of the Arab Spring

The First phase of the post- Arab Spring regional order can be characterised as that which began with the stepping down of Hosni Mubarak and ended with the 3 July 2013 military takeover/popular 'coup' in Egypt. This phase is characterised by Islamist domination of parliaments in North Africa and a Qatari – Turkish – Egyptian alliance in its formative stages. The second phase of the post- Arab Spring regional order is that in which Saudi Arabia reigns supreme. The second phase started with the July 3 2013 military takeover in Egypt and ended with the accession of King Salman. This phase is characterised by a rolling back of Qatari diplomatic and political gains in the post- Arab Spring political arena, coupled with Saudi regional dominance and the GCC rift that placed Qatar in semi-diplomatic isolation. The third phase of the post- Arab Spring regional order began with the accession of King Salman and as of May 2015 is ongoing. This phase is characterised by increased Saudi-Qatari cooperation, a softening of Saudi stance towards the Islamists and Turkey and relations with Egypt not being as central as they were in the last two phases to regional dynamics. The third phase marks the beginning of Saudi Arabia asking what Egypt can and will do to help solve regional issues and not only what Saudi Arabia can do to stabilize Egypt.

The relations between Qatar, Saudi Arabia and Egypt in the Arab Spring and post Arab Spring period followed the pattern of a zero sum game, with the improvement in the bilateral relationship between two countries would harm relations with the third country. This was demonstrated by the fact that as Saudi – Egyptian relations improved those between Saudi Arabia and Qatar suffered culminating with the withdrawal of the Saudi Ambassador to Qatar, and again following the accession of King Salman when Saudi relations with Qatar improved and Saudi relations with Egypt faced a setback.

Phase One

Qatar Policy Towards the Arab Spring

Qatari policy was pro- Arab Spring in Tunisia, Libya, Egypt and Syria. The Qatari governments support was limited to political statements and media support in cases where the regimes did not use force against the protesters; in Libya where the protesters were, killed Qatar intervened militarily as part of an Arab-NATO Coalition. In Syria, from the start of the protests until August 2011 Qatar originally urged the regime to reform[3], Calls for non-violence were ignored by the regime the Qatari government called for Bashar Al Assad to step down[4], when President Bashar failed to step down and atrocities were committed against protesters, Qatar called first for an armed Arab Military Intervention.[5]

Strategically the Qatari government was well placed to play a decisive role in the Arab Spring, as diplomatically the Qataris had a strong relationship with the Muslim Brotherhood and many other opposition movements. The Qatari media was also well placed to take advantage of the momentum as the Qatari Al Jazeera channel was the most viewed Satellite channel in the Arab World.[6] With these tools at its disposal, the Qatari government decided to bet on the fact that the youth protesters would succeed in toppling the government. When this investment came to fruition the Qatari government offered these new governments the hand of friendship as Qatar's Arab Spring policy was to 'financially and politically support the group it perceived as having the best chance of getting to power'.[7]

Strategically Qatar sought to build a new alliance between itself, Turkey, Egypt and Tunisia. The goal was not to build an Islamist alliance as was feared by some but to find a role for Qatar outside of the regional struggles of Saudi Arabia and Iran. Qatar also worried that 'if neither of the large Arab countries fill the leadership vacuum in the region, the Arab sphere will be sliced between Iran and Turkey'.[8] The Qatari search for a third alliance in the region can be demonstrated by Qatari foreign policy in the period 2005-2011 when it played the role of the mediator in many conflicts, seeking to reduce regional tension in Yemen, Lebanon, Sudan and Palestine, the conflicts in Yemen and Lebanon were strongly related to the Saudi- Iranian tensions and the conflict in Palestine was somewhat related. Qatar at the time was strongly against Iranian policy in Iraq but had a less hostile view of the Iranian relationship with Hezbollah and maintained strong relationships with Hamas. Qatar thus saw itself as best suited to play the role of the mediator and bridge the divide between Iran and Saudi Arabia, as was demonstrated by the fact that Qatar invited Iranian President Mahmoud Ahmadinejad to the GCC summit in Doha in an effort to force dialogue.[9]

Qatar's strategic goals were best summed up as being 'to guarantee security and project soft power in a neighbourhood of jealous regional powers such as Saudi Arabia, Iran, and Iraq'.[10] The new Egyptian Government appeared to share Qatar's policy of maintaining a privileged relation with Saudi Arabia without being overtly anti-Iranian. The motivations were not antagonistic to Saudi Arabia as some have claimed but were based on Qatar making its voice heard and playing an active role in an active alliance.

Financially Qatar extended the hand of friendship to the new governments in post Arab Spring Tunisia, Egypt and Libya. This policy was not ideologically, as is evidenced by the fact that Qatari support for Egypt began under the transitional period that was led by the Egyptian Military.[11] The policy of financial aid was driven by Qatar's understanding that in order for the unrest in North Africa to stop funds were needed to tackle the increasing youth unemployment and simulate growth, by the mutually beneficial need of the Qatari Sovereign Wealth Fund for stable markets with high growth to invest in and by the understanding that in order for this new regional alliance to succeed the new states cannot be allowed to collapse financially.

Qatari - Egyptian relations peaked during the tenure of the Muslim Brotherhood in Egypt, Qatar supported Egypt with loans, investment projects, the providing of energy and its media. The Qatari financial support for Egypt government began under the transitional government when Qatar provided the new government with loans and increased dramatically with time, culminating in the announcement in Cairo by the Qatari Prime Minister Hamad Bin Jassim Bin Jabor Al-Thani that Qatar would invest $18.5 billion in Egypt over 5 years. Qatari financial aid made to Egyptian government under the tenure of the Brotherhood was worth at least $ 8 billion by April 2013, including $ 3 billion that was provided in aid at a time that Egypt was struggling to receive a loan from the IMF.[12]

In order to avoid large-scale power outages in Egypt, Qatar promised Egypt five free cargoes of LNG each containing 3.2 billion cubic feet.[13] Qatar also agreed to meet all Egypt's gas export obligations for the summer of 2013, as the Egyptian energy export infrastructure could not cope.[14] Qatari media especially Al Jazeera had a favorable relationship with Egypt this is demonstrated by the fact that shortly after the resignation of Mubarak in early 2011, Al Jazeera launched an Egyptian TV channel Al Jazeera Mubasher Misr.[15]

Saudi Arabian Policy Towards the Arab Spring

Saudi Arabian Policy towards the Arab Spring rested on the two pillars of balancing Iran, by preventing Iranian alliances with the new governments and cementing existing Saudi alliances and partnerships. The second pillar was preventing the unrest from affecting the Saudi interior especially and the GCC generally. Saudi Arabia's primary tool to face the risk of popular unrest at home and the possibility of Iranian expansion abroad was financial, Saudi Arabia's secondary tool was its media, primarily Al Arabiya which though significant was not as prominent as Al Jazeera in disseminating its message at the outset of the Arab Spring.

Saudi Arabia was steadfast in its determination to guarantee that the Arab Spring did not adversely affect the GCC states, the Saudis thus created aid packages worth $10 billion dollars each for both Oman and for Bahrain, over a ten-year period.[16] When street protests in Bahrain demonstrated that, the financial aid was not enough to maintain stability the Saudis along with the Emiratis sent in troops under the auspices of the Peninsula Shield to maintain order. Saudi Arabia maintained the same financial relationship with Jordan and Morocco, pledging $ 2.5 billion in aid to each over five years[17], Morocco only received the aid two years later.[18] Saudi Arabia also sought to provide Jordan and Morocco with a form of junior partner membership of the GCC in what some analysts believed to be a finance for security arrangement that sought to stabilize Jordan and Morocco on the one hand and provide Saudi Arabia with Jordanian and Moroccan troops to defend against Iran on the other.[19] Saudi Arabia may have also considered expanding the GCC in order to 'transform the GCC into a more cohesive, politically dependable alternative to the Arab League'.[20]

Saudi Arabia was at first not actively hostile towards the new Egyptian government; with time the strategic view in Saudi Arabia shifted to the view that interpreted the Brotherhood as having a quest to reshape the balance of power in the region, as part of a Qatari - Egyptian - Turkish axis that supported and promoted the interests of Islamists in the region and in which 'Riyadh would find itself isolated'.[21] The revolution in Egypt became extremely troublesome for Saudi Arabia for 3 reasons, firstly Egypt had been Saudi Arabia's closest regional ally and it was thus understandably uneasy at what policy the new government would take towards it, secondly Egyptian overtures to Iran caused Saudi Arabia to worry that not only had it lost a regional ally but Iran might gain one and thirdly the Saudi Arabians were worried that the Muslim Brotherhood might seek to export the Arab Spring into Saudi Arabia,[22] this led President Morsi to announce that Egypt had no intention of exporting the revolution and that the security of the Gulf States was a red line.[23] Saudi Arabia was not satisfied with these reassurances as Egypt was mending fences with Iran and Hamas and Islamists at home seemed to be encouraged by the Muslim Brotherhood coming to power in Egypt, the Egyptian revolution thus struck the twin pillars of Saudi Arabia's post Arab Spring policy and had to be countered.

Saudi – Egyptian relations were not overtly antagonistic during the Morsi era, this may be interpreted by the fact that Saudi Arabia had no guarantee that the Muslim Brotherhood government would be toppled and thus did not want to make an enemy of Egypt. Saudi Arabia also did not want to push Egypt too far into the hands of Iran. Signs of Saudi attempts at building bridges with Egypt, a $2.7 billion aid package was pledged, that included a $1 billion transfer to the Egyptian Central Bank and other grants for development and energy.[24] The mass protests that erupted over the summer of 2013 in Cairo provided the Saudis with the reassurance they needed to place all their bets with the military and not focus on building bridges with the Muslim Brotherhood led government.

Phase Two

In phase two the momentum turns against Qatar as it was not well placed to maintain its regional position due to 'a mismatch between leadership intent and diplomatic capacity'.[25] 'The events of July 3, 2013 brought the Arab Spring full circle'[26], the volte-face of the Arab Spring swept aside Qatar's new alliance in Egypt and in September 2013 the Al Nahdah party in Tunisia, who were also closely allied with Qatar, were pressured into stepping down.[27] The rapid turn of events marked a major shift in the Arab Spring that took the advantage away from Qatar and handed it back to Saudi Arabia. The Middle East was moving past its revolutionary/ Islamist phase and towards a new order that firmly favoured Saudi Arabia. The new order differed from the old in that Tunisia and Libya now had elections. However, Saudi Arabia's twin pillar policy of preventing the exportation of revolutionary ambition and new strategic alliances with Iran was secure.

The military takeover in Egypt can be seen as the point the momentum in the Arab Spring turned against Qatar and in favor of Saudi Arabia. The fall of Morsi and the ascendance of General Al Sisi can be seen as a direct factor in the isolation that Qatar faced in the GCC.

The Impact of the Military Taking Power on Qatari-Egyptian Relations

The Military takeover in Egypt occurred on the (3rd of July of 2013) only one week after the Emir of Qatar Sheikh Hamad Bin Khalifa Al-Thani abdicated in favour of his son Sheikh Tamim (on the 25th June 2013), analysts expected the new Emir to abandon his father's policies and adopt a less independent and less assertive foreign policy.[28]

Qatar's initial response seemed to vindicate this opinion, as following the military takeover an official statement released by the Foreign Ministry and circulated by the Qatar News Agency declared Qatar's support for the 'will of the brotherly Egyptian people and their options for achieving their aspirations towards democracy and social justice'.[29] At the time, local and international media interpreted this as a sign that Qatari- Egyptian relations would not be affected by the military takeover.[30]

It is unclear whether Qatari overtures were made to Egypt after the military takeover, three factors contributed to their deterioration the hostile tone taken by Al Jazeera against what it described as a military coup, Qatar's hosting of members of the Brotherhood who had fled Egypt and the Egyptian imprisonment of former President Mohammed Morsi[31]. In September 2013 Egypt returned the $ 2 billion it had borrowed from Qatar in a sign of strained relations,[32] that only deteriorated further after the Qatari Foreign Minister criticized the Army's crackdown on street protests[33].

Although Egypt returned the loan it received from Qatar, Qatar upheld its pre–military takeover commitment to provide Egypt with LNG and supplied the Egyptians with 'five giant shipments' of LNG free of charge.[34] The deterioration in relations between Egypt and Qatar was manifest in three forms of confrontation: media confrontation, diplomatic confrontation and judicial confrontation.

Media confrontation between Qatar and Egypt was characteristic of their relationship dynamic post–military takeover in Egypt. The Media confrontation began during the second phase of tertiary relations and continued through the third phase. Al Jazeera played host to a plethora of Brotherhood figures who criticized the military takeover and provided the group with much airtime[35], this was especially important to the Brotherhood as they were not welcome on most satellite channels in the Gulf and Egypt. Al Jazeera Mubasher Misr broadcast scenes of the protests, until it was banned by the Egyptian authorities in August 2013.[36] The channel continued to broadcast from Doha, until Qatari authorities suspended it in December 2014 in what some regarded as a reconciliatory gesture.[37] The official reason given for the suspension of Al Jazeera Mubasher Misr's broadcasts was the lack of the relevant permits.[38] The Egyptian Media was relentless in its attacks on Qatar[39], conspiracy theories involving Qatar were given much airtime on Egyptian television and fabricated stories of turmoil in Qatar were treated as serious news stories and promoted by the Egyptian media, including a story about a coup d'etat in Qatar.[40] President Sisi defended these Media attacks against Qatar as being a 'reflection of public opinion'.[41]

Media confrontation between Qatar and Egypt escalated to the point that in June 2014 an Egyptian sentenced three journalists of Al Jazeera English to terms ranging from seven to ten years imprisonment 'on charges of aiding terrorists and endangering national security'.[42] The journalists spent over six months in jail with one being deported in January 2015 and the other two released on bail in February 2015[43]. The detention of the journalists marked the only instance of direct judicial confrontation. Indirect judicial confrontation occurred during the trials of former Egyptian President Morsi, when one of the charges leveled against him was committing espionage on behalf of Qatar, by 'providing Qatari intelligence with a trove of classified documents with a direct bearing on Egypt's national security'.[44] Judicial confrontation was thus led by the Egyptians and not reciprocated by the Qataris.

Diplomatic tension between Egypt and Qatar escalated when Egypt withdrew its ambassador from Qatar on 6 March 2014 citing the need to 'correct the path of the Qatari Government'.[45] Shortly after, Saudi Arabia, the UAE and Bahrain withdrew their ambassadors. In February 2015 Qatar recalled its ambassador to Egypt 'for consultation' after the Egyptian delegate at the Arab league accused Qatar of supporting terrorism because of its objection to the uncoordinated nature of Egyptian airstrikes against ISIL in Libya, with Qatar maintaining the need for "consultations before any unilateral military action against another member state"[46]. The Qatari Ambassador returned to Egypt in March 2015, the Egyptian Ambassador has not returned to Doha since he was withdrawn in March 2014.[47]

High-level official rhetoric of Qatar regarding Egypt and of Egypt regarding Qatar was much more nuanced and balanced. Qatar's Foreign Minister declared at a speech given to a Chatham House audience in December 2014 that *Qatar's policy toward Egypt remains the same, and is anchored in full respect of the country's national sovereignty and territorial integrity. This policy is based on the following principle: to work with the country's legitimate government, not with a party or a group; to provide assistance as needed and upon request by the government; to encourage dialogue between all parties; to promote inclusion into the national political framework; and to never resort to force against peaceful protesters. It is ultimately beyond question that the stability of Egypt is in the interest of everyone*[48]. The references to Qatar's respect for Egyptian sovereignty, working with the legitimate government and not with any particular group, provides a clear indication that Qatar accepts Sisi's government as the legitimate government in Egypt, does not believe in partnering with the Muslim Brotherhood against the Egyptian government and will not interfere in Egyptian internal affairs.

Signaling no official stance against President Sisi. The speech by the Emir of Qatar at the 69 session of the United Nations (September 2014) did not refer to Egypt once, when discussing Qatar's regional priorities and focused instead on Palestine and Syria.[49] Similarly, the speech of the Egyptian President at the 69th session of the UN did not refer to Qatar.[50] The lack of reference by Qatar of Egypt in the UN speech and vice versa, implies that they regard the issues discussed as being of a graver concern and this may be seen as a sign that both sides were attempting back from their stronger stances vis-à-vis one another.

The Impact of the Military Taking Power on Saudi-Egyptian Relations

Bilateral relations between Egypt and Saudi Arabia improved almost instantly. Saudi Arabia welcomed the Egyptian military takeover with open arms and could not have been more enthusiastic about the turn of events. The Saudi King Abdullah praised General Sisi for having 'saved the country from a dark tunnel'. In another speech in August 2013 the king declared "Let the entire world know, that the people and government of the Kingdom of Saudi Arabia stood and still stand today with our brothers in Egypt against terrorism, extremism and sedition, and against whomever is trying to interfere in Egypt's internal affairs."[51] The high level Saudi interest in supporting the military government lasted all through the reign of King Abdullah; with the Saudi King visiting Egypt just weeks after Sisi became President officially in June 2014[52], only a few weeks before the death of the Saudi king. King Abdullah took a personal interest in mending Qatari - Egyptian relations, personally sponsoring a summit that was to take place in Riyadh in December 2015 between Emir Tamim and President Sisi, in what was expected to be the summit that resolved the tension between Qatar and Egypt.[53] The timing of the meeting (scheduled for just one month after the GCC rift was resolved) raises the possibility that this meeting was as a direct result of the resolution and may have even been part of the reconciliation agreement.

Saudi Arabia was a crucial financial supporter of Egypt after the military takeover. In August 2013, barely one month since the military takeover Saudi Arabia along with the UAE and Kuwait pledged $12.5 billion in aid to Egypt and reassured the Egyptians that it would 'compensate Egypt for any aid that Western Countries might withdraw'.[54] In March 2014 in a sign of solidarity with the Egyptians, the Saudi Arabians and the Emiratis listed the Muslim Brotherhood as a terrorist organization.[55]

The importance of Egypt to Saudi Arabia was demonstrated by the fact that for the first time in the history of the GCC, relations with an outside power caused a rift within the GCC. Saudi Arabia, the UAE and Bahrain explained, that this step was as a result of Qatari refusal to comply with their demands, to not support "anyone threatening the security and stability of the GCC whether as groups or individuals - via direct security work or through political influence, and not to support hostile media".[56] In a thinly veiled reference to the Muslim Brotherhood and Al Jazeera. The GCC rift lasted until November 2014.[57] It is likely that some understanding was reached regarding the normalization of relations with Egypt. High level meetings took place between the Qatari government officials and President Sisi, including one with the Emir of Qatar[58], and another with a special envoy from Qatar and the head of the Saudi King's Diwan.[59] It is yet unclear what understanding, if any was reached between the Qatari's and the Egyptians.

Phase Three

The Accession of King Salman

The Accession of King Salman to the throne of Saudi Arabia marked the beginning of the third phase in the dynamic of Qatari – Saudi – Egyptian relations post – Arab Spring. The volte – face of Saudi Arabia's policy was sudden and unexpected, many analysts were misled by the fact that King Salman declared that: "We will remain, with God's support; maintain the straight path that this country has advanced on since its establishment by the late King Abdulaziz".[60] One of King Salman's first foreign policy decisions was to host the Turkish President in Riyadh in March 2015[61], which marked the second meeting between the two leaders in two months (the first was at the funeral of King Abdullah in January 2015.[62] Hamas also moved to improve relations with Saudi Arabia after the accession of King Salman, at first testing the waters by Khalid Meshaal personally offering condolences at the Saudi Embassy in Qatar[63], by March reports emerged that Saudi Arabia had asked Hamas to mediate on its behalf with the Islah party in Yemen.[64] Hamas officially denied the report[65] but in April 2014 the Islah party in Yemen officially announced its support for operation decisive storm.[66] King Salman's policies can be viewed through the lens of Saudi Arabia's first pillar with regard to the Arab Spring, not to let Iran fill the void created by any post Arab- Spring vacuum. The Saudis were more worried by the Houthi occupation of Sanaa than they were by Islamists in the region. The Islamists no longer posed a threat to the second pillar of Saudi Arabia's Arab Spring policy as the momentum of the early days of the Arab Spring had long passed and the Islamists were now viewed as a potential partner in combating Iran's proxies. There was a feeling among some Saudi academics that the isolation of the Islamists had gone too far and that King Salman as opposed to King Abdullah does not view all the Muslim Brotherhood as terrorists.[67]

Is there a divergence of Opinion Between Saudi Arabia and Egypt With Regard to Regional Issues?

Egypt and Saudi Arabia's views diverge on many regional and international issues including Yemen, Syria and Russia. The divergence of opinion is not a result of the accession of King Salman, however during his reign the Yemeni and Syrian dossiers gained importance relative to the Egyptian portfolio. Egypt was a reluctant supporter of the military campaign in Yemen, sending four warships to join the blockade of Aden, but not participating in any combat, Egypt also lost investments from Russia and China due to its decision.[68] In May following President Sisi's visit to Saudi Arabia[69], the foreign minister of Egypt announced Egypt's willingness to send ground troops to Yemen.[70] President Sisi personally replied that although no Egyptian troops were in Yemen at present: "An announcement will be made if any other forces were deployed in the operation".[71] The Egyptian Foreign Minister's remarks may be interpreted in the light of increased Saudi pressure on Egypt to play an active part in the Yemeni operations specifically and to bring its strategic priorities closer to those of Riyadh in general. The Egyptian Media which Riyadh regards as being influenced by the Egyptian State have been harsh critics of Riyadh since the beginning of operation decisive storm.[72] It is unclear whether Egypt is using these as a soft power bargaining chip as was the case with Qatar in the past or if the objective is to create the illusion of popular discontent over the war at home. Further tension my arise if Saudi Arabia decides to arm the Muslim Brotherhood in Yemen.

Egyptian relations with Russia, never an issue for Saudi Arabia under King Abdullah, are becoming more problematic for Saudi Arabia under King Salman. President Sisi first visited Russia as President in August 2014[73], when King Abdullah still ruled Saudi Arabia. During the reign of King Abdullah in November 2013, the Russians began negotiations to establish a naval base in Egypt.[74] In March 2014, Russia began exporting sophisticated weaponry to Egypt.[75] Sisi's second visit to Moscow was in May 2015[76], which followed a visit by President Putin to Egypt in February 2015.[77] In a possible sign of Putin leveraging Russian relations with Egypt to reconcile with the Arab countries, the Russian President penned a letter addressed to Arab leaders attending the Arab League Summit at Sharm El Shiekh in March 2015. In what the Russians termed a message of "greetings and solidarity", Putin expressed willingness to help resolve regional crisis. His message was rebuked by the Saudi Foreign Minister who stated that Russia has been supplying the Syrian regime with the weapons that Bashar Al-Assad uses to kill his own people. The contrast between King Abdullah's stance regarding Egyptian- Russian relations and that of King Salman demonstrates that Egypt has moved down the list of Saudi Arabian strategic priorities and is no longer viewed as the sine qua non of Saudi Arabia's regional policy. Given Saudi Arabia's strong reaction to the Russian message of 'greetings and solidarity', the damage that a Russian Naval Base in Egypt would do to Saudi-Egyptian relations would certainly be severe.

Egypt has been quiet regarding the Saudi rapprochement with Turkey and it is yet unknown whether the rapprochement with Turkey will bring Turkey closer to Egypt or Saudi Arabia further away from Egypt. Turkey has an important role to play in Syria and Riyadh announced increased cooperation with Ankara with regards to backing the rebels who seek to remove Al Assad from power[78]. There is a possibility that Qatar may have brokered the Saudi – Turkish rapprochement.[79] The fact that instead of Saudi Arabia brokering a Qatari-Egyptian reconciliation, Qatar brokered a Saudi – Turkish reconciliation is possibly the best indication of the fundamental state and policy reorientations that have occurred during phase three of the Qatari-Saudi Egyptian relation post-Arab Spring.

Economic relations have not taken the same trajectory as political relations. In February 2015 there was a regional tour by the Egyptian foreign minister in the Gulf, designed to measure and encourage the Gulf States support of the economic conference in Sharm El Sheikh, as there was some fear that the Gulf States would not be as supportive as they once were.[80] At the Sharm El Sheikh conference, Egypt received pledges of $12.5 billion, of which $4 billion came from Saudi Arabia[81]. The continued Saudi economic support of Egypt, is likely a tie that keeps Saudi Arabia and Egypt strategically bonded.

The Future Trajectory of Relations

Egypt maintains economic and military importance to Qatar and Saudi Arabia, as the largest Arab Army, the Egyptian Military is in a unique position to cooperate with Qatar and Saudi Arabia in Yemen against the Houthis and in Syria and Iraq against ISIL. Intelligence sharing and officer training are potential avenues for increased security cooperation. As the largest Arab country by population, Egypt (if stability increases) can offer the Qatari and Saudi Arabian Sovereign Wealth funds with a destination for investments. Egyptian skilled and unskilled labour has long been in high demand in the Gulf, in spite of the tense relations between Qatar and Egypt after the military takeover, the Egyptian community in Qatar grew by over 30%. Food Security is another area in which the Egyptians can play a vital role, Egypt currently supplies the Gulf region with food exports, the food security cooperation could be expanded to renting out or selling arable land to Qatar and Saudi Arabia as was done by Brazil, Sudan and Pakistan among others.

Qatar and Saudi Arabia are important to Egypt in the Energy, Economic and Labour sectors. Egypt currently faces an energy crisis, Qatar and Saudi Arabia are well placed to enter into long term contracts to supply Egypt with energy and meet any potential shortfall. Qatar and Saudi Arabia can offer Egypt much needed Foreign Direct Investment, as currently the UAE is the only GCC country to provide Egypt with large-scale FDI investments. The Egyptian Government is heavily reliant on foreign loans and Qatar and Saudi Arabia could continue to provide Egypt with some loans. Qatar and Saudi Arabia could also increase the size of their respective Egyptian work forces, thus providing Egypt with a means to reduce unemployment, relieve some of the strain on government resources and increase remittances from the gulf to Egypt.

The fact that Egypt officially joined the coalition against the Houthis and has not reacted negatively to Saudi Arabia's reconciliation with Turkey and Hamas, indicates that the Egyptians still value their relationship with Saudi Arabia. Economically, Egypt once stable offers very clear opportunities to Qatar and Egypt. Financially Qatar and Saudi Arabia could offer Egypt much needed financial aid, foreign direct investment and an outlet for some of its large number unemployed youth. This mutually beneficial arrangement could draw Egypt and the Gulf closer together if diplomatic issues are resolved rather than escalated.

Diplomatically and politically, the possibility of increased tensions remains. It is clear that following phase three of the relationship dynamic of Qatar, Egypt and Saudi Arabia, some diplomatic and political avenues are blocked. The Saudi sponsored Qatari-Egyptian rapprochement is no longer on the agenda. Egypt's ties to Russia are becoming a concern for Saudi Arabia. The Egyptian media is mounting an anti- Saudi campaign in 2015 similar to the one started against Qatar in 2013 and at a time when Saudi Arabia is looking to assert itself militarily in Yemen and by proxy in Syria, Turkey and the Islamist are increasingly proving more useful than the Egyptians. The execution of former President Morsi is likely to be troublesome for Qatari-Egyptian relations, as Qatar objects to the fact that he is imprisoned in the first place. Saudi Arabia may be troubled by the execution as it would likely setback Saudi Arabia's rapprochement with Turkey, Hamas and the Islah party in Yemen and provide one more area in which the Saudi-Egyptian strategic outlooks do not complement one another. Throughout the Arab Spring, Egyptian policy towards Syria has been ambiguous, if the Damascus falls to the rebels and a pro-Turkey government takes over, there is a possibility that tension between Egypt on the one hand and Saudi Arabia and Qatar on the other increases. Egyptian reluctance to take a firm stance diplomatically in Yemen, Syria and concerning the Saudi-Iranian tensions following the execution of Nimr Al Nimr could cause Saudi policy makers to question the wisdom of further supporting the Egyptian government, especially considering the current economic environment of falling oil prices and the sizeable economic assistance required by Egypt.

The trend must be analysed *ceteris paribus*, as the possibility of an unexpected and sudden event, changing the dynamics once more is always a possibility in the Middle East. As things stand at the time of writing, political and diplomatic crises appear to dominate centre stage, as they are all imminent or short term issues. The economic opportunities are longer term issues and require much more planning and a sustained period of stability in Egypt. It is likely that Egypt is aware of the need to avoid tension with Saudi Arabia, as in spite of Egypt's privileged relationship with Russia, it took part in operation 'Decisive Storm' even though it did not participate in the conflict; another indicator that it acted more out of necessity than conviction. If Egypt's willingness to avoid tension coupled with the more nuanced Qatari stance towards Egypt continue, then the future trajectory of relations in the third phase will be more positive.

Conclusion

Trilateral relations between Qatar, Egypt and Saudi Arabia have changed trajectories three times since the beginning of the Arab Spring. The first shift occurred in phase one of the relationship dynamic, with the fall of Mubarak and the increase in Qatari aid to Egypt followed by signs of an emerging Qatari-Turkish-Egyptian axis during the tenure of the Muslim Brotherhood. The second shift in trilateral relations occurred after the military takeover in Egypt, Egypt's relationship with Turkey and Qatar took a turn for the worst and Saudi-Egyptian relations improved dramatically. The third shift brought Qatar and Saudi Arabia closer together and Saudi Arabia closer to Turkey, while some divergence of opinion occurred between Saudi Arabia and Egypt. The chapter explored avenues for potential cooperation and the possibility of increase tension. The avenues of cooperation were shown to be more balanced against the possibility of increased tension as time progressed. To conclude, signs of tension were mainly short-term, whereas the potential for cooperation surrounding economic and longer term issues could be developed upon by the three countries and will help to avoid confrontation in future.

Notes

1   Guido Steinberg. *Leading the Counter-Revolution Saudi Arabia and the Arab Spring.* (Berlin: SWP Research Paper, 2014).

2   The key difference between the twin track policy and the two pillar policy is that the twin track consists of balancing Iran and stabilizing monarchies abroad, the two pillar policy replaces stabilizing monarchies abroad with preventing the Arab Spring from entering Saudi Arabia and the GCC from abroad, this is demonstrated by the lack of follow up commitments from Saudi Arabia which indicates Morocco and Jordan were not part of the long term policy.

3   The Peninsula, "Qatar Urges Syria to Stop Violence and Start Reforms". 23 August 2011: http://tinyurl.com/zojze4z

4   BBC News, 'Syria Unrest: World Leaders Call for Assad to Step Down'. 18 August 2011: http://tinyurl.com/hd9zahv

5   Al Jazeera, "Qatari Emir: Arabs Must Intervene in Syria", 26 September 2012.

6   The Economist. "More Powerful than Ever." May 29, 2010.

7   Lina Khatib, *Qatar and the Recalibration of Power in the Gulf.* Rep. Carnegie Middle East Center, September 2014: 4.

8   Khalid Hroub, "Qatar and the Arab Spring", Henrich Böll Stiftung, 3 March 2014: 37: http://tinyurl.com/zsfam8e

9   Reuters, "Ahmadinejad to Attend Gulf Summit, Iran Says." 2 December 2007.

10 Andrew Hammond, *Qatar's Leadership Transition: Like Father, Like Son.* February 2014, Vol. 95., European Council on Foreign Relations: 2.

11 Jamil Al-Ziabi, "Qatari FM: We Do Not Support the Muslim Brotherhood", *Al-Monitor.* 22 February 2015.

12 Bloomberg, "Egypt to Get $3 Billion More From Qatar Amid IMF Loan Bid.", 10 April 2013.

13 Summer Said, "Qatar Promises Free Fuel to Egypt." *Wall Street Journal.* 10 June 2013.

14 Robert Tuttle and Tarek El-Tablawy. "Egypt to Get $3 Billion More From Qatar Amid IMF Loan Bid." *Bloomberg*, 10 April 2013.

15 "Al Jazeera Mubasher Misr Channel Banned from Egypt." *al-Ahram*, 29 August 2013: http://tinyurl.com/jdoglou

16 Tarek Al-Tablawy, "GCC Pledges $20 Billion in Aid for Oman, Bahrain." *The Washington Post*, 10 March 2011.

17 Michael Theodoulou, "GCC Agrees Five-year Aid Plan for Morocco and Jordan", *The National*, 13 September 2013.

18 Gulf News, "Morocco Gets First Instalment of Aid Package." 2 February 2013: http://tinyurl.com/gmheopt

19 Ahmad El-Din, "The Stream: GCC Courts New Kingdoms", *Al Jazeera*, 1 June 2011; Curtis Ryan, "Jordan, Morocco and an Expanded GCC", MERIP, 15 April 2014.

20 Mehran Kemrava, "The Arab Spring and the Saudi Led Counterrevolution in Foreign Policy", *Foreign Policy*, Winter 2012: 96-104.

21 Sherif El-Ashmawy. *The Foreign Policies of Saudi Arabia and Qatar Towards the Arab Uprisings The Cases of Egypt, Libya and Bahrain.* (Cambridge: Gulf Research Meeting, August 2014): 8.

22 Rene Rieger, *In Search of Stability: Saudi Arabia and the Arab Spring.* (Cambridge: Gulf Research Meeting, August 2013).

23 The Daily Star, "Morsi Visit to Saudi Signals Continuity in Relations", 10 July 2012.

24 Al-Akhbar, "Saudi Finalizes Egypt Aid Package", 22 May 2012.

25 Kristian Coates Ulrichsen, *Qatar and the Arab Spring Policy Drivers and Regional Implication*, (Washington D.C.: Carnegie Endowment for International Peace, 2014): 6.

26 Kristian Coates Ulrichsen, "Egypt-Gulf Ties and a Changing Balance of Regional Security", *The Cairo Review*, 12 January 2015: http://tinyurl.com/j3rqan7

27 Ibid.

28 Kristian Coates Ulrichsen, *Qatar and the Arab Spring Policy Drivers and Regional Implication*: 19

29 Gulf Times, "Congratulatory Messages", 4 July 2013.

30 Amena Bakr and Regan Doherty, "Qatar Hails New Egypt Leader in Apparent Policy Shift", *Reuters*, 4 July 2013; The Peninsula, "Qatar to Continue Supporting Egypt", 5 July 2013.

31 Andrew Hammond, *Qatar's Leadership Transition: Like Father, Like Son*: 6.

32 Yasmine Saleh and Patrick Werr, "Egypt Returns $2 Billion to Qatar in Sign of Growing Tensions", *Reuters*. 19 September 2013.

33 Rania Al Gamal and Asma Alsharif, "Egypt Summons Qatari Envoy after Criticisms of Crackdown", *Reuters,* 4 January 2014.

34 Jamil Al-Ziabi, "Qatari FM: We Do Not Support the Muslim Brotherhood", *Al-Monitor*, 22 February 2015.

35 Paul Farhi, "Al Jazeera Faces Criticism in Egypt over Its Coverage of Muslim Brotherhood", *The Washington Post*, 5 January 2014; Greg Carlstrom, "Why Egypt Hates Al Jazeera", *Foreign Policy*, 19 February 2014.

36 Ahram Online, "Al Jazeera Mubasher Misr Channel Banned from Egypt", 29 August 2013.

37 Shabina Khatri, "Al Jazeera Mubasher Misr Taken off Air amid Qatar-Egypt Reconciliation", *Doha News*, 23 December 2014.

38 BBC News, "Al-Jazeera Suspends Egyptian Channel Mubasher Misr", 23 December 2014: http://tinyurl.com/gtpkeoj

39 Walaa Hussein, "Media Wars Hamper Qatari-Egypt Relations", *Al-Monitor*, 3 November 2014: http://tinyurl.com/hrvqrns

40 Maysar Yaseen, "أين ذهب أمير قطر؟" "تميم" يختفي عن وسائل الإعلام.. Translated 'Tamim' Disappears from the Media Where Did the Emir of Qatar Go." *El-Watan News*, 22 May 2015: http://tinyurl.com/zzjlwkj

41 Ahram Online, "Sisi Says Media Attacks on Qatar Reflection of Public Opinion", 28 February 2015: http://tinyurl.com/jg59wld

42 Patrick Kingsley, "Al-Jazeera Journalists Jailed for Seven Years in Egypt", *The Guardian*, 23 June 2014: http://tinyurl.com/khbuozq

43 Patrick Kingsley, "Al-Jazeera Journalists Leave Egyptian Prison on Bail", *The Guardian*, 13 February 2015: http://tinyurl.com/kp5noba

44   Laura King and Amro Hassan, "Egypt Levies Additional Espionage Charges against Ex-President Morsi", *Los Angeles Times*. 6 September 2014: http://tinyurl.com/hw82yov

45   David Kirkpatrick, "Egypt Pulls Ambassador From Qatar", *The New York Times*, 6 March 2014: http://tinyurl.com/zafw9q5

46   Al Jazeera, "Qatar Recalls Ambassador to Egypt over ISIL Row", 19 February 2015: http://tinyurl.com/qdc5hhs

47   Al Arabiya, "Qatar Ambassador Returns to Egypt after Rift over Libya", 31 March 2015: http://tinyurl.com/jecgl4t

48   Khalid AlAttiya, "Qatar's Foreign Policy" Chatham House, 4 December 2013: http://tinyurl.com/j3z9lol

49   Qatar Tribune, "Emir Addresses UN General Assembly", 25 September 2013: http://tinyurl.com/z2vh7jl

50   UN News Center, "Débat Général, United Nations, Main Body, Main Organs, General Assembly", 24 September 2013: http://tinyurl.com/zjmjbk6

51   David Hearst, "Why Saudi Arabia Is Taking a Risk by Backing the Egyptian Coup", *The Guardian*, 20 August 2013: http://tinyurl.com/kvjgu6e

52   Al Jazeera, "Saudi King Abdullah Visits Egypt's Sisi", 20 June 2014: http://tinyurl.com/oxud3hr

53   Ahmad Jamaleddine, "Saudi-Sponsored Summit to Mend Ties between Egypt and Qatar", *Al Akhbar*, 22 December 2014: http://tinyurl.com/hjcht4h

54   Liz Sly, "Backing Egypt's Generals, Saudi Arabia Promises to Fill Financial Void", *The Washington Post*, 19 August 2013: http://tinyurl.com/mlcl4ea

55   BBC News, "Saudi Arabia Declares Muslim Brotherhood 'terrorist Group'", 7 March 2014: http://tinyurl.com/lpdy8xo

56   BBC News, "Gulf Ambassadors Pulled from Qatar Over 'Interference'", 5 March 2014: http://tinyurl.com/lale6c8

57   Al Jazeera, "Gulf States Reinstate Ambassadors to Qatar", 17 November 2014: http://tinyurl.com/kbl648k

58   Gulf Times, "Emir Meets Arab Leaders in Sharm El Sheikh", 28 March 2015: http://tinyurl.com/go5nzhc

59   Turkish Press, "Egypt Sisi Meets Qatari Envoy in Cairo", 20 December 2014: http://tinyurl.com/j989myf

60   Reuters, "Saudi King Salman Vows to Maintain Same Approach as His Predecessors", 23 January 2015: http://tinyurl.com/j5nj4uf

61   Al Arabiya, "King Salman and Erdogan Hold Talks in Riyadh", 2 March 2015: http://tinyurl.com/jjrzyhe

62   Harriyet Daily News, "World Leaders Head to Saudi Arabia to Meet New King Salman", 1 June 2015: http://tinyurl.com/j5hctp8

63   Adnan Abu Amer, "Hamas Reaches out to New Saudi Leadership", *Al-Monitor*, 5 February 2015: http://tinyurl.com/z45dtht

64   Alaraby, "Brothers Again: Saudi Arabia and Hamas Patch up Differences", 19 March 2015: http://tinyurl.com/zpp2gja

65   Middle East Monitor, "Hamas Denies Mediating between Saudi and MB in Yemen", 18 March 2015: http://tinyurl.com/jn95ezr

66   Ahmed Fouad, "Muslim Brotherhood Split on Saudi Strikes in Yemen", *Al-Monitor*, 13 April 2015: http://tinyurl.com/heve68p

67   "كاتب سعودي: الملك سلمان لا يعتبرجماعة الإخوان إرهابية", Freedom and Justice Gate, "King Salman Does Not Consider The Muslim Brotherhood to Be a Terrorist Organisation", 21 April 2015: http://tinyurl.com/zw785sh; "السعودية تقترب من تغيير سياستها تجاه الإخوان المسلمين"، Altagreer، "صحيفة التقرير. "Saudi Arabia Approaches Changing Its Policies to the Muslim Brotherhood", 18 February 2015: http://tinyurl.com/hgkaw2z

68   Dina Ezzat, "Egypt's Foreign Policy Worries Mount after Yemen CrISIL", *Ahram Online*, 24 April 2015: http://tinyurl.com/hajct4o

69 Middle East Eye, "Egypt's Sisi Makes Unexpected Visit to Saudi Arabia, After Royal Shake-up", 2 May 2015: http://tinyurl.com/jlu52w6

70 Aya Nader, "Egypt Will Launch Ground Intervention in Yemen If Necessary: Foreign Minister", *Daily News Egypt*, 25 May 2015: http://tinyurl.com/j8zcpej

71 Anadolu Agency, "No Ground Troops Deployed in Yemen: Egypt's Sisi", 17 April 2015: http://tinyurl.com/jotof22

72 Middle East Monitor, "Saudi Ambassador to Egypt: Egypt Is Suffering from a Media Breakdown", 1 May 2015: http://tinyurl.com/hy22ydf

73 Mustafa Bassiouni, "Sisi's Visit to Russia Is Message to the West", *Al-Monitor*, 13 August 2014: http://tinyurl.com/j5duuhy

74 Middle East Monitor, "Russia Seeks Naval Base in Egypt", 20 November 2013: http://tinyurl.com/gq37rdn

75 David Schenker and Eric Trager, "Egypt's Arms Deal with Russia: Potential Strategic Costs", The Washington Institute for Near East Policy, 4 March 2014: http://tinyurl.com/ooderx3

76 Al Arabiya, "Egypt's Sisi Keen on Cooperating with Russia", 10 May 2015: http://tinyurl.com/mp2k8t4

77 Al Jazeera, "Putin Seeks to Expand Russian Influence in Egypt Visit", 9 February 2015: http://tinyurl.com/map274g

78 Hurriyet Daily News, "Turkey, Saudi Arabia Agree to Boost Support to Syria Opposition", 2 March 2015: http://tinyurl.com/jybaz2m

79 Ryan Grim, Jessica Schulberg, Sophia Jones and Burak Sayin, "Saudi Arabia, Turkey Discussing Unlikely Alliance To Oust Syria's Assad" *The Huffington Post*, 4 December 2015: http://tinyurl.com/lwnzz4q

80 Ayah Aman, "Gulf States to Cut Aid to Egypt", *Al-Monitor*, 17 February 2015: http://tinyurl.com/gwqnvpq

81 Al Arabiya, "Gulf States Offer $12.5 Billion Aid to Egypt", 13 March 2015: http://tinyurl.com/zggtflx

5

Egypt-Turkey Relations in Context: What Role for the GCC States?

Robert Mason

Introduction

Egypt first exchanged ambassadors with Turkey in 1925, and since then the bilateral relationship has experienced a number of highs and lows. In 1954, president Nasser expelled the Turkish ambassador for statements which were critical of the Free Officers' movement. In 1961, the Turkish ambassador was expelled again for criticism about the United Arab Republic between Egypt and Syria. Turkey has remained under suspicion for maintaining close ties to the West, including with Israel. However, Egypt's relations with Turkey improved after Egypt signed the Camp David Accords with Israel in 1979.

A joint Turkish - Egyptian committee was set up in 1988 to explore common interests and areas for cooperation and by 1993 the Turkish - Egyptian Business Council was established. Both states were part of the Barcelona Process which was designed to promote economic ties around the Euro-Med region. Bilateral trade negotiations began in 1998 and formed the basis of the Turkish - Egyptian Free Trade Agreement of 2005. From 2011, the Arab Spring contributed to domestic unrest and regime change in Egypt that led, temporarily, to a Muslim Brotherhood affiliated president. Turkey's support for Mohamed Morsi, and his subsequent removal through a military backed popular 'coup' has created an enduring rift in Egypt-Turkey relations.

This chapter analyses the Egypt-Turkey relationship and assesses what prospects there are for the current frosty relations to thaw. Reference is made to Turkey and Egypt's economic and political relations with each other and the GCC states[1], Turkey's 'zero problems with neighbours' foreign policy and its abandonment of it; opposing policies in Libya; criticism over Gaza and terrorism; the re-election of the Erdoğan's Justice and Development Party (AKP) in November 2015; and in particular, the role that third parties such as Saudi Arabia and Kuwait might play in facilitating a rapprochement. Already both Egypt and Turkey support the Saudi-led operations in Yemen and there could well be behind the scenes diplomatic tracks aimed at slowly mending fences. Although Erdoğan is maintaining a strong line against Cairo, it is questionable how long this can be sustained given the number of challenges facing the Sunni camp and the subsequent necessity for unity.

Economic Relations

The precipitous decline in Egyptian - Turkish relations is somewhat perplexing since as recently as 2007 Egypt and Turkey had signed a Memorandum for a Framework for a Turkish - Egyptian Strategic Dialogue which aims to strengthen bilateral political, economic and cultural cooperation.[2] In addition, due to a Free Trade Agreement signed between the two states in 2005 which came into force in 2007, bilateral trade jumped two and a half times to reach $1.5 billion in 2007 and $2.3 billion in 2008.[3] By 2013, the figure for total bilateral trade rose to $4.2 billion, which although dwarfed by Turkish trade with other partners such as Iran, amounting to $14.6 billion in 2013, was still growing quickly.[4] Furthermore, investments must also be taken into account: Turkey invests $2 billion in Egypt and employs 52,000 workers.[5] These figures could of course be higher if political relations improved.

The Egyptian decision to let the so-called Roll-on/Roll-off agreement lapse after 2014 because it did not provide Egypt with any significant benefit is one example of politics appearing to undermine economic linkages. It gave rise to speculation that the FTA (which is a separate deal) was in trouble.[6] The Ro-Ro agreement was negotiated in 2012, before the Morsi presidency, contrary to popular perception, and was designed to facilitate Turkish foodstuffs and textiles from the northern Mediterranean port of Damietta into the Gulf via Al-Adabiya on the Red Sea thereby compromising Egypt's own position vis-à-vis the GCC states.[7] It did have some advantages for Egypt though, in cutting the amount of time it takes to export wheat to an important export market, Russia. The Turkish government appears to have responded to the Egyptian move by imposing a "dumping fee" on imports of Egyptian polypropylene, justifying the move by saying the imports were exceptionally low price and were hurting Turkey's chemical manufacturing industry.[8]

Turkey will no doubt maintain its strong economic relations with the GCC states, including bilateral trade which stood at $16 billion in 2014[9] with great growth potential Turkish consumer good exports and construction projects. Turkey has been successful in securing $10 billion in investments from GCC states across a range of industries, from health to Islamic banking.[10] This, compared with Egyptian - GCC trade which stood at $ billion the same year. However, Egypt has been successful in attracting $12 billion in Gulf investments during its Sharm El Sheikh economic conference in 2014 and plans to establish a Free Trade Zone with the GCC states in order to boost its economy further.[11]

Turkey and Egypt are also equally engaged with the GCC states at the political level. Saudi Arabia has built its largest embassy in Cairo and both states continue to consult one another over issues in which they have a direct state such as the Middle East Peace Process and counterterrorism. Turkey has also managed to maintain its relations with the GCC states largely within the framework of its original 'zero problems with neighbours' policy and implemented a GCC-Turkey High Level Strategic Dialogue.

Although Egypt only represents a small export market for Turkey, after the financial crisis of 2008, the Gulf became the number one export market for Turkey. Similarly after the Arab Spring in Egypt, the GCC states, and Saudi Arabia, Kuwait and the UAE in particular, are vital partners with which Egypt is interested in securing close economic and political relations. This manageable competition over access to the GCC states became a broader and more contentious political issue after the popular 'coup' on 3 July 2013 which ousted president Morsi from power.

Turkey's 'Zero Problems with Neighbours' Policy and its Demise

Under Abdullah Gul, a western educated pragmatist, a new foreign policy initiative, commonly dubbed 'zero problems with neighbours', was introduced in 2004. This was partly a response to the convergence of the launch of Turkey's new EU accession negotiations, its backing of the "Annan plan" for the reunification of Cyprus and part of a normalisation process with Armenia. However, its main principles, which consisted of fostering peace and security in the region[12] could also be applied to Turkey's relations to other potentially problematic states such as Israel, Libya and Syria, Greece, Iran and the Kurdish Regional Authority.

The approach was based on the realisation that whenever conflict broke out in the neighbourhood, it was Turkey that was often directly affected it, through for example, refugees spilling across its border.[13] It was also based on a more assertive stance following Turkey's rapid economic growth and expanding soft power capabilities. The policy was shaped by the necessity of establishing and maintain regional stability to support economic growth, largely based on attracting inward investment and increasing bilateral trade relations. The policy was maintained by Ahmet Davutoglu when he became foreign minister in 2009.

However, the policy quickly gave way to fast changing facts on the ground and unprecedented challenges to Turkey's relationship with authoritarian regimes at the onset of the Arab Spring. Due to its Islamist agenda and support for Gaza, Turkey's stance on Israel had become increasingly critical even before the Flotilla incident in 2010 in which nine activists were killed by Israeli naval commandos. Turkey subsequently downgraded diplomatic relations and severed military relations in September 2011. Even after president Obama intervened in 2013, forcing an apology from Israeli prime minister Netanyahu, relations had not improved in the absence of recompense being paid. By December 2015, Turkey and Israel looked finally ready to restore relations after a visit by Erdoğan to Israel and an agreed framework of compensation was hammered out.[14] However, Turkey seems to have balked at the imminent normalisation of relations and has instead preferred to add the removal of the Gaza blockade to its list of demands.[15] Turkey has also used Gaza (under control of Hamas; a branch of the Muslim Brotherhood) as another tool by which to criticise Egypt and bolster his own Islamist credentials at home.[16]

The main reason for the about turn in Turkish policy, however, was its over-optimism over the fall of Assad. As soon as it became clear that Turkish support for the protestors in Damascus would not be enough to oust Assad from power, the 'zero problems with neighbours' policy became null and void. The deterioration in official relations is also having a knock on effect to Turkey's relationship (and possibly NATO's relationship, since Turkey is a member) with other powers such as Russia, especially after it shot down a Russian jet in November 2015.[17] Turkey had 1.9 million Syrian refugees on its territory in 2015 according to the UNHCR and further airstrikes will likely increase that figure.[18] Ankara is thus concerned on a number of levels about the Syrian crisis, from the effect it is having from a regional and national security perspective, including a loss of influence in Damascus, to the way an international alliance against Islamic State can play into the hands of Kurdish Workers' Party (PKK) separatist ambitions. Erdoğan was also quick to label PKK in the same terms as Islamic State in order to erode Kurdish support before the Turkish General Election in 2015.

Although Turkey's relationship with the Kurdish Regional Government seems counter-intuitive given Ankara's struggles with the PKK, the relatively peaceful and oil-rich Kurdish autonomous region in northern Iraq has been ripe for investment and trade. The relationship cannot be studied in isolation however, and following an escalation in the conflict between Turkey and the PKK, the Turkish air force launched an attack on what it called a safe house on the border between Iraqi Kurdistan and Iran in August 2015, leading to civilian casualties and a Kurdish backlash.[19] This could yet undermine economic relations, including oil exports worth billions of dollars. The future bilateral relationship depends on a number of factors: the maintenance of the personal relationship between Erdoğan and Barzani (the KRG President), the war against Islamic State which could still threaten Kurdish control over vital oil-rich cities such as Kirkuk, and the KRG's relationship with the Iraqi central government in Baghdad and the Iranian leadership in Tehran.

In Egypt, Erdoğan went from being feted around the world for being the first world leader to call on president Mubarak to step down in 2011, to being shunned by Cairo for a spate of rhetorical attacks against the Egyptian leadership for its alleged state terrorism, including comparing Sisi to Assad.[20] Egypt and Turkey have traded barbs over issues from democracy to meddling in Egypt's internal affairs, including Erdoğan flashing a Rabba sign at supporters. This quickly culminated in the Egypt expelling the Turkish ambassador in November 2013 and pledging not to send its own ambassador and downgrade diplomatic relations to charge d'affaires. Turkey's (along with Qatar's) support of deposed president Morsi has done little to enamour Turkey to the Sisi presidency. Further comments by President Tayyip Erdoğan that Mohamed Morsi should be released from jail and the death sentences against his supporters lifted being pre-requisites to improving diplomatic relations have fallen on deaf ears in Cairo and are simply prolonging poor relations.[21]

There is a clear interpretation in Cairo that Erdoğan's comments are reflective of his bias towards a fellow Islamist party. It seems that Erdoğan feels that he has nothing to lose by pursuing this provocative course of action even if it is unlikely to lead to any tangible benefits. Many Egyptian Muslim Brotherhood figures now live in Turkey and have opened satellite TV stations.[22] Turkish Islamists are keenly aware of the works by Brotherhood intellectuals such as Hassan al Banna, Sayed Qutb and Yousuf Al-Qaradawi. The removal of Morsi from power also equated in the minds of Turkish Islamists as part of their own history and forced removal from power. However, support for these texts are dwindling in the Gulf. For example, in December 2015, 80 books, including those from the above authors were banned in Saudi Arabia.[23] It is possible that other states in the GCC follow suit, and given Turkey's increasing focus on the GCC states for trade and investment, pressure could be put on Turkey to moderate its rhetoric vis-à-vis overt support for the Muslim Brotherhood. A change in leadership could also achieve the same result.

Opposing Policies in Libya

Turkey had a significant historical and economic interest in Libya, based largely on construction projects. Before the NATO intervention, Erdoğan appears to have been concerned that Libya would become a "second Iraq" and offered to mediate between Gaddafi and NATO forces. However, following the onset of airstrikes against the Libyan regime in 2011, Turkey was forced to abandon its potential mediation role and close its embassy. It's policies towards Libya thereafter again reflect a transition from 'zero problems with neighbours' to going 'all in' in support of Islamist groups. Some of these groups such as Ansar al-Sharia (a faction which is loyal to Al-Qaeda), which are intent on destabilising the recognised Libyan government, are allegedly being funded by individuals with links to the Turkish business elite.[24] Further accusations have been made about Turkish and Qatari aircraft flying in and out of the Mitiga air base which is controlled by the rebel Libyan Dawn coalition, amounting to what has been term "clear and explicit support" for terrorism.[25] It is perhaps no surprise, following the reports of intercepted vessels bound for Libya, including four containers of weapons found by the Egyptians in December 2013, that diplomatic relations were downgraded at that time.

It must have been an important contributing factor since Egypt is firming on the side of the recognised government and its attempts to re-establish stability and security in the country. Indeed, Egypt and the UAE were so concerned about the lack of U.S. action in support of the Libyan government that they resorted to carrying out their own airstrikes against violent Islamist groups in August 2014.[26] With the spectre of a rising threat from Islamic State, the onus has been on securing a political agreement that will bring the factions together. This was achieved through the Skhirat agreement which was inked in December 2015, but since there are armed hardliners against the deal, it is questionable whether it will stick.[27] Until it does, Libya will remain in effect, a proxy battleground between states such as Turkey and Qatar who support Islamist groups vying for control over the state and the recognised government back by the West and other Middle Eastern states such as Egypt.

The Re-Election of the Erdoğan's Justice and Development Party (AKP)

An important question in Turkey's relationship with Islamists is whether, following an electoral victory, Erdoğan will moderate a foreign policy which is creating enemies and the 2015 undermining Turkish influence. The vote itself holds clues as to the diminishing attraction of an Islamist leaning government. The AKP failed to secure an outright majority; the first time since coming to power in 2002.[28] Even before the election took place, there was criticism of raids against media groups considered hostile to the AKP and the jailing of journalists critical of the ruling party in government.[29] Whether this crackdown at home will translate into a more authoritarian style after the election remains to be seen. However, it could become harder to criticise Egypt if Ankara is pursuing similar security-centric policies domestically. Already, there are accusations of double standards.[30]

Certainly, the AKP is trying to maintain focus on its Islamist base of support. Yet this cannot be guaranteed going forward for two main reasons. The first is what started as a non-violent protest to save Gezi Park, has rolled into a broader and more popular anti-government protest. This is specified as including political corruption (the destruction of an already small central park epitomised alleged corruption in the country), police brutality (a feature of perceived authoritarianism), journalist self-censorship and an ineffective political opposition.[31] Some of these points may have been contributing factors in the partial military backed coup attempt in July 2016. The second is that Turkey may actually be becoming more secular and less conservative according to Volkan Ertit in his book: *The Age of Anxious Conservatives: Turkey, That Moves Away from Religion.*[32] If these trends continue along the lines of more public protests no matter what suppressive measures are employed, and greater liberalisation; the AKP could be undermined in future elections. In terms of foreign policy, since the current foreign minister, Mevlut Cavusoglu, is a founding member of the AKP, there is likely to be more continuity than change for the time being.

The Syrian Refugee Crisis and Turkish EU Accession: A Lynchpin to Normalised Turkish-Egyptian Relations?

On the face of it, the Syrian crisis appears to have little consequence to Turkey - Egyptian relations. As discussed above, Turkey is involved in the conflict at multiple levels, including hosting a large proportion of Syrian refugees. Egypt however, has sat out of direct intervention in the conflict, preferring to work through the Arab League, calling for a political settlement with other Arab leaders[33], and supports its GCC allies in their more immediate objectives in Yemen. However, it is precisely the European migrant crisis, of which Syria is a major part, that makes Turkey more relevant and attractive as a prospective new EU member state, which could in turn have a major bearing on Turkey - Egyptian relations. By facilitating Turkey's accession to the EU, negotiations which form part of a common EU - Turkey Joint Action Plan on migration, Turkey could form an integral part of a solution that disperses the number of migrants and refugees across all EU member states.[34] Although Germany has generally been welcoming to Syrian refugees, taking in up to 1.5 million in 2015[35], this situation is unsustainable and could create problems for Chancellor Merkel in her bid for re-election in 2017.[36]

So, indirectly and subject to the outcome of ongoing accession negotiations, the EU could have a significant bearing on Turkish foreign policy in the not too distant future. What this would mean for Turkey - Egyptian relations remains somewhat unclear, but generally EU accession provides constraints on political parties in terms of establishing secularism through normative behaviour, encouraging civil society through various policy initiatives, and ensuring legislative compliance with EU legal rules through cases brought before the European Court of Justice. Conceivably, all this could mean that Ankara must tone down its Islamist discourse in order to integrate more effectively with the EU. By doing so, it may find that it not only becomes a bridge between east and west within the EU and a considerable ally on the migrant crisis, but is able to restore and build more pragmatic relations with Egypt. The negotiations could yet be thwarted by fears of a creeping Islamisation of Europe at the political level; for example if Nicholas Sarkozy runs for, and wins, the next French presidential election which takes place in 2017. He has been an arch advocate for Turkey not joining the EU since it does not share the same history and culture.[37]

If Turkey is ultimately successful, accession could serve to re-orientate its foreign policy away from the Gulf and back towards Europe, which remains Turkey's biggest export market. By reconciling its Islamist discourse in a European framework and adopting a common agenda with other European allies, Turkey could end up as a quintessential hybrid state: European and Middle Eastern, majority Muslim in a Christian dominated bloc, Islamist and secular. Whilst most Turks support EU accession (53% in favour in 2014[38]), the AKP has thus far been unable to deliver on accession. EU accession could boost the AKP and provide a chance for reinvention.

Saudi Arabia and Kuwait as Catalysts for a Rapprochement?

In December 2015, Riyadh announced a new multinational Islamic military alliance to fight terrorism, including Turkey and Egypt.[39] Although the listing of some members such as Pakistan and Lebanon may have taken them by surprise, it is clear that both Turkey and Egypt have a vested interest in being involved. King Salman has maintained King Abdullah's focus on Egypt, saying they have strategic links and a "shared future".[40] On Turkey, since 2005, Saudi Arabia and Turkey have been trying to preserve regional stability on a pragmatic basis given their general policy divergence over political Islam.[41] In December 2014, Egypt cautiously accepted a Gulf initiative - in effect tying Egypt into a Saudi-led reconciliation effort aimed at normalising relations with Qatar after the ambassadors of Saudi Arabia, UAE and Bahrain were recalled. The reason for the diplomatic tension was Qatar's vocal criticism of its fellow GCC members in its official media outlets and continued support for extremist groups such as al-Nusra Front and newly banned groups such as the Muslim Brotherhood.[42]

Although, Egypt consented to its inclusion in this rapprochement, some analysts believe it is a reconciliation in name only.[43] Therefore similar attempts by Saudi Arabia to leverage Egypt into more pragmatic dealings with Turkey could also be limited or come unstuck at a later point in time. Saudi Arabia was exhorting both sides to improve their relationship from February 2015 during an official Egyptian visit to the Kingdom through to May 2015[44], but in the run up to the General Election in Turkey, that process has been complicated by the AKP needing to maintain or even elaborate on its Islamist credentials. As long as Ankara remains focused on projecting pro-Islamist rhetoric at Cairo, the time may not be right for the two to come together bilaterally.

The rationale for a Saudi - Turkish - Qatari axis is much stronger and immediate than a Turkish - Egyptian reconciliation. Turkey is a NATO member and given Saudi Arabia's 2010 proposal for creating an Arab force back by the U.S. and NATO to destroy Iranian-backed Hezbollah in Lebanon, Turkey will remain a useful ally.[45] The three states are cooperating on military responses to Iranian intervention in Syria. The three regional powers are collaborating on funding, arms and other forms of support to rebel groups and maintain a belief that Assad must go. Regional tensions are also exacerbated by the conclusion of the Joint Comprehensive Plan of Action (JCPOA) with Iran which the GCC states feels will embolden Iran in the Levant and Gulf and so Iran must be contained at all costs. There is no similar alignment of Egyptian and Turkish national security interests in the region: their divergent policies on Libya is testament to that. However, the regional and international dynamic is changing so quickly, there soon could be, especially is the Arab League undertakes a more active role in Syria or if events in Libya and Gaza spur more cooperative responses.

Conclusion

The Egypt-Turkey relationship hit rock bottom in late 2013 with the expulsion of the Turkish ambassador from Cairo due to Turkey's perceived interference in the internal affairs of Egypt, including ongoing support for the Muslim Brotherhood. The fundamental elements of a more constructive relationship do appear to be there: the potential for growing trade and investment and a common interest in regional stability and security. However, a number of issues have coalesced to form a barrier to further cooperation. A better relationship is therefore likely to be premised on the following: Turkey reinstating some new form of 'zero problems with neighbours' policy since it's abandonment has seriously damaged Turkey's regional position, especially with regard to relations with Egypt. Turkish support for Islamist groups in Libya and Gaza is a source of grievance for the Sisi government. Ankara might therefore consider channelling more support through multilateral efforts, such as UN attempts to broker a unity government in Libya.

If a unity government in Libya holds, it may prove to be the foundation for a broader alliance between Turkey, the GCC states, Egypt and other states to cooperate more fully on a common agenda. The conflict in Syria has illustrated that when there is sufficient converge of interests, as between Turkey, Saudi Arabia and Qatar, there is room for close cooperation. It would certainly benefit both sides if the Free Trade Agreement with Turkey can be maintained and not undermined by allowing other economic agreements to lapse. However, in order to fully take advantage of it, Egypt should develop other more value-added industries in its economy in order to avoid the agreement favouring one side over the other. This will also help to enhance its economic relationship with Turkey and the GCC states.

The future of the Turkey-Egyptian relationship is dependent on a constellation of dynamic factors, but tends to centre around Turkish government support for the Muslim Brotherhood as a mechanism to boost its domestic popularity. Whilst this might not change in the short term, the AKP could tone down its rhetorical opposition to the Sisi government and allow the GCC states to continue to build opportunities for a Turkish - Egyptian reconciliation in the same vein as Egypt's reconciliation with Qatar. This might not be effective at first, but will still constitute a significant step towards a normalisation of relations. Longer term, relations will be determined by the net effect of all the internal and external dynamics affecting both the AKP after their electoral victory and the Sisi government.

For the AKP in particular, the ground of public opinion appears to be shifting against what is considered to be an imposing Islamist government with growing authoritarian tendencies. Should there be new mass protests or major advances in negotiations with the EU over Turkish accession, either of these eventualities could serve to reshape Turkish foreign policy. However, as an EU member state, Ankara may find that it is distancing itself further from Egypt and taking a more ambivalent view of a state which has had as many problems with EU democratisation efforts as it has with Turkish support for Islamists. If Turkey accedes to the EU, it may confirm Cairo's worst fears: that Turkey was always a European state more than a Middle Eastern one and that its interests are not compatible. A rosy future for the bilateral relationship is therefore far from certain

References

Ataman, Muhittin. "Turkish - Saudi Arabian Relations During the Arab Uprisings: Towards a Strategic Partnership?" *Insight Turkey*, Vol. 14, No. 4 (2012)

Davutoğlu, Ahmet. "Turkey's Mediation: Critical Reflections from the Field", *Middle East Policy*, 20 (1), (Spring 2013)

Mason, Robert. "Towards a Strategic Partnership? Turkish Foreign Policy and GCC Alliance Building in the Era of the Arab Revolutions" in Ozden Oktav (ed.), *GCC - Turkey Relations: Dawn of a New Era*, (Geneva: GRC Publishing, 2015)

Notes

1   For a discussion on Turkey - GCC relations see Robert Mason, 'Towards a Strategic Partnership? Turkish Foreign Policy and GCC Alliance Building in the Era of the Arab Revolutions' in Ozden Oktav (ed.), *GCC - Turkey Relations: Dawn of a New Era*, GRC Publishing, 3 June 2015

2   Republic of Turkey Ministry of Foreign Affairs, 'Relations Between Turkey-Egypt': http://tinyurl.com/zftctsg

3   Republic of Turkey Ministry of Foreign Affairs, 'Turkey - Egypt Economic and Trade Relations': http://tinyurl.com/mwoosmm

4   Mehmet Cetingulec, 'Turkey, Iran Seek to Boost Trade as Mistrust Lingers', *Al-Monitor*, 30 August 2014: http://tinyurl.com/z86kpcq

5   Tamer Hafez, 'Egypt, Turkey on the Rocks After Ro-Ro Scuttled', Business Monthly Magazine of American Chamber of Commerce in Egypt, December 2014.

6   ibid.

7   ibid.

8   ibid.

9   Jay Rosenbaum, 'Turkey and the GCC: 'A Win-Win Dynamic', *Middle East Monitor*, 13 August 2015: http://tinyurl.com/ocx37nc

10   ibid.

11   Nigel Wilson, 'Egypt Seeks Free Trade Zone Talks with Gulf States in Bid to Boost Economy', *International Business Times*, 29 August 2014: http://tinyurl.com/hrpe6us

12   Scott MacLeod, 'The Cairo Review Interview: Strategic Thinking', Cairo Review of Global Affairs: http://tinyurl.com/zjnk2v2

13   Ahmet Davutoğlu, 'Turkey's Mediation: Critical Reflections from the Field', *Middle East Policy*, 20 (1), Spring 2013: 83

14   John Reed, Israel and Turkey Poised to Restore Ties After 5-Year Rift', *Financial Times*, 17 December 2015: http://tinyurl.com/hkuvpk4

15   Reuters, 'Turkey Sees No Normalisation of Israel Ties Without End to Gaza Blockade - Spokesman', 28 December 2015: http://tinyurl.com/zmjlogr

16   Josh Levs, 'This Time, Gaza Fighting is 'Proxy War' for Entire Mideast', *CNN*, 1 August 2014: http://tinyurl.com/n28wnwz

17   Mark Galeotti, 'Why did it Take Turkey just 17 Seconds to Shoot Down a Russian Jet?', *The Guardian*, 26 November 2015: http://tinyurl.com/okbvc7s

18   UNHCR, '2015 UNHCR Country Operations Profile - Turkey': http://tinyurl.com/ohazmzd

19   Amberin Zaman, 'The Iraqi Kurds' Waning Love Affair with Turkey', *Al-Monitor*, 1 September 2015: http://tinyurl.com/qgulnbq

20   Piotr Zalewski, 'How Turkey went from 'Zero Problems' to Zero Friends', *Foreign Policy*, 22 August 2013: http://tinyurl.com/j46sqxw

21   Humeyra Pamuk, 'Turkey's Erdogan Says Egypt Should Free Morsi Before it can Restore Ties', *Reuters*, 9 April 2015: http://tinyurl.com/h66z4dj

22   Ahram Online, 'Muslim Brotherhood 'Rabaa' Channel Launched, Airing from Turkey', 21 December 2013: http://tinyurl.com/jpwnl7k

23   Arab News, '80 Books Promoting Brotherhood Banned', 2 December 2015: http://tinyurl.com/hhp2hx5

24   Jonathan Schanzer, 'Turkey's Secret Proxy War in Libya?', *National Interest*, 17 March 2015: http://tinyurl.com/zl3y3t8

25   ibid.

26   Simon Henderson, 'U.S. Allies Bombing Islamists: The UAE Airstrikes on Libya', The Washington Institute for Near East Policy, 25 August 2015: http://tinyurl.com/jdskh5d

27   Aziz El Yaakoubi, 'Libyan Factions Sign UN Deal to Form Unity Government', *Reuters*, 17 December 2015: http://tinyurl.com/qczf3xr

28   Jon Henley, Kareem Shaheen and Constanze Letsch, 'Turkey Election: Erdogan and AKP Return to Power with Outright Majority', *The Guardian*, 2 November 2015: http://tinyurl.com/ngbyflz

29   ibid.

30   Pinar Tremblay, 'Erdogan's Biggest Fear: The 'Concerned' Islamists', *Al-Monitor*, 15 August 2015: http://tinyurl.com/hzd2gd4

31 The Guardian, 'What's Causing the Protests in Turkey?', 4 June 2013: http://tinyurl.com/jjea9dv

32 See Mustafa Akyol, 'Turkey is Becoming More Secular, Not Less', *Al-Monitor*, 2 March 2015: http://tinyurl.com/gp5f25f

33 Ahmed Fouad, 'Could Egypt be Key to Political Solution in Syria?', *Al-Monitor*, 25 October 2015: http://tinyurl.com/htmagot

34 Nick Tattersall and Paul Carrel, 'Merkel, in Bind on Migrants, Ready to Back Faster Turkish EU Bid', *Reuters*, 18 October 2015: http://tinyurl.com/gwd65ml

35 Justin Hugger and Matthew Holehouse, 'Germany Expects up to 1.5 Million Migrants in 2015', *The Telegraph*, 5 October 2015: http://tinyurl.com/qcz925y

36 Erik Kirschbaum, 'Merkel to Run for Fourth Term in 2017: Der Spiegel', *Reuters*, 1 August 2015: http://tinyurl.com/go4s9oa

37 Jasper Mortimer, 'France Says Blunt 'Non' to Turkey', *France 24*, 25 February 2011: http://tinyurl.com/z2xnz8e

38 Kadri Gursel, 'Turks Turn to EU with Renewed Enthusiasm', *Al-Monitor*, 10 September 2014: http://tinyurl.com/hbln65x

39 Elekhbariya, 'Saudi Arabia Announces 34-Member Islamic Military Alliance to Fight Terrorism', 15 December 2015: http://tinyurl.com/zmp2f4t

40 Al Alarabiya, 'King Salman Hails Strong Saudi, Egypt Ties', 9 February 2015: http://tinyurl.com/z7lcvwq

41 For details see: Muhittin Ataman, 'Turkish - Saudi Arabian Relations During the Arab Uprisings: Towards a Strategic Partnership?' *Insight Turkey*, Vol. 14, No. 4: http://tinyurl.com/gu744wm

42 BBC News, 'Gulf Ambassadors Pulled From Qatar Over 'Interference'', 5 March 2014: http://tinyurl.com/lale6c8

43 Walaa Hussein, 'Egypt Cautiously Accepts Reconciliation with Qatar', *Al-Monitor*, 8 December 2014: http://tinyurl.com/gu3jefz

44 Semih Idiz, 'Ankara's Relations with Cairo Still Frosty Despite Saudi Mediation', *Al-Monitor*, 5 May 2015: http://tinyurl.com/jheegt6

45 Ewan MacAskill, 'Wikileaks Cables: Saudis Proposed Arab Force to Invade Lebanon', *The Guardian*, 7 December 2010: http://tinyurl.com/jpmpcrh

6

Saudi Arabia and Egypt's Strategic Relationship: Continuities and Transformations After King Abdullah's Death[1]

Sebastian Sons

Introduction

The Saudi leadership under late King Abdullah bin Abdulaziz bin Sa'ud (r. 2005-2015) perceived the fall of Egypt's Hosni Mubarak in 2011 and the subsequent electoral victories of the Muslim Brotherhood (*al-Ikwhan al-Muslimun*, MB) under President Muhammad Morsi from June 2012 until July 2013 with great concern. Since the 1970s, the moderate, pro-U.S. Mubarak regime had been one of Saudi Arabia's most important allies for several reasons[2]: (1) Together, they contained the regional influence of states such as Saddam Hussein's Iraq, Hafiz and Bashar al-Assad's Syria, Iran as well as non-state actors such as Hamas; (2) Egypt offered Saudi Arabia military backing and support in times of external crisis; (3) Saudi Arabia still served as an important job market for Egyptian migrants[3]; (4) in turn, Egypt's economy required the remittances coming from Saudi Arabia in order to tackle domestic socio-economic challenges.[4] Domestically, Mubarak excluded the MB from the political process. This strategy was supported by King Abdullah due to the Saudi leader's traditional skepticism towards the Islamist movement even before 2011 and Saudi Arabia's "emergence as [an] assertive regional power"[5] since 2011. Thus, the removal of Mubarak put the preservation of the following pillars of Saudi foreign policy under pressure:

Safeguarding the Domestic Power of the Al Sa'ud

Since the foundation of the Kingdom of Saudi Arabia in 1932 by King Abdulaziz Ibn Sa'ud (r. 1932-1953), Saudi foreign policy was profoundly driven by the primary political interest in saveguarding the domestic power of the Al Sa'ud as the only legitimate ruler of the kingdom.[6] This decision-making process is based on "elite-level alliance networks"[7] and was shown again after the late King Abdullah died and the power transition to his successor King Salman took place relatively smoothly.

Safeguarding Saudi Arabia's Business Interests

Saudi Arabia's increased role as an influential economic player on a regional and global level has also driven its foreign policy in recent years.[8] The Saudi economy is characterized by patronage and clientele networks based on "segmented clientelism"[9] that have been established over time in order to integrate the merchants and tribal players into the bureaucratic system.[10] However, the Saudi business community has been only to a small extent co-opted and controlled directly by the ruling family.[11] Thus, both players – business community and royal family – could cooperate either as allies or compete each other as rivals i.e. business families can act either as promoters of Saudi foreign policy or as veto powers as far as they perceived their own business interests at risk due to the Al Sa'ud's political decisions.[12]

Safeguarding the Saudi Alliance with the Wahhabi ulama

Third, Saudi foreign policy is characterized by an ideological and rhetorical policy based on Wahhabism. In this regard, political decision-makers need to take the interests of the Wahhabi clergy into consideration in order to satisfy them but also to legitimize political decisions ideologically.[13] Since King Faisal's rule (r. 1964-1975), religious scholarship was transformed into a co-opted state clergy. Certainly, the more the religious establishment was integrated into the state apparatus, the more it lost its influence as a veto power and thus became only a "junior partner".[14] This grows particularly apparent when the anti-Shia foreign policy[15], mostly directed against Iran, is taken into consideration.

After the outbreak of the "Arab Uprisings", Saudi Arabia shifted its foreign policy strategy from a non-interventionist, mediating policy towards a status quo policy aiming at the stabilization of allied regimes in Egypt in order to preserve these foreign policy pillars.[16] Of course, the "Arab Uprisings" came as a shock for the Kingdom which was reflected in an evolution of its foreign policy from a "consensual pattern to a confrontational assertive one."[17] However, the death of King Abdullah and the shift to new King Salman in January 2015 reconfigured the means of Saudi policy on Egypt in different fields of action. While Egypt's government under General Abd al-Fattah Sisi served as a reliable partner for the old king who supported Egypt with financial assistance and political support, King Salman has shown more reluctance to continue with this pro-Sisi stance. This shift in Saudi Arabia's policy on Egypt is driven by a general reconfiguration of the Kingdom's foreign policy from "Ikhwanoia" to "Iranoia".

In its first part, the chapter will thus focus on the pillars of Saudi Arabia's policy on Egypt under King Abdullah and its efforts between 2011 and 2014. Secondly, the new King Salman's policy on Egypt since spring 2015 will be analyzed. Finally, a short outlook will be given. Mainly based on experts' interviews conducted in Saudi Arabia and Egypt in 2014 and 2015, the chapter highlights remaining continuities and possible transformations of the bilateral relationship by comparing the political strategies of King Abdullah and his successor Salman.

Abdullah's Policy on Egypt Since 2011: Saudi Arabia's "Ikhwanoia"

Islamist Democracy Versus Saudi Monarchy

The close Egyptian-Saudi partnership came to an abrupt end when Mubarak was ousted from power in February 2011. The following transition process which resulted in the election of Muhammad Morsi in April 2012 as new President worried the Saudi ruling family who was concerned of losing an important ally in the regional balance of power.[18] From the Saudi perspective, a model of Islamist democracy established by the MB as a political alternative could have attracted parts of the Saudi population and thus challenged the leadership claim of the Saudi regime within the Islamic world.[19] More precisely, political Islam causes a challenge to the ideology of Saudi-Wahhabi rule.

This "Ikhwanoia" dated back to the 1950s and 1960s. At that time, the bilateral relations cooled down due to the pan-Arab, anti-monarchical policy of Egypt's President Gamal Abd el-Nasser[20] (r. 1952/1954-1970) followed by a massive influx of internal Egyptian dissidents to Saudi Arabia who were persecuted at home and thus flew abroad to countries such as Saudi Arabia. Especially members of the banned MB found asylum in Saudi Arabia and formed the backbone of the education system in the kingdom.[21] The young Saudi generation was subsequently educated by school curricula inspired by the ideology of the MB.[22] Their ideology of activist political Islam became appealing also for many Saudis who began to see the MB as a pure and clean antipode to the Saudi political elite, and as a suitable alternative to the Saudi religious and political leadership. Meanwhile, the MB started to establish a Saudi-based network – often with official Saudi support.[23] However, the Saudi leadership subsequently began to perceive the growing sympathies for the MB with suspicion and as a challenge for its own legitimacy; after all, the MB's ideology has from the start aimed at the removal of Arab monarchies and hereditary dynasties and their replacement by an Islamist transnational political system.[24] As a consequence, Egyptian migrants were expelled due to these ideological and political tensions. The Saudi rulers' perception of the MB further deteriorated after the Iraqi invasion of Kuwait in 1990 was supported by the Islamists.[25] In addition, a rising Islamist opposition within Saudi Arabia (*al-Sahwa al-Islamiya*, 'Awakening movement') was accused of being influenced by the Saudi MB.[26] This influence continues to be a domestic challenge to the Saudi leadership until today: Prominent Sahwa leaders condemned the ousting of Morsi publicly by signing petitions and indirectly criticized the Saudi rulers.[27]

Possible Egyptian Rapprochement with Iran

Second, the cautious rapprochement of Morsi with Iran seriously worried Saudi Arabia as this conflicted with Saudi geo-political reasoning in which the religious and political rivalry with Iran plays a dominant role. This rapprochement was demonstrated by successive high-level meetings between officials of both states[28] and the allowed passing of two Iranian battle ships through the Suez Canal in February 2011.[29] In addition, Morsi constituted mutual cooperation with Qatar that presented itself as a strong supporter of the MB for decades and especially since 2011 which was perceived with strong concern by the Saudi rulers and led to inner-GCC disunity[30] shown by the recall of the Saudi, Emirates' and Kuwait's ambassadors from Qatar in March 2014.[31] In November 2014 on the GCC summit in Doha, Qatar was demanded by the other GCC members to stop its support for the MB and the pro-Islamist propaganda of *Aljazeera*. Qatar agreed to reduce its assistance for the MB, to support the new Egyptian government, and to limit Saudi-critical reporting on *Aljazeera*.[32] In January 2015, Qatar closed the Egyptian branch of *Aljazeera*.[33]

While the political relations further deteriorated under Morsi's presidency, the Saudi leadership became aware that the current Egyptian government has to be removed. Finally, the *coup d'état* of General Abd al-Fattah Sisi and his military comrades in July 2013 – in Egyptian public discourse labeled as "Second Revolution"[34] – was to some extent prepared together with Saudi Arabia in advance.[35] Immediately after the fall of Morsi, King Abdullah congratulated Sisi and granted him full support. The message was clear: Saudi Arabia will stand at the side of Egypt's army – no matter what this support will cost.[36] This strong cooperation became significant during several visits of high-ranking delegations from Egypt to Saudi Arabia and *vice versa*.[37] It was quiet obvious that Sisi, who served as a military attaché in the Egyptian embassy in Saudi Arabia during Mubarak's reign, showed keen interest in reinstalling the full Saudi support on a political and economic level whereas Abdullah supported Sisi's political strategy due to four main reasons:

1. The change from an Islamist democracy under the MB to a military regime proved that the MB's ideology was no success model for the Arab world and, thus, did not harm the legitimacy of the Saudi monarchy.
2. With the fall of the MB, the rapprochement between Morsi and Iran was stopped.
3. The fall of the MB meant also the end of Qatar's strong influence in Egypt.
4. Saudi Arabia presented itself as the savior of the Egyptian destiny which helped the kingdom to improve its image in the Arab-Sunni world.

Saudi Business Interests at Stake

Besides these political struggles, the turmoil in Egypt and the election of Morsi as new president also caused severe consequences for the Saudi business community's interests in Egypt. Saudi businessmen have been very active in Egypt for decades due to the fact that the country is the largest consumer market in the region, geo-strategically well situated as a logistical and economic hub to the Sub-Saharan countries and Europe, and geographically close to the Western Saudi Hijaz region, which includes the city of

Jeddah, the Kingdom's most important trade center. Some bilateral business networks can be traced back to the end of the 19ᵗʰ century when members of important Egyptian merchants' families came to the Hijaz in order to visit Mecca and Medina for pilgrimage (*hajj*), and then settled in and started trade activities from Jeddah.[38] These longstanding ties have stood the test of time no matter which political conflicts occurred between both states. Saudi businessmen, especially entrepreneurs who are operating from Jeddah, have been following their business interests on their own, hardly determined by political decisions or governmental interests. They often used direct access to Egyptian political decision-makers. Of course, Saudi Arabia's business community was not specifically interested in saving the political regime from collapse and in keeping the MB from power but to keep Egypt as an important market stable and secure its return on investments. This demand is mainly based on investments in real estate, energy, petrochemicals, tourism, agriculture and agribusiness, and infrastructure. In total, 3,302 Saudi companies are said to have been active in the Egyptian market in 2014, most of them working via local sub-contractors, middlemen or branches of multi-sectoral conglomerates.[39] When it comes to trade, the volume reached $3.25 billion (exports: $420 million, imports: $2.83 billion) in fiscal year 2013/2014 and has risen to $3.31 billion in fiscal year 2014/2015 (exports: $595.2 million, imports: $2.71 billion). Saudi Arabia is thus the main Gulf trade partner of Egypt. Total Saudi investment in Egypt amounts to $5.7 billion in 2014 (or 27 percent of the Arab total investment in Egypt) in 2,743 projects.[40] In addition, influential non-governmental or semi-governmental players are exerting their influence via their long-standing connections with members of the old elites within the Egyptian business community, the military, and the current government. Among them are the Chambers of Commerce, the bilateral Egyptian-Saudi Business Association (ESBA) founded in December 2013 by the Jeddah Chamber of Commerce and Industry (JCCI) and the General Federation of Egyptian Chambers of Commerce (FEDCOC)[41], and Saudi business conglomerates owned by influential merchant families such as az-Zamil, Bin Ladin, Salih Kamil, or al-Juffali.

However, several Saudi infrastructure and construction projects implemented under Mubarak were brought to a halt when the Morsi government decided to nationalize them – a situation unacceptable for both the Saudi business community and the Saudi political elite. In total, 28 legal disputes between the Morsi government and Saudi entrepreneurs came to the surface, resulting in bitter resentment from the Saudi side. These firms controlled nearly $2.15 billion in assets, accounting for around 61.6% of the total stalled Saudi investments in Egypt.[42] The businessmen were accused of bribery to manipulate Egypt's tenders and auctions law. However, economic activities went on, and the new Egyptian government showed strong willingness to settle the disputes with important Saudi partners by establishing a special committee in April 2012 presided by the prime minister. By 2014, 19 cases were settled out of court with strong involvement of the Egyptian Ministry of Investment and the Ministry of Defense and the Saudi Chambers of Commerce.[43]

Despite these legal struggles, the majority of the Saudi business community watched the new economic policy of the MB favorably. Its pronounced fight against non-transparency, corruption and Mubarak-fashioned networks of patronage by putting long-lasting contracts under test was generally expressed with sympathy by the Saudi businessmen. They hoped to strongly benefit from ongoing transitional processes within the economic and bureaucratic structure at the cost of traditional Egyptian business elites.[44] At the end of 2013, Saudi investments in Egypt amounted to $2.5 billion while the trade volume was $5 billion which means no fundamental decrease in comparison to pre-2011.

Financial Assistance: Preserving the Saudi Interests

In order to preserve the Saudi interests, Saudi Arabia disbursed tremendous sums in financial assistance in form of loans, grants, and energy subsidies in order to prevent Egypt's insolvency.[45] Since 2011, Egypt's economy was hit by a severe economic crisis. Thus, Sisi was in utmost need of foreign capital in order to overcome the acute budget deficit and Saudi Arabia served as one of the most reliable and generous donors of grants, loans, and energy subsidies for the Sisi government but also for the Supreme Council of the Armed Forces (SCAF) which was granted soft loans in 2011 and 2012 such as $500 million for financing development projects in Egypt in different sectors from the Saudi Fund for Development (SDF). These included housing, water, irrigation, sanitation, supply, electricity, energy, health and a credit line to finance non-oil products worth $750 million. Saudi Arabia also provided $750 million as a line of credit to bridge the budget deficit in May 2011, a deposit of $1 billion to the Central Bank in May 2012, and a further $500 million as treasury bonds and bills in June 2012. A sum of $1.45m was also provided by the Saudi Fund in the Egyptian Development Programme supervised by the Ministry of International Cooperation as well as $200 million aimed at fostering SME establishments and $250 million as oil subsidies.[46] After Morsi's fall, Saudi Arabia pledged financial assistance of $5 billion in form of a non-interest deposit of $2 billion (with the duration of five years) to the Central Bank of Egypt (CBE), donations of $1 billion, and gas and oil support of $2 billion in order to stabilize Egypt's deteriorating economy.[47] On the Egyptian Economic Development Conference (EEDC) in March 2015, further $4 billion has been pledged by Saudi Arabia.[48] One main goal of the financial assistance was to slow down the dramatic decrease of Egypt's foreign currency reserves which stood at some $36 billion in January 2011, and have decreased to $18.1 billion at the end of 2011 and to $12.3 billion in February 2012. By the end of February 2014, net international resources grew again to $17.3 billion.[49] In addition, the depreciation of the Egyptian pound has improved from 10.4% in the first half of 2013 to 0.9% in the second half due to the financial assistance from the Gulf.[50] Already in February 2014, the Egyptian administration stated that the influx of Gulf financial assistance will increase the economic growth to 3.5% while the economic growth was only 1% in the second half of 2013.[51]

From a political perspective, the financial assistance was not delivered unconditionally: Instead, the influx of Saudi money was to a large extent part of a political understanding between Saudi Arabia's and Egypt's leaderships as both were interested in cracking down on the MB. The representation of the MB as "the bogeyman (…) has been the single most important factor deferring protest and keeping the disparate actors within the regime united."[52] Sisi's anti-MB strategy was totally supported and to some extent demanded by King Abdullah in order to prevent the establishment of a Mubarak-like Islamist deep state "within three months in comparison to Mubarak who created such as system within 30 years."[53] However, taking money from abroad became a "double-edged sword" for Egypt's economic recovery: On the one hand, Sisi bought time to manage the currency depreciation and the economic recession smoothly but on the other, the future economic recovery could be hampered if Egypt's government is to avoid cutting subsidies and making other economic reforms.[54] Furthermore, criticism has spread among Egyptian social media activists who accused the government of selling the country to the Gulf region.[55] Similar reservations towards the ongoing financial support emerged also in Saudi Arabia. In September 2013 former Foreign Minister Saud al-Faisal (died in July 2015) clarified that the Kingdom will (and has to) decrease or even cease its financial assistance.[56] Challenged by decreasing oil revenues due to the sinking oil price[57] and rising discontent from the domestic population who suffers from high youth unemployment rate of 30% and limits of the welfare system, unconditional assistance to the Sisi administration was seen as a "financial burden" from the Saudi perspective.[58] Every year, 550,000 young Saudis enter the job market and cannot be absorbed anymore.[59] Thus, Saudi policymakers may find that the tradeoff between financial assistance abroad and spending on social programs at home becomes progressively harder to justify.[60] There is a degree of alarm at the extent of Saudi financial and economic assistance and a sense that Egypt may turn out to be a "bottomless pit" requiring constant and long-term support.[61]

Salman's Policy on Egypt: Shift from "Ikhwanoia" to "Iranoia"

Although Saudi Arabia's relationship to Egypt will probably not undergo a dramatic change, some gradual modifications in King Salman's policy on Egypt can be observed since his inauguration: While Abdullah fostered the installation of Sisi and the ousting of Morsi due to his animosities towards the MB and its cautious reconciliation with Iran, King Salman is working on establishing a more pragmatic foreign policy strategy which may include to reshuffle the Saudi stance towards Sisi's Egypt. This new policy agenda is based on a general shift of Salman's foreign policy from "Ikhwanoia" to "Iranoia". The deteriorating security situation in neighboring Iraq, Syria, Bahrain, and Yemen is considered as an expansion of Iranian power at the cost of the Kingdom. Although this perception is often exaggerated and can be thus labeled as "Iranoia"[62], the anti-Iranian discourse and the strong feeling of being surrounded by pro-Iranian enemies became a predominant pattern of Saudi Arabian public discourse and the main driving force in Saudi Arabia's foreign policy even under Abdullah. However, this "Iranoia" has even intensified after Abdullah passed away in January 2015 and his half-brother Salman was inaugurated as new Saudi king on January 23, 2015.[63]

Animosities Regarding the Saudi Military Action in Yemen and Syria

In comparison to his predecessor's policy, King Salman's military action in Yemen indicates this foreign policy shift towards a more interventionist and non-diplomatic approach.[64] With regard to the Saudi-Egyptian relationship, operation "Decisive Storm" (renamed in April 2015 operation to "Restoring Hope") has also caused animosities between both governments: While Egypt favors a joint military force under the supervision of the Arab League (AL) with strong Egyptian leadership, King Salman is more interested in forming ad-hoc coalitions under his control. The establishment of the joint AL military force, comprising roughly 40,000 soldiers, was announced on the summit in Sharm el-Sheikh in March 2015 on Sisi's initiative. As the largest army in the region with 400,000 active soldiers and 500,000 military reservists, Egypt is seeking to recover its regional importance by commanding the joint military force.[65]

King Salman's Interest in the Possible Re-Integration of the MB

Saudi Arabia's new leadership is skeptical of Sisi's radical anti-MB policy. The crackdown policy of Egypt's president has excluded the MB from the political decision-making process and even from social life.[66] This has widened the inner-Egyptian societal rift between pro-MB and anti-MB forces. Although Sisi still enjoys widespread public support, the deteriorating security situation especially on the Sinai peninsula may further destabilize the political situation. This might lead to further frustration among the Egyptian people and to more radicalization among the young generation of the MB. While Saudi Arabia is interested in a stable Egypt, King Salman is watching this development very cautiously.

On a regional level, Sisi's definition of terrorism which is based only on fighting Sunni Islamists such as the MB contradicts the Saudi approach of fighting pro-Iranian and pro-Shiite forces like those in Yemen.[67] Furthermore, King Salman wants to cooperate with Turkey and Qatar in order to fight the "Islamic State" (IS, *Da'ish*) in Iraq and Syria and might be thus interested in a re-integration of Egypt's MB in order to appease pro-MB Qatar and Turkey.[68] This was also shown by the integration of these both countries in the Saudi-initiated anti-terrorism alliance, consisting of 34 Islamic states, which was founded in December 2015.[69] This more pragmatic policy towards the several MB branches across the region are not rooted in more trust in the movement by the new Saudi king but by the assessment that the threat of IS is even higher than the threat of the MB.[70]

Personal Animosities

Furthermore, the leaking of telephone conversations of Sisi with his advisers in February 2015 blaming Saudi Arabia and other Gulf states in an abusive way caused tremendous reactions in Gulf media and social networks. In the alleged recording, a man identified as Sisi stated: "We need 10 billion to be put in the army's account (…) and we want 10 like them from the Emirates, and from Kuwait another 10, in addition to a couple of pennies to be put in the central bank and that will complete the 2014 budget" continuing "Man, they [the Gulf states, S.S.] have money like rice."[71] Although the authenticity of these talks is not proved yet and Sisi tried to calm the waves by calling King Salman immediately, the *Twitter* campaign "Sisi ridicules the Gulf" started stating to abandon the Saudi financial support of Egypt.[72] For sure, these reactions will not cause a general political turnaround of Saudi Arabia's strategy towards Egypt but have spread anti-Egyptian animosities in Saudi and Gulf societies.[73] Furthermore, King Salman and other high-ranking Saudi members of the royal family are worried about Sisi's decreasing popularity among his own people. Since the beginning of his reign, he has raised tremendous expectations to solve the economic crisis, to create jobs for the unemployed youth, and to reinstall security. None of these has been realized yet. Thus, the image of Sisi in Saudi Arabia has further decreased. He is considered a weak leader without charismatic attitudes who does not have a real vision for his country.[74]

Conclusion

Under King Salman, the bilateral relationship with Egypt has undergone several modifications. Whereas his predecessor King Abdullah supported Sisi on both a financial and personal level in order to reinstall the pre-2011 *status quo ante*, King Salman is following a different approach: Being more skeptical about Sisi's political course, the Egyptian-Saudi relationship has cooled down to some extent. Financial assistance will not be pledged unconditionally anymore and the Saudi political support for Sisi's strict anti-MB crackdown campaign has its limits.[75]

Instead, it became obvious in recent months that King Salman's foreign policy is more focused on nearby hot spots such as Yemen, while Egypt as well as other North African countries are of less interest and will only be prioritized in the case of a deterioration of security or a serious economic crisis in these countries that might harm Saudi interests.[76] King Salman's foreign policy priority is to contain Iran's and IS's regional impact in neighboring countries. In this regard, the fight against the regional clout of the MB became less important. In general, King Salman is diversifying external alliances in order to prove his ability to act as a sovereign regional power. Although the U.S. remains a reliable ally, other coalitions (such as the anti-Houthi alliance and the new anti-terrorism alliance) and ad-hoc partnerships will become more important. In addition, with oil prices having dropped by almost 60% since June 2014, Saudi new leaders have also to reassess their economic policy towards more inward spending, towards cutting financial support for traditional Sunni allies such as Egypt, and diversifying and liberalizing the private economy in order to prevent social frustration and further jihadist radicalization.[77]

References

Aarts, Paul and Gerd Nonneman, pp. 111-143, London: Hurst & Company, 2006.

Abir, Mordechai. *Saudi Arabia. Government, Society and the Gulf Crisis.* (London: Routledge, 1993).

Attiya, Ahmad. "Beyond Labor. Foreign Residents in the Persian Gulf States." In: *Migrant Labor in the Persian Gulf,* edited by Mehran Kamrava and Zahra Babar, (London: Hurst & Company, 2012): 21-40.

Al Tamamy, Saud Mousaed. "Hegemonic or Defensive? Patterns of Saudi Foreign Policy in the Era of the Arab Spring." *ORIENT* IV (2012): 14-21.

Albers, Henry. *Saudi Arabia: Technocrats in a traditional society.* (New York: Peter Lang International Academic Publishers, 1989).

Al-Rasheed, Madawi. "Circles of power: Royals and society in Saudi Arabia". In: *Saudi Arabia in the Balance. Political Economy, Society, Foreign Affairs,* edited by Paul Aarts and Gerd Nonneman. (London: Hurst & Company, 2006): 185-213.

Coates Ulrichsen, Kristian. "Egypt-Gulf Ties and a Changing Balance of Regional Security." *The Cairo Review on Global Affairs* (January 12, 2015).

Cordesman, Anthony H. "Saudi Stability in a Time of Change." Center for Strategic and International Studies, (April 21, 2011).

Darwich, May. "The Ontological (In)security of Similarity: Wahhabism versus Islamism in Saudi Foreign Policy". *GIGA Working Papers* no 263 (December 2014).

Dazi-Heni, Fatiha. "Saudi Leadership in a Chaotic Middle Eastern Context." *ISPI Analysis* 279 (November 2014).

El Houdaiby, Ibrahim. "Beyond the Crisis. A Roadmap for Reconciliation in Egypt." *DGAPstandpunkt* 9, German Council on Foreign Relations (June 2014).

Field, Michael. *The merchants: The big business families of Saudi Arabia and the Gulf.* (New York: The Overlook Press, 1984).

Gause III, F. Gregory. "Saudi Arabia's Regional Security Strategy". In: *The International Politics of the Persian Gulf,* edited by Mehran Kamrava. (Syracuse: Syracruse University Press, 2011): 169-183.

Henderson, Simon. "Riyadh Looks to Moscow." *Policy Alert,* The Washington Institute for Near East Policy (June 17, 2015).

Hertog, Steffen. "Modernizing without democratizing? The introduction of formal politics in Saudi Arabia". *International Politics and Society* 3 (2006): pp. 75-78.

Hertog, Steffen. "Segmented Clientelism: The political economy of Saudi economic reform efforts". In: *Saudi Arabia in the Balance. Political Economy, Society, Foreign Affairs.*

Hertog, Steffen. "The Costs of Counter-Revolution in the Gulf." *Foreign Policy* (May 31, 2011).

Hertog, Steffen. *Princes, Brokers, and Bureaucrats: Oil and the State in Saudi Arabia.* London, Ithaca: Cornell University Press, 2010.

Kapiszewski, Andrzej. "De-Arabization in the Gulf: Foreign Labor and the Struggle for Local Culture." *Georgetown Journal of International Affairs* 8, no. 2 (2007): pp. 81-88.

Khatib, Lina. "Qatar and the Recalibration of Power in the Gulf". Carnegie Middle East Center (September 2014).

Knauerhase, Ramon. *The Saudi Arabian economy.* New York: Praeger, 1977.

Lacroix, Stéphane. "L'Arabie Saoudite au défi du printemps arabe". CERI, Sciences Po Paris (September 2011).

Lacroix, Stéphane. "Saudi Arabia's Muslim Brotherhood predicament." *POMEPS Studies* 25 (March 25, 2014).

Lacroix, Stéphane. *Awakening Islam. The Politics of Religious Dissent in Contemporary Saudi Arabia.* Cambridge: Harvard University Press, 2011.

Lucas, Viola and Thomas Richter. "Arbeitsmarktpolitik am Golf: Herrschaftssicherung nach dem ,Arabischen Frühling'." *GIGA Focus Nahost* 12 (2012).

Luciani, Giacomo. "Saudi Arabian business: From private sector to national bourgeoisie". In: *Saudi Arabia in the Balance. Political Economy, Society, Foreign Affairs*, edited by Paul Aarts and Nonneman, Gerd, pp. 144-184, London: Hurst & Company, 2006.

Malik, Monica and Tim Niblock. "Saudi Arabia's Economy: the Challenge of Reform". In: *Saudi Arabia in the Balance. Political Economy, Society, Foreign Affairs* edited by Paul Aarts and Nonneman, Gerd, pp. 85-110, London: Hurst & Company, 2006.

Niblock, Tim. *Saudi Arabia. Power, legitimacy and survival.* London: Taylor & Francis, 2006.

Ranko, Annette and Najwa Sabra. "Sisis Ägypten – Vollendung der Revolution oder zurück auf Null?" *GIGA Focus* No. 1 (2015).

Reibman, Max. "The IMF in Egypt, Act Two." Carnegie Endowment for International Peace (April 24, 2014).

Roll, Stephan. "Al-Sisis Entwicklungsvisionen. Großbauprojekte und Herrschaftssicherung in Ägypten." *SWP-Aktuell* 35, German Institute for International and Security Affairs (May 2014).

Said Aly, Abdel Monem. "Post-Revolution Egyptian Foreign Policy," *Middle East Brief* No. 86, Brandeis University (November 2014).

Seznec, Jean-Francois. "Changing Circumstances: Gulf Trading Families in the Light of Free Trade Agreements, Globalization and the WTO." In: *The Gulf Family: Kinship Policies and Modernity*, edited by Alanoud Alsharekh, pp. 57-82, London: Saqi, 2012.

Sons, Sebastian and Inken Wiese, "The Engagement of Arab Gulf States in Egypt and Tunisia since 2011: Rationale and Impact," *DGAPanalyse* No. 9, October 2015.

Soubrier, Emma. "Regional Disorder and New Geo-economic Order: Saudi Security Strategies in a Reshaped Middle East", *GRM Papers*, Gulf Research Center (September 2014).

Steinberg, Guido. "Leading the Counter-Revolution. Saudi Arabia and the Arab Spring". *SWP Research Paper*, German Institute for International and Security Affairs (June 2014).

Steinberg, Guido. "Saudi-Arabien: Sicherheit für Öl". In: *Außenpolitik mit Autokratien: Jahrbücher des Forschungsinstituts der Deutschen Gesellschaft für Auswärtige Politik 30*, edited by Josef Braml, Wolfgang Merkel and Eberhard Sandschneider, pp. 136-44, Berlin: De Gruyter, 2014.

Steinberg, Guido. "The Wahhabiya and Shi'ism, from 1744/45 to 2008." In: *The Sunna and Shi'a in History: Division and Ecumenism in History*, edited by Ofra Bengio and Meir Litvak, pp. 163-182, New York: Palgrave Macmillan, 2011.

Steinberg, Guido. Saudi-arabische Religionspolitik nach 2001. Instrument zur Fortsetzung eines Zweckbündnisses. In: *Staatliche Religionspolitik in Nordafrika/Nahost. Ein Instrument für modernisierende Reformen?* Edited by Sigrid Faath, pp. 175-196, Hamburg, 2007.

Sunik, Anna. "Alte Ziele, neue Taktik – Saudi-Arabiens außenpolitischer Aktivismus." *GIGA Focus Nahost* 3 (2014).

Teitelbaum, Joshua, "Is the GCC in Peril?" *BESA Center Perspectives Paper* No. 240 (March 12, 2014).

The Washington Institute for Near East Policy "Who Is Steering the House of Saud?" (August 10, 2015).

Trager, Eric and Marina Shalabi. "Egypt's Muslim Brotherhood Gets a Facelift." *Foreign Affairs* (May 20, 2015).

Tsebelis, George. "Decision making in political systems: Veto players in presidentialism, parlamentarism, multicameralism and multipartyism". *British Journal of Political Science* 25, no. 3 (1995): pp. 289-325.

Wehrey, Frederic. "The Authoritarian Resurgence: Saudi Arabia's Anxious Autocrats." Carnegie Endowment for International Peace (April 15, 2015).

Westphal, Kirsten, Marco Overhaus and Guido Steinberg. "Die US-Schieferrevolution und die arabischen Golfstaaten. Wirtschaftliche und politische Auswirkungen des Energiemarkt-Wandels" *SWP-Studie* 15, German Institute for International and Security Affairs (September 2014).

Wright, Steven. "Foreign Policy in the GCC States". In: *The International Politics of the Persian Gulf*, edited by Mehran Kamrava, pp. 72-93, Syracuse: Syracuse University Press, 2011.

Notes

1   From November 2014 until July 2015, the author participated in a project of the German Council on Foreign Relations (DGAP) on the economic and political activities and engagement of the Gulf states: Saudi Arabia, Qatar and United Arab Emirates in Egypt and Tunisia, funded by the German Federal Foreign Office. The findings of this chapter are based on the outcomes of the project. See Sebastian Sons and Inken Wiese, "The Engagement of Arab Gulf States in Egypt and Tunisia since 2011: Rationale and Impact," *DGAPanalye* No. 9, October 2015.

2   Said Aly, "Post-Revolution Egyptian Foreign Policy".

3   Today, 1.3-3.0 million Egyptian migrants are working in Saudi Arabia. See *Saudi Gazette*, "85 percent expatriates are from 8 countries," September 10, 2015: http://tinyurl.com/pfjda4k (accessed July 6, 2016), Dina Ezzat, "Egypt-Saudi ties: What is in store?" *Ahram online*, August 10, 2014, http://tinyurl.com/zkk5965 (accessed July 6, 2016), Lucas, Richter, Arbeitsmarktpolitik am Golf, Ahmad, "Beyond Labor", Kapiszewski, "De-Arabization in the Gulf: Foreign Labor and the Struggle for Local Culture".

4   In 2012, $5.7bn has been remitted to Egypt. See *Al-Arabiya online*, "Saudi Arabia world's second top remittance-sending country," 27 October 2013: http://tinyurl.com/ha9e5n5 (accessed July 6, 2016)

5   Coates Ulrichsen, "Egypt-Gulf Ties and a Changing Balance of Regional Security".

6   Gause III, "Saudi Arabia's Regional Security Strategy": 169, Wright, "Foreign Policy in the GCC States": 78, Al-Rasheed, "Circles of power: Royals and society in Saudi Arabia": 185-213, Knauerhase, *The Saudi Arabian economy*.

7   Wright, "Foreign Policy in the GCC States": 79.

8   Luciani, "Saudi Arabian business: From private sector to national bourgeoisie": 144-184, Niblock, *Saudi Arabia. Power, legitimacy and survival*.

9   See Hertog, *Princes, Brokers, and Bureaucrats: Oil and the State in Saudi Arabia*: 5: "'Clientelism' denotes unequal, exclusive, diffuse, and relatively stable relationships of exchange within and around the state apparatus (…). It is 'segmented' because of the parallel and often strictly seperate existence of institutions and clienteles in the Saudi distributional system (…)." See also Hertog, "Modernizing without democratizing? The introduction of formal politics in Saudi Arabia": 75-78, Hertog, "Segmented Clientelism: The political economy of Saudi economic reform efforts": 111-143.

10 For instance, this is shown by the non-participation of members of the royal family in boards or boards of trustees of many Saudi business conglomerates. See Abir, *Saudi Arabia. Government, Society and the Gulf Crisis*, Albers, *Saudi Arabia: Technocrats in a traditional society*, Field, *The merchants: The big business families of Saudi Arabia and the Gulf*, Steinberg, "Leading the Counter-Revolution. Saudi Arabia and the Arab Spring".

11 Seznec, "Changing Circumstances: Gulf Trading Families in the Light of Free Trade Agreements, Globalization and the WTO,": 65.

12 Tsebelis, "Decision making in political systems: Veto players in presidentialism, parlamentarism, multicameralism and multipartyism": 289-325.

13 Darwich, "The Ontological (In)security of Similarity: Wahhabism versus Islamism in Saudi Foreign Policy."

14 Steinberg, "Saudi-arabische Religionspolitik nach 2001. Instrument zur Fortsetzung eines Zweckbündnisses": 175.

15 Steinberg, "The Wahhabiya and Shi'ism from 1744/45 to 2008": 163-182.

16 Sunik, "Alte Ziele, neue Taktik – Saudi-Arabiens außenpolitischer Aktivismus", Soubrier, "Regional Disorder and New Geo-economic Order: Saudi Security Strategies in a Reshaped Middle East", Nawaf Obaid, "Saudi Arabia Shifts to More Activist Foreign Policy Doctrine" (op-ed), *Al-Monitor*, 17 October 2013: http://tinyurl.com/zabhy8z; Lacroix, "L'Arabie Saoudite au défi du printemps arabe."

17 Al Tamamy, "Hegemonic or Defensive? Patterns of Saudi Foreign Policy in the Era of the Arab Spring": 14.

18 Soubrier, "Regional Disorder and New Geo-economic Order: Saudi Security Strategies in a Reshaped Middle East".

19   Steinberg, "Saudi-Arabien: Sicherheit für Öl": 142.

20   Saudi Arabia's ruling family watched his hegemonic and expansionist foreign policy with high concern. Taking Saudi Arabia's primary goal of prevailing the rulers' legitimacy into consideration, at these times, Egypt posed a viable threat to Saudi Arabia. As a monarchy based on the religious legitimacy of the Wahhabi *ulama*, the Saudi establishment felt threatened by the non-religious and pan-Arab ambitions of Nasser.

21   Wehrey, "The Authoritarian Resurgence: Saudi Arabia's Anxious Autocrats".

22   Interview in Riyadh in December 2014.

23   The official assistance of Saudi Arabia to the MB took various forms, including funding the creation of Islamic charities in which the MB played a major role, as with the Muslim World League, founded in Mecca in 1962, and the World Assembly of Muslim Youth, created in Jeddah in 1972.

24   In addition to that, the MB 'betrayed' the Saudis by siding with Saddam Hussein following his invasion of Kuwait in August 1990. See al-Rasheed, *A History of Saudi Arabia*: 100.

25   While Saudi Arabia relied on the U.S. and Egyptian troops to liberate the occupied emirate and to ensure its own security against the threat of Saddam Hussein, the MB opposed Western intervention.

26   Interview in Riyadh in December 2014. See also Lacroix, *Awakening Islam. The Politics of Religious Dissent in Contemporary Saudi Arabia*.

27   Lacroix, "Saudi Arabia's Muslim Brotherhood predicament".

28   Michael Theodoulou, "Quartet's Chances for Syria Peace May Be Bleak", *The National*, 19 September 2012: http://tinyurl.com/jhbyqsd

29   Harriet Sherwood, "Iranian warships cross Suez canal", *The Guardian*, 22 February 2011: http://tinyurl.com/j9nv7xq

30   Khatib, "Qatar and the Recalibration of Power in the Gulf", Teitelbaum, "Is the GCC in Peril?".

31   *Aljazeera*, "Saudi, UAE, Bahrain withdraw Qatar envoys," 6 March 2014: http://tinyurl.com/jqjwf7t. Riyadh did not even have an ambassador in Qatar between 2002 and 2007.

32   *Al-Arabiya*, "Gulf leaders gather in Doha for GCC summit," 9 December 2014: http://tinyurl.com/jo4l2a3

33   Amr Abdelatty, "Al Jazeera's Egypt closure deals blow to MB," *Al-Monitor*, 8 January 2015: http://tinyurl.com/hg3kpmc

34   Ranko, Sabra, "Sisis Ägypten – Vollendung der Revolution oder zurück auf Null?".

35   See Lacroix, "Saudi Arabia's Muslim Brotherhood predicament": "In fact, there are even indications that Saudi officials had been in touch with Egyptian officers and some anti-Brotherhood Egyptian businessmen weeks before the coup, and that they had made it clear that they would welcome Morsi's ouster."

36   Interview in Riyadh in December 2014.

37   *Asharq Al-Awsat*, "King Abdullah pays visit to Egypt," 21 June 2014: http://tinyurl.com/zu6jdp4, *Al Arabiya News*, "Egypt's Sisi meets Saudi King Abdullah on first official visit to kingdom," 10 August 2014: http://tinyurl.com/zez7cxe

38   Telephone interview in November 2014.

39   Ibid.

40   General Authority for Investment and Free Zones, "Saudi Arabia accounts for 27% of Arab Investments in Egypt," March 3, 2015: http://tinyurl.com/j7cj4yl

41   *Amwal Al Ghad*, "Egypt, Saudi Arabia to Launch Business Association in Cairo on Sunday," 28 December 2013: http://tinyurl.com/hxb9dwy

42   *Emirates 24/7*, "28 Saudi investment problems in Egypt cleared," 17 March 2014: http://tinyurl.com/jhccj5v

43   Interviews in Cairo in February 2015.

44   Interviews with Saudi businessmen in Jeddah and Riyadh in December 2014. This was shown e.g. by the inauguration of Hassan Malek, a leading businessman of the MB, as head of the Egyptian-Saudi Business Council, and the foundation of the Egyptian Business Development Association (EBDA) in March 2012, bringing together chief executives from Saudi Arabia, Turkey, and the U.S., as well as old-guard non-MB Egyptian financiers.

45 Roll, "Al-Sisis Entwicklungsvisionen. Großbauprojekte und Herrschaftssicherung in Ägypten."

46 Doaa Farid, "New roadmap for Egyptian-Saudi economic relations under development: Abdel Nour," *Daily News Egypt*, 16 November 2013: http://tinyurl.com/j76cste

47 Rebecca Spong, "Saudi Arabia and UAE prop up Egypt's economy," *Middle Eastern Economic Digest*, 11 July 2013: http://tinyurl.com/jcnhj3m, *Ahram online*, "Egypt receives Saudi $2 bn deposit," 21 July 2013: http://tinyurl.com/j6uz334

48 Doaa Farid, "Saudi Arabia, Kuwait, UAE pledge $12bn to Egypt, Oman contributes $500m in Economic Summit," *Daily News Egypt*, 13 March 2015: http://tinyurl.com/zg7ujeb

49 Michael Marks, "Ägypten erhält ausländische Darlehen für Infrastrukturprojekte." Germany Trade and Invest, 19 April 2012: http://tinyurl.com/heak4f3

50 Reibman, "The IMF in Egypt, Act Two".

51 *Ahram Online*, "Egypt relies on Gulf aid to energise economy: Finance minister," 2 February 2014: http://tinyurl.com/h6ctd24

52 El Houdaiby, "Beyond the Crisis. A Roadmap for Reconciliation in Egypt."

53 Interview in Cairo in February 2015.

54 Nasser Saidi, "GCC Should Aid-For-Trade," *Gulf Business*, 6 July 2014: http://tinyurl.com/z3usgum

55 Interviews in Cairo in February 2015.

56 *Middle East Monitor*, "Al-Faisal warns: Saudi Arabia will not support Egypt forever," 4 September 2013: http://tinyurl.com/h7hxtxd

57 Several estimations predict that Saudi Arabia will become a net oil importer by 2030 due to rapidly increasing oil and gas consumption on a private and commercial level. In 2014, one third of the oil production was consumed on the domestic market. See Westphal, Overhaus, Steinberg, "Die US-Schieferrevolution und die arabischen Golfstaaten. Wirtschaftliche und politische Auswirkungen des Energiemarkt-Wandels": 27.

58 Hertog, "The Costs of Counter-Revolution in the Gulf"

59 See Cordesman, "Saudi Stability in a Time of Change": "Successful governance and the search for stability must change an economy that now draws on petroleum income for 80% of its budget revenues, 45% of its GDP, and 90% of its export earnings."

60 Telephone interview in December 2014.

61 Interview in Riyadh in December 2014.

62 On Iranoia, see Sebastian Sons, "Riad setzt auf Risiko", *Zenith online*, 2 April 2015: http://tinyurl.com/hwn5but; and Sebastian Sons, "Sugardaddy wird geizig," *Zenith* (Autumn 2015): 58-59.

63 Sebastian Sons, "Tod eines Wandlungsreisenden," *Zenith online*, 23 January 2015: http://tinyurl.com/lck2u89

64 Sebastian Sons, "Der Junge schafft das nicht", *Zenith* (Winter 2015): 34-35.

65 Dazi-Heni, "Saudi Leadership in a Chaotic Middle Eastern Context".

66 In May 2015, Morsi has been sentenced to death, 2,500 members or supporters of the Muslim Brotherhood were killed, and 16,000 imprisoned. See Trager, Shalabi, "Egypt's Muslim Brotherhood Gets a Facelift."

67 Interview in Cairo in February 2015.

68 Matthias Sailer, "Conditional support," *Qantara*, 18 March 2015: http://tinyurl.com/z2j7xgl

69 *Aljazeera*, "Saudi Arabia forms Muslim 'anti-terrorism' coalition," 15 December 2015: http://tinyurl.com/ognkvvk

70 Interviews in April and May 2015 in Cairo and Berlin.

71 Yara Bayoumy, "Egypt's Sisi reassures Gulf leaders after alleged derisive audio leaks," *Reuters*, 9 February 2015: http://tinyurl.com/zug32nn, *Middle East Eye*, "Egypt's Sisi makes brief visit to Saudi Arabia, as new alleged leak to be aired," 1 March 2015: http://tinyurl.com/zho78w9; See also: http://tinyurl.com/zfkqpud

72 *Middle East Monitor*, "New hashtag ridicules Sisi following audio leak," 13 February 2015: http://tinyurl.com/h4moj6n

73 Interview in June 2015 in Berlin.
74 Interviews in Riyadh and Jeddah in December 2014.
75 However, investment will continue as Saudi Arabia has announced in December 2015 to invest further $8 bn and support Egypt with subsidized oil exports over the next five years. See Abdel Latif Wahba, Ahmed Feteha, "Saudi Arabia Promises Egypt More Aid, Could Buy Local Debt," *Bloomberg*, 15 December 2015: http://tinyurl.com/zch83st
76 Interviews in June 2015 in Berlin.
77 Ismaeel Naar, "What to expect from the new Saudi king," *Aljazeera*, 27 January 2015: http://tinyurl.com/l9wew6k; Malik, Niblock, "Saudi Arabia's Economy: the Challenge of Reform,": 102-103.

7

Tactical Alliance?: The Relationship between Egypt under El-Sisi, Saudi Arabia and the UAE[1]

Eman Ragab

Introduction

The strategic transformations in the Middle East five years after the Arab Spring, as well as the developments in Egypt following 30 June 2013 revolution[2] have redefined Egypt's relationship with UAE and Saudi Arabia. Analysts in Egypt and the Gulf usually consider this type of relationship as a "new axis" taking place in the region; an "economic and military axis"[3]; a "strategic partnership"[4]; or a "strategic alliance"[5]. However, the complexities of the bilateral interactions between Egypt under El-Sisi, Saudi Arabia, and the UAE regarding many regional issues, reveals that these concepts are somewhat inaccurate in that they overlook the continuation of tensions among them, and their different or contradictory visions regarding the future of the region and their regional ambitions.

This chapter argues that the bilateral relationship between Egypt under El-Sisi, UAE, and Saudi Arabia since the 2013 revolution till the Jan 2015 leadership change after the death of King Abdullah[6], was taking the shape of a "tactical" alliance that served their national interests through a pragmatic coordination of their policies to counter the perceived common threats posed by the MB. The construction of theses perceptions after 2013 can be traced back to the victory of the Egyptian MB in the presidential elections in 2012 and the policies it adopted since then towards Saudi Arabia and UAE. These perceptions were articulated in the official discourse and the policies adopted by both countries towards Egypt as will be examined in the first section.

The policies pursued in the framework of this alliance are not only economic. It includes providing political and diplomatic support to enhance the Sisi regime's regional and international legitimacy, in exchange for Egypt's commitment to reduce the two countries vulnerability to threats originating from the political activism of the MB in Egypt and in its neighboring countries.

By definition, the informal alliance, or what Jeremy Ghez calls a tactical alliance[7], is dependent on countries sharing the same perceptions of a threat or an enemy. Stephen Walt[8] defines alliances as a "formal or informal commitment for security cooperation between two or more states". In the case of informal or *ad hoc* alliance, it is "based either on tacit understandings or some tangible form of commitment, such as verbal assurances or joint military exercises".[9] Perceptions of threats and of the interests being served, is very crucial factor for the tactical alliance to endure. According to Walt, "when there is an imbalance of threat, states will form alliances or increase their internal efforts in order to reduce their vulnerability"[10], and once the threat disappears the alliance disappears as well.[11]

In the case of the Middle East, the historical analysis of the interactions in the region reveal few important remarks that is useful in analyzing the bilateral relationship between Egypt after 2013, Saudi Arabia and UAE. First, historically alliances have been one of the debatable issues among politicians and academics. Arab countries historically refrain from officially supporting any alliances that entails long term commitments especially if they are engineered by the United States. For instance, the 24 February 1955 Baghdad Pact was rejected by Egypt under Nasser, Syria, Lebanon, and to a lesser degree by Jordan and Saudi Arabia.[12] During Mubarak era, as argued by Ahmad Yousef there was a gap between the official discourse of Mubarak and his policies towards regional alliances including those engineered by the Arab countries.[13] For instance, since the 2006 war between Israel and Hezbollah, the Bush Administration reframed the conflict in the region through promoting the 'two axes' idea: the "moderate axis" represented by GCC countries, Jordan, Egypt, Lebanon, Iraq and Palestine, and the "axis of fear" represented by Iran, Hezbollah, Hamas and Syria.[14] Mubarak stated clearly on 6 October 2006 that Egypt is against "dividing the region into moderates and radicals".[15] In practice, Egypt was keen to be part of the 6+2+1 meetings that included the six GCC countries, Jordan, Egypt and the USA.[16]

Second, in most of the cases studied by Walt, the state was the main actor, and the main source of threat. Thus the threat is being defined by the geographic proximity, the military capability of the state, and the perceived aggression. However, The increasing influence of Violent Non State Actors (VNSAs) in the Middle East turns them into a source of threat, and in this case balancing or countering the threat posed by the MB after 2013 is more difficult than that is posed by a country like Iran.

Third, the strategic transformations in the Middle East caused by the Arab spring, and the increasing complexities and uncertainty in the region makes the formation of a rigid alliance or traditional-ideology based alliances very risky and make the tactical alliance the dominant type in the region. The countries in the region become more willing to seek tactical alliances as a realistic option that will not require abroad or a strategic shift in their foreign policies[17]. Also, they are becoming more pragmatic in pursing their interests, willing to cooperate with their "enemy" in specific issues. For instance, Turkey, Saudi Arabia under King Abdullah, as well as Qatar adopted contradictory policies towards Egypt after the 2013 revolution, but agreed on the importance of toppling the Assad regime in Syria through arming the opposition groups and calling the international community to intervene militarily.[18]

The last remark is that, despite the historical relationship between Egypt and Saudi Arabia, the different and sometimes conflicting interests each pursues drive them to seek flexible mechanisms for coordinating their policies and for facing common perceived threats posed by the MB after the 2013 revolution. This historical relationship is based on understanding the strategic importance of each other in pursuing any regional policy, avoiding the escalation of differences regarding many regional issues into overt conflicts or overt objection[19], and the continuation of military-to-military cooperation regardless the regime type in Egypt.[20] Ali Eldean Hilal argues that this pattern of relationship serves as a "dynamic tenuous alliance", based on conversions and in the same time on divisions regarding their regional ambitions and the model of Islam each represents.[21]

In the case of UAE, the bilateral relationship is dynamic and shaped by contextual factors stemming from shifting regional environment, rather than historical calculations as in the case of Riyadh. During Mubarak era as argued by Hilal and Yousef the bilateral relationship was "personal". Mubarak considered Sheikh Zayed as the "wise of the Arabs". Although the Emerati rulers historically weighs the importance of maintaining good relations with Egypt, they lack active relationship with it as part of their inactive regional role in the pre-Arab Spring period.[22] The toppling of the MB in Egypt has triggered a new phase in the relationship.

This chapter also argues that the continuation of the tactical alliance between Egypt, Saudi Arabia under King Salman and the UAE, is conditioned by whether these countries continue to share the same perceptions of the MB as a threat to their national security, and whether they find that the tacit bilateral cooperation in the framework of this alliance is serving their interests amidst a shifting regional environment.

Based on this background, this chapter is divided into two sections. The first section examines the construction of the bilateral tactical alliance between Egypt, Saudi Arabia and UAE through analyzing the perceptions in the three countries regarding the MB following June 2013 in comparison to that prevailed during the MB's era in Egypt June 2012 - June 2013.

The second section examines the tactical alliance in action by analyzing the policies followed by these countries towards the MB, the corner stone of this alliance, and other regional issues namely the conflicts in Libya, Yemen and Syria. The conclusion analyzes the future of this alliance in the light of the changes in leadership in Saudi Arabia, and the continuation of differences/rivalries among them when it comes to their regional ambitions.

Shifting Perceptions: the Tactical Alliance Under Formation

Five years after the Arab revolutions that swept the region sine Dec 2010, it become clear that what would affect the GCC countries in general is not the change triggered by these revolutions, but the new structure of power in the countries affected by the revolutions, the attitudes of the 'new' ruling elites, and accordingly the shifts in the state's identity, foreign policies, and perceptions of its regional roles and how it would affect GCC countries' roles in the Middle East.

Egypt after the 2011 revolution became a controversial issue for Saudi Arabia and the UAE, as well as for other GCC countries. Both asserted the historical relationship with Egypt and the importance of maintaining "good" relationship with it. Many articles and columns in Gulf local newspapers appreciated the importance of Egypt in the region.[23] For example _Al-Riyadh_ and _Al-Jazeera_ newspapers have portrayed the Saudi announcement of providing grants to Egypt after the fall of Mubarak's regime as a "duty".[24] The Saudi Foreign Minister, Saud al-Faisal, said that Egypt is "the captain of the Arab world and we care about its stability."[25] _Okaz, Al-Riyadh_, and _Al-Jazeera_ newspapers described Egypt as a "large Arab shield."[26]

Following this prompt response to the 2011 revolution, the Saudi and Emirati elite's approaches to the election of Mohamed Morsi as a president of Egypt since June 2012 was underpinned by two perceptions, perceptions of fear as well as of "possibility".[27] The first perception considered the regime change in Egypt as a source of threat to these countries' national security, due to the spillover effect when it comes to the activists seeking "change" in the GCC countries, either the Gulf version of the MB, or liberals, who are the drivers of reform and change. They were concerned about that it could lead to a new form of the "export of the revolution" that they feared after the 1979 Iranian revolution. For instance, one of the columnist in the Emirati newspaper _al-Bayan_ was warning against the "Egyptian/Ikhwani agenda" that is to be applied in the Gulf.[28]

Maintaining the Relationship During the MB's Era?

Some officials in UAE, although they do understand the importance of the historical relationship with Egypt, based on the will of Sheikh Zayed to his sons, they considered Egypt under the MB a source of threat to their security and thus preferred not to engage with it, especially in terms of economic assistance and investments. It was concerned about the possible links between the Emeriti version of the MB and its Egyptian counterpart.

This fear is based on two factors. First, the UAE as other Gulf countries did not seem willing to embark on a process of political change even as revolutions were spreading in the region. The suppression of the protests in Bahrain in 2011 revealed that these countries more or less reject change led by the people, sticking to the idea of change led by the ruling elite. Second, the MB in Egypt, which considers itself a transnational movement, tends to espouse the idea that harming the MB in one country requires a reaction from the MB in other countries. The statements of Sheikh Yusuf al-Qaradawi, who condemned the stripping of citizenship of seven Brotherhood members in the UAE, angered the then Dubai Police Chief, Dhahi Khalfan.[29] Khalfan threatened to arrest Qaradawi. In response, Mahmoud Ghezlan, the official spokesman of the MB in Egypt, threatened to move the Islamic world against the UAE if Qaradawi was arrested.[30]

This triggered a reaction from the general secretary of the GCC, who noted that these statements are "irresponsible, lacking wisdom, and conflicting with the links and common ties that connect the Arab and Islamic peoples." He emphasized that "these statements work against the efforts of GCC states and Egypt to enhance their strong relations over the years".[31]

UAE's perceptions of the MB as a threat to its national security was reflected in its official discourse and its policies towards Egypt. For instance, Khalfan pointed out at on January 18, 2012, that the MB threat to Gulf security is equivalent in importance to the Iranian threat[32]. Also, the Emirati foreign minister, Abdullah bin Zayed, criticized the MB for not respecting national boundaries and accused them of plotting to undermine state sovereignty. He called upon all GCC countries to cooperate to confront this threat.

There was a trend among the ruling elite in UAE considered the success of the MB in the presidential elections as an event that would according to the wordings of one Emeriti officials "build Berlin Wall" between Egypt and UAE[33], and redirect its investment to Morocco and Jordan. Although the UAE promised to provide $3 billion to Egypt in the form of loans, deposits, and grants, but it did not take any real step to fulfill this promise. It also restricted the renewal of residence permits of Egyptian workers that estimated to be 400 thousands, to avoid revolutionary contagion from these workers. Meanwhile the UAE renewed the residency for workers of other nationalities. Mohammed Jamal Heshmat, a MB's leader and deputy of the Foreign Relations Committee at the People's Assembly in Egypt, called attention to this issue.[34] This restriction was based on the uncovering of a cell of 11 Egyptian MB members acting through administrative offices in UAE in order to recruit Egyptian workers to join the MB, and to collect money to the mother organization in Egypt that mounts to $2 million.[35]

In the case of Saudi Arabia, the dominant perception among the ruling elite was a bet on Morsi that he would work to secure Egypt's interests and respect the rules that have governed Egypt's relations with Saudi Arabia, namely the policy of non-interference in their domestic affairs, along with cooperation against any Iranian threats as part of Egyptian security, and a supportive stance on its positions towards the Syrian crisis and the Iranian nuclear program.[36] Thus, for the Saudi regime, Egypt was perceived as an asset, while the ruling MB was seen as a threat that can be contained. This was very well shaping the containment policies of Saudi Arabia followed till the 2013 revolution. Saudi Arabia paid $500 million on May 16, 2011, while it had promised to offer a package amounting to $3.75 billion.

The debate in the Saudi newspapers was reflecting these policies. For instance, many opinion columns in *Asharq Al-Awsat* and Gulf newspapers discussed Morsi's speech in Tahrir Square after his victory in the elections, indicating how he sent reassurances to the West while forgetting about Gulf countries. However, President Morsi visited Saudi Arabia on July 12, 2012, and it was his first official visit after taking over power. The visit was a sign of the strategic nature of Egypt's relations with Saudi Arabia. Morsi's speech after meeting

King Abdullah confirmed the Kingdom's religious importance for Egypt and the Islamic world as the cradle of Sunni Islam. Politically, his visit to Riyadh was a clear message to other Gulf countries which did not welcome his coming to power as a member of the MB. During the visit, Saudi newspapers confirmed the importance of continuing strategic relations with Egypt and suggested ignoring the fact that Morsi belongs to the MB in order to promote and protect Saudi interests.

Saudis cautious engagement with Egypt under the MB, enabled them to maintain the military cooperation with Egypt in the form of joint maneuvers. It was a sign that the Saudis are serious in maintaining their historical relationship with the state institutions in Egypt represented by the army, irrespective of the attitudes of the MB. Joint Saudi - Egyptian military exercises took place with the Royal Saudi Air Force under exercise name 'Faisal' (in June 2011[37]), between the navies - called 'Morgan-13' (conducted in September 2012[38]) and between the biggest joint military exercise in their history, called 'Tabook-3' (which took place on 3 May 2013[39]). However, the economic aid as was promised by Riyadh after the 2011 revolution was not fulfilled.

In response, Morsi followed two type of policies, but they were ineffective in reassuring the Saudis and persuading them to pump more cash in Egypt, or in containing the fears of the Emiratis which led to a troubled relationship with UAE that was hard to be managed[40]. First, Morsi strengthened the relationship with Qatar, as it was the one that was willing to support the MB's regime. However, depending on the Qatari investments was not enough to revive the economy. According to Yasser Ali, a MB leader and the then spokesman of the presidency during Morsi, Qatar's increasing influence in Egypt was a concern for the Saudis and Emiratis as it deducted from the influence they had during Mubarak's era.[41]

Second, Morsi has adopted an "indirect reassurance policy" to address the Saudis and Emiratis concerns. He mentioned in his speech at Cairo University that Egypt will not work on exporting its revolution to any other country.[42] The aforementioned cell of the Egyptians arrested in the UAE was a test to this stance.[43]

2013 Revolution: the Game Changer?

The 2013 revolution was a game changer in Egypt's relationship with Saudi Arabia and with UAE. The nationalist and independent attitudes of the new Egyptian ruling elite, that seeks the interests of the state including stability in the region and the spread of the modern civilian state model were praised by UAE and Saudi Arabia. King Abdullah was the first to congratulate the interim president Adly Mansour, and in his letter he praised the role of the armed forces in ending the era of the MB that was taking the country into " a dark tunnel, God only could apprehend its dimensions and repercussions".[44] The Emirati foreign minister Abdullah bin Zayed was the first to tweet supporting this change, considering the army a "strong shield" and a "protector" which embraced all components of the people.[45]

Based on these stances, it can be argued that the three countries in the aftermath of the 2013 revolution, perceived the MB as a threat to their national security. This shared perception was the cornerstone of a tactical alliance being formed bilaterally between Egypt, UAE and Saudi Arabia, aiming at weakening the political influence of the MB in Egypt and in other Arab countries going through political change, and spreading the model of the strong civilian state in the region.

Different strategic statuses of the three countries, as well as their contesting regional ambitions affected the policies adopted in the framework of this alliance. Having Saudi Arabia as the most stable wealthy country seeking to play a leading role in uncertain environment in the region, and to contain the destructive impact of the Arab revolutions, defined ceilings for the available and acceptable regional policies to be adopted by Egypt, and to lesser degree by UAE towards regional issues.

In the case of the UAE, it is one of the small countries benefited from the power vacuum in the region caused by Egypt's inactive regional role due to the complex transitions it is going through, by Syria as it is torn up by violent conflict since 2011, and by Saudi Arabia as it was more concerned with containing the impact of the Arab Spring internally and in its surrounding neighbors, namely in Yemen and Bahrain.[46]

For Egypt, suffering from economic stagnation and increasing violence by the MB and active terrorist organizations in Sinai and the mainland, make its activism in the realm of foreign policy directed to serve its economic and security needs. In other words, its relationship with UAE and Saudi Arabia is interest based, and this pragmatic nature make it more cautious in following policies towards issues that doesn't serve its national needs and interests.

This tactical alliance is based on the verbal support provided by the Saudi and Emirati Sheikhs to the new regime in Egypt, as well as on set of policies aims at materializing the alliance. These policies on one hand aimed at stabilizing the new regime in Egypt, assuring its legitimacy through using their international networks of relations to ease the criticisms of the new regime in Egypt, to counter the campaign led by Qatar and Turkey depending on western think tanks and media outlets to defame the new regime. For instance, the Saudi foreign minister Saud al-Faisal visited the French president on August 18, 2013 to stress the importance of "giving the roadmap in Egypt a chance"[47], and he announced that if the west cut its aid to Egypt," the Islamic and Arab *Omma* is wealthy enough to help Egypt"[48]. The UAE foreign minister Abdullah bin Zayed met with the US secretary of State John Kerry to discuss the situation in Egypt, and to make sure no further criticism be directed towards the new regime.[49]

Second, it aimed at establishing the legitimacy of the new regime to be based on economic achievements. The economy suffered during MB's era from increasing external debts and shrinking foreign reserves that affected directly the day to day life of regular citizens[50], which was an important motive to more than 30 million people to go to the streets on 30 June.[51] Saudi Arabia supported the new regime with $5 billion. After the dispersal of the MB's sit-in in *Raba'a and Nahda* on August 14, 2013, it was keen on supporting the Egyptian government in countering the violence that took place in the aftermath. King

Abdullah in August 17, 2013, said that "The World needs to know that the government and the people of the Kingdom of Saudi Arabia, stands today with their brothers in Egypt against terrorism, misguidance, and sedition, and against all those who try to interfere with its domestic affairs".[52]

The UAE provided three billion$ after June 2013[53]. In October 2013, it promised package of 4.9 billion$ aimed at developing living conditions for the Egyptians.[54] In addition, both countries played a role in facilitating the purchase of Russian arms by the Egyptian army.[55] The total aid provided by Saudi Arabia, UAE and Kuwait was $12 billion that is more than the economic and military aid of the U.S. to Egypt that mounts annually to $1.5 billion.[56]

This financial support continued after the election of president Abdel Fattah el-Sisi in June 2014. The UAE provided $9.6 billion, besides Emirati private sector investments of $7 billion. During the Economic Development Conference held in *Sharm el Sheikh* on March 2015, the UAE and Saudi Arabia each provided $4 billion, along with Kuwait $4 billion, Oman $500 million.[57]

The UAE is more welling to implement projects directly through partnerships in the framework of the Emirati -Egyptian fund, or in cooperation with the army. They also appointed a minister of state responsible for following up the investments and aids to Egypt, Minister *Soltan al Jaber* who has a permanent office in Egypt[58]. Having an alliance with Egypt enabled UAE to intervene in Egyptian politics through supporting the new regime in its fight against the MB, and to build constituencies that favor strengthening relations with it depending on its developmental aid. On the other hand, these policies aimed at redirecting the Egyptian foreign policies to be in line with the Saudi and Emirati policies, but that was hard to be assured as examined in section two.

Egypt on its part, reiterated its commitment to the security of the Gulf region, and considered it as part of its national security. El-Sisi during his electoral campaign, and in his inaugural address showed his readiness to deploy the Egyptian army to protect any Arab country including the Gulf countries if the "Arab national security" is being threatened by a "real threat" and if such deployment was "requested". He also reiterated that deploying the Egyptian troops is only a "short distance".[59] In line with these commitments, for the first time Egypt initiated joint exercises with UAE in 2014. Air exercises Zayed-1 was conducted in February 2014[60], Khalifa-1 and *Seham al Haq* in October 2014.[61]

It is worth noting that Egypt's commitment to the security of the Gulf includes three caveats. First, the shifting security perceptions of UAE and Saudi Arabia, including Egypt's status and stability as well as Iranian actions in the regional environment, creates expectations regarding the Egyptian role in parallel with this alliance. The internal dimension of their security is increasingly important. This challenges the Egyptian policies in the framework of the alliance, as it can't rely exclusively on the projection of military power to support its allies, and must also consider the red lines of not interfering in their internal affairs.

Second, GCC countries in general are sensitive towards any permanent existence of the Egyptian troops on their lands. Attempts of forming Arab Peace Forces have been attempted in the past, most notably according to the 6 March 1991 Damascus Declaration, but have failed for a number of reasons mainly to do with mistrust amongst members and the prior exclusion of Iran and Iraq.[62] Third, the military capabilities of Saudi Arabia and the UAE have been upgraded since the invasion of Kuwait 1990-1991. Both managed to develop their armies depending primarily on the U.S., UK and France to rebuild their military capabilities through arms imports, training programmes and joint exercises with the West. Since the 1990s, they took part in many armed operations abroad, including the 2003 Free Iraq Operation, The Dawn Operation against Gaddafi regime in 2011[63], the military operation against ISIL in Syria since September 2014[64], and the military operation in Yemen since March 2015.

The Tactical Alliance in Action

This section argues that the threat posed by the MB is the only issue that Egypt, Saudi Arabia during King Abdullah's reign, and the UAE has a common perception about. They hold different and sometimes contradictory positions towards other regional issues. However, the UAE could become closer to Egypt in its assessments of other regional issues in compared to Saudi Arabia, especially after the death of King Abdullah.

The Muslim Brothers Transitional Unifying Threat?

The shared perceptions among the three countries regarding the MB were reflected in the policies adopted. The Egyptian government's December 25, 2013 designation of the MB as a terrorist organization, was followed by Saudi Arabia designation of the group as a terrorist entity since March 2014[65]. Since November 2014, the UAE[66] announced its list of 83 terrorist organizations that includes MB after three years of arresting *ikhwan* leaders[67] and banning its local version *al-Islah* organization[68], as they are according to Abdullah bin Zayed "doesn't believe in the nation state, or respect the national sovereignty".[69] King Abdullah was keen to show his support of Egypt in its fight against terrorism as being carried out by the MB as aforementioned.

Besides, Saudi Arabia and UAE were keen on coordinating their policies in order to track the activities of the MB's members in the Gulf. Saudis in Sep 26, 2012 arrested an Emeriti national for being member of *al-Islah*, and the UAE government released information of uncovering a cell in cooperation with the Saudi government.[70] They attempted to expand this coordination to include the other GCC countries through the GCC security agreement, that was ratified in 2012. It aimed at enhancing intelligence cooperation between the six GCC countries in order to counter terrorism and radicalism and any other threats to national security.

However, the continuation of the MB as the core issue that the tactical alliance between Egypt and Saudi Arabia and Egypt and UAE is based on, is going through changes due to: 1) the shifting perceptions of the new ruling elite in Riyadh that is considering the MB as a threat that can be contained and not countered as was during King Abdullah, 2) the limited reverse back effect of the 2013 revolution. Despite the toppling of the MB regime in Egypt, they continue to be important political power in many other countries. In Bahrain and Kuwait they are part of the national parliaments and governments. Also, in Libya, Syria and Yemen they are an important political power that can't be ignored if the political settlement of the conflicts is considered.

Analyzing the Saudi policies after the death of King Abdullah, indicate that the perceptions it shared with UAE and Egypt regarding the MB is going through revisions. These revisions were reflected in number of policies adopted since Salman took power, that in practice overlook Saudi designation of the MB as a terrorist organization. First, Saud al-Faisal statement that the Kingdom does have issues with the *ikhwan* who have *Baia'a* to the General Guidance, and not the MB in general. Second, the communications between Saudi Arabia and Egyptian MB leaders in London, al-Nahda in Tunisia,and Hamas.[71] Third, Riyadh hosted the meeting for the World Federation for Muslim Scholars that is designated by UAE as a terrorist organization, and in response the UAE boycotted the meeting. Fourth, the Saudis were becoming more willing to support the *Ikhwan* in Yemen represented by *al-Islah* party in order to weaken the Houthis.[72] For Egypt, having more conservative leaders in Saudi Arabia who preferred the inclusion of the MB in the political system in Egypt[73] instead of weakening them would be problematic. In this regard, Hilal argues that Saudi Arabia is becoming pragmatic in dealing with the MB in Egypt and in other Arab countries. It supports Egypt in its policies towards the MB as long as it doesn't drag Riyadh into a uncalculated regional confrontation, and as long as it serves its national interests.

Also, the UAE position towards the political future of the MB in Egypt is dependent on the stability of the new regime. Being hard towards the Emerati MB doesn't mean that the UAE will stand against any calculated political reconciliation in Egypt as long as it will serve the regime's stability. This position has been very well articulated by many Emeriti experts. On Egypt's side, there is a conviction as articulated by the ex minister of foreign affairs, that UAE is concerned about the reconciliation but "doesn't have a veto power".[74]

Conflicts in Syria and Yemen

Since the eruption of the Syrian conflict in March 2011, the countries in the region were divided regarding this conflict. GCC countries led by Qatar and Saudi Arabia, supported by Turkey provided military and financial support to the armed groups in their conflict against al-Assad regime in order to shift the balance of power on the ground through weakening the regime. They also called for international military intervention in Syria to topple al-Assad regime, paving the way for new transitional period led by the civilian opposition group. The UAE was supporting this direction, with a slight difference when regarding the type of the opposition group it supported. Its funding was channeled to the moderate Free Syrian Army that turned out to be very weak on the ground.

On the other hand, Egypt has a very well defined position as being expressed by the interim government following the fall of the MB's regime. This position is based on the peaceful settlement of the conflict through a national dialogue, and Nabeel Fahmy, the then minister of foreign affairs, was keen on expressing that: "Egypt has no intent for jihad in Syria" to refute what was announced by Morsi in June 2013.[75]

The military operations in Yemen led by Saudi Arabia is another case that shows the different calculations of UAE, Egypt and Saudi Arabia. The Houthis that managed to control Sana'a in February 2015, is classified by Saudi Arabia and the UAE as a terrorist organization. While Egypt considers it a part of the Yemeni people. The decision of Saudi Arabia to launch the 'Decisive Storm' operation in Yemen on 26 March 2015 was supported by the UAE which contributed both troops and fighter aircraft. El-Sisi issued a statement supporting the operation but at the same time made any participation from Egypt pending the approval of the parliament, the SCAF or the Cabinet, as mentioned in article 152 of the constitution.

Egypt is adopting a clear policy towards the conflict in Yemen based on the importance of the political settlement of the conflict, through an inclusive dialogue that include the Houthis. The Saudis are more keen on assuring their leading role in the transition in Yemen, building on what they achieved after the February 2011 revolution. But their mediation is not welcomed by Houthis and Ali Saleh, thus they are relying on the military operations that may shift the balance on the ground and pressure the Houthis to accept a dialogue under their sponsorship.

The UAE is more pragmatic, especially when it comes to the influence exerted by Houthis and Saleh. Although it has designated the Houthis as a terrorist organization, it is also trying to promote a political solution based on having Ahmed, the son of Saleh, as the interim president for Yemen, to the exclusion of the MB. These differences, were responsible for the UAE's low level of representation in the Arab Summit held few days after operation 'Decisive Storm', as the UAE didn't want to show full support for the operation. Meanwhile, the Saudis were represented at the highest level, by King Salman.[76]

Countering Terrorism: The Libya Question

Countering terrorism in the region, especially in Libya, is another issue where the Egyptians don't share the same perceptions with the Saudis, but instead have more in common with the Emiratis. Both states prefer supporting the Tobroq government instead of supporting Islamist groups. In August 2014, *The Guardian* published a report that the UAE, supported by Egypt, launched air strikes against the Islamist militias to prevent them from controlling Tripoli.[77] These strikes were part of the proxy conflict among the UAE, Qatar and Turkey in Libya, where the latter support Islamist militias. Indeed, Qatar hosts Ali Salabi, the most influential Islamist and backer of the MB, while the UAE hosts Mahmoud Jibril.

These differences were crystallized after the killing of 21 Egyptians by ISIL in Libya in February 2015. Egypt launched air strikes targeting ISIL in Daranha the same month. The

UAE supported the operation as part of its policy of weakening the militias supported by the MB. When Egyptian president called for an international military intervention in Libya[78], the UAE supported the call and tried to secure the support from France; whilst Saudi Arabia was concerned, it preferred to pursue a similar policy to Qatar, Turkey, and the United States, which all expressed their desire for a peaceful settlement of the conflict. The Egyptian and Emeriti efforts, supported by France and Italy, managed to separate out the political settlement of the conflict in Libya and the fight against terrorist organizations included in the UNSCR 2214.

The Egyptian air strikes were thus followed by a proposal for forming a joint Arab force for countering terrorism in 23 February 2015. This call aimed at forming an umbrella alliance to fight terrorist organizations in Libya and ensure the task would not fall to Egypt alone. The call was not supported by the United States, European countries or Russia. Although Egypt supported the International Coalition for fighting ISIL in Syria and Iraq led by the USA since September 2014, it failed to broaden out the campaign to include other terrorist organizations in the Middle East.

The Egyptian proposal lacked much detail, including specifying a clear relationship with the International Coalition. However, the troop size for the task is estimated to range between 20,000 and 40,000 troops, whereby the backbone of the force would be Egyptian troops, and the rest from other Arab countries. These forces will be formed in the framework of the Arab League, and will carry out joint exercises every three months for building capacity and transferring experience.[79]

Regionally, the reactions to Egypt's proposal was based on the political and strategic consequences of forming these forces, as it would grant Egypt a leading regional role in fighting terrorism. The UAE shares the same perceptions with Egypt especially regarding the future of the conflict in Libya and therefore supported the initiative. So did Jordan. Saudi Arabia was more conservative, along with other Arab countries like Algeria. King Salman favours a regional Sunni axis led by Saudi Arabia and aims at "achieving Arab and Islamic Solidarity".[80] The broadening of the coalition supporting the 'Decisive Storm' led by Saudi Arabia in Yemen to include Pakistan and Turkey, was an attempt to put the Saudi vision into action. Indeed, Saudi leadership on Yemen has been followed by the establishment of its own 34-member alliance to fight terrorism, launched in December 2015.[81]

For Egypt, taking part actively in the 'Decisive Storm' operation was a risk as there is no genuine threat posed by the conflict in Yemen to Egypt's national security, unlike the case of Libya. President el-Sisi in his speech in the Arab Summit reiterated Egypt's position towards the conflict in Libya. He criticized those who link supporting the legal government in Libya and political dialogue, and emphasized the importance of fighting terrorism and in the same time seeking political settlement of the conflict, and reiterated his call for the international community to carry out its responsibility in countering terrorism in Libya[82] He even warned against slipping towards providing political concessions to the terrorist groups in exchange for putting its arms down. On his part, King Salman in his speech avoided talking about Libya, and focused mainly about the Saudi operation in Yemen.[83]

These differences between the Egyptians and Saudis, make the idea of proposing Egypt itself as the leader of the region, an issue that challenges Saudi Arabia's own regional ambitions. Due to that the meetings of the Chiefs of Arab Armed Forces following the Arab League summit to discuss the Arab Joint Forces, Egypt's proposal didn't reach any genuine step leading to the formation of these forces.[84]

Conclusion: Enduring Alliance?

The durability of the tactical alliance between Egypt and the UAE and Saudi Arabia to counter the threats posed by the MB is challenged by four main limitations: First, is the personalization of this alliance. It relies on the perceptions of the ruling leaders in the three countries. Despite the historical importance of Egypt for both UAE and Saudi Arabia as aforementioned, the pattern of relationship following the 2013 was a reflection of the perceptions of King Abdullah and Mohamed Biz Zayed of the importance of supporting the new regime in Egypt in order to curb the political activism of the MB in the region, and to spread the model of the civil modern state. The durability of these perceptions among the generations of princes in the ruling families in both countries is questionable, in light of the existence of new young generations that consider Egypt as a liability rather than an asset[85], less adherent to the will of Sheikh Zayed and King Sa'ud, and even questions the MB as a threat to their national security. Besides the revision of the threat posed by the MB by the Saudi new leaders, the regime tends to rely on the MB leaders in supporting internal policies to counter the threats posed by ISIL and the Houthis, and by extension, Iran.

On the other hand, the transitional nature of this pattern of relationships is not very well institutionalized in Egypt among the academic and political elites, or the media. They are more concerned about what Egypt needs to pay in return for the Emirati and Saudi support.[86] For instance, increasing Emirati funding to Egyptian think tanks is considered by a former minister of foreign affairs as a "danger" that the government in Cairo is aware of, but can't curb".[87] Also, Saudi pressure on Egypt to take part in 'Decisive Storm' in Yemen was criticized in many talk shows in Egypt, and some of which called for the rethinking of the relationship with the Saudis instead of being forced to take part in a conflict that doesn't serve any interest of Egypt.[88]

In addition, not much attention is being paid in Egypt to the "new Gulf" which is being shaped in the aftermath of the Arab spring by younger princes, or the increasing pragmatism of these countries on regional issues, or in terms of their increasing influence in shaping and redirecting change in many Arab countries.[89] Second, the three countries still need to develop policies that enable them to manage their differences regarding many regional issues to avoid escalation. Egypt and Saudi Arabia managed their differences through discussions behind closed doors in the case of Yemen, with Egypt adopting an official policy that is careful not to contradict Saudi policies, except in the case of Libya as mentioned. Egypt and Saudi Arabia emphasized the importance of institutionalized consultation in order to reduce differences regarding regional issues through forming the Saudi-Egyptian Coordination Council in 11 November 2015.[90]

Third, this type of alliance defines for Egypt ceilings for pursuing independent policies towards crucial issues for the UAE or Saudi Arabia, or for playing a leading regional role. Hilal argues that el-Sisi is a leader with a vision and wants to act as a leader, unlike Mubarak who considered Egypt's regional role as an intrinsic feature of Egypt's existence. As a reflection for these ceilings, Egypt doesn't have freedom to normalize its relationship with Iran, not because of the financial aid it gets from Riyadh[91], but due to the strength of the historical relationship. Besides the security concerns, any positive movement towards Iran would risk its relationship with Saudi Arabia.

It become clear also that it is not only Saudi Arabia that matters for el-Sisi, but also the UAE that follows more independent bilateral policies in supporting the new regime in Cairo, not only through the developmental aid provided to the people of Egypt, but also through diplomatic and security cooperation. Due to the regional rivalry between UAE and Qatar, any normalization of the relationship between Egypt and Qatar could risk the investments in Egypt as well as the diplomatic support it offers. Also, despite Egypt's willingness to use force to protect the security of the Gulf as been repeatedly mentioned by president el-Sisi, the deployment of Egyptian forces will be more assured in the case it serves the Egyptian interests and to counter any attack on the territory of any of the GCC countries. This explains Egypt's policies towards Yemen.

The attitudes within the Egypt government are very important in defining the future of the relationship with the UAE and with Saudi Arabia, as well as the perceptions of the Saudis and Emiratis towards Egypt. In other words, there is "duality" of Egypt's relationship with the GCC states: it is both an asset and as a threat. Mustafa el Feqy, former head of Arab relations committee in the people's assembly during Mubarak era, described this status by stating that Egypt's neighbors "love it and are concerned about it", but it causes them a "feeling of inferiority" due to its "civilizational tradition, its strategic location, its national character, its large population size, and its limited wealth".[92]

References

al-Shahaby, Omar, et al, "The Constant and the Shifting 2014:the Gulf between Societal Disintegration and the linkage between Money and Power (in Arabic)", 2014 Report, Gulf Center for Development Policies.

Baskan, B., "The Police Chief and the Sheikh," The Washington Review of Turkish & Eurasian Affairs, April 2012.

Colombo, Silvia, et al, "The GCC in the Mediterranean in Light of the Arab Spring", Mediterranean Paper Series 2012, Istituto Affari Internazionali IAI -Rome and the German Marshall Fund of the United States.

Dwivedi, Sangit Sarita, "Alliances in International Relations Theory", International Journal of Social Science & Interdisciplinary Research,Vol.1 Issue 8, August 2012.

Farouk, Yasmine,"More than Money: Post-Mubarak Egypt ,Saudi Arabia, and the Gulf",GRC GULF PAPER, April 2014.

Fürtig, Henner (ed.), Regional Powers in the Middle East: New Constellations After the Arab Revolts, (New York: Palgrave Macmillan, 2014).

Ghez, Jeremy, "Alliances in the 21st Century: Implications for the US-European Partnership", Occasional Paper, Rand Corporation, 2011.

Korany, Bahgat and Ali E. Hillal Dessouki (eds.), The Foreign Policies of Arab States: The Challenge of Globalization, (Cairo:American University Press in Cairo, 2008).

Mahmood, Ahmed Ebraheem, "The War in Lebanon and the Illusion of Rebuilding the Regional Axis(in Arabic)", al-Ahram Strategic File, issue 141, Sept 2006.

Morris, Mary E., "New Political Realities and the Gulf: Egypt, Syria, and Jordan", PROJECT AIR FORCE-Arroyo Center, RAND, 1993.

Ragab, Eman, "A New Gulf?: Implications of Camp David Summit between the GCC Countries and the United States" (in Arabic), Afaq Seyasiya (The Arab Center for Studies and Researches), Issue no 19, July 2015.

Ragab, Eman, "The Gulf after the Arab Spring: the Challenge and the Response" (in Arabic), Democracy Journal (peer reviewed), Jan 2015.

Ragab, Eman, "Tactical Alliances: Shifting Regional Alliances in the Middle East after the Arab Revolutions (in Arabic)", the State of the Region, a monthly periodical issued by the Regional Center for Strategic Studies in Cairo, Issue no.9, July 2014.

Ragab, Eman Ahmed, The Arab Regional System in the Aftermath of the Occupation of Iraq (in Arabic), (Beirut: Center for Arab Unity Studies, 2010).

Telci, İsmail Numan, "Overcoming the Regional Stalemate: Understanding the Politics of the Gulf States and Turkey during the Egyptian Coup", POMEAS BRIEF, No.8, Project on the Middle East and the Arab Spring POMEAS, April 2015.

Walt, Stephen. "Why Alliances Endure or Collapse", Survival: Global Politics and Strategy, 39:1.

Notes

1   In writing the final version of this paper, I had a deep discussions with Ali Eldean Hilal Dessouki, Professor of Political Science- Faculty of Economics and Political Science, Cairo University. I extend my sincere thanks to him.

2   The Preamble to the 2014 Egyptian constitution states that both 30 June 2013 and 25 January 2011 are revolutions supported by the Egyptian army.

3   Marzooq al-Ghanem suggested the formation of this axis during president Abdel fattah El-Sisi's visit to Kuwait during Jan 2015. See: "The Gulf-Egyptian axis is lifeline" (in Arabic), *al-Bayan*, 8 January 2015.

4   This term was widely used by Emeriti local newspapers and think tanks. See for instance: "The four Gulf countries and Egypt Thwart the Second Drive a Wedge (in Arabic)", 2 February 2015, *al Mezmah*: http://tinyurl.com/j2xtvld

5   This term has usually been used by the Egyptians and the Emiratis. See the statements of the Egyptian minister for industry and commerce Fakhry Abdelnoor in: "Egypt and UAE: Historical Relations (in Arabic)", *al Bayan*, 12 November 2014.

6   King Abdullah bin Abdelazeez death was announced on 22 Jan 2015. Salamn, the then crown prince, became the King of Saudi Arabia, Muqrin bin Abdelazeez was appointed as the Crown Prince, and Mohamed bin Salman the Deputy Crown Prince. See: *al-Riyadh* (in Arabic), 23 January 2015.

7   Jeremy Ghez, "Alliances in the 21st Century: Implications for the US-European Partnership", *Occasional Paper*, Rand Corporation, 2011: 8-9.

8   Balance of Power theory was developed by Liska, Morgenthau, and Kaplan, while the Balance of Threat was developed by Stephen Walt.

9   Stephen Walt, "Why Alliances Endure or Collapse", *Survival: Global Politics and Strategy*, 39:1, (1997): 157.

10 Sangit Sarita Dwivedi, "Alliances in International Relations Theory", *International Journal of Social Science & Interdisciplinary Research*, Vol.1, Issue 8,(August 2012): 230.

11 Walt discusses why alliance dissolve in: Stephen M. Walt, "Why Alliances Endure or Collapse", *Op.Cit.*

12 For more details on this point please see: Eman Ahmed Ragab, *The Arab Regional System in the Aftermath of the Occupation of Iraq (in Arabic)* (Beirut: Center for Arab Unity Studies, 2010), pp. 77-78.

13 Ahmad Yousef Ahmad, interview by the author, 6 December 2015, Cairo. He is Prof of Political Science-Cairo University, and was the head of the Arab Institute for Arab Researches and Studies 1993-2011. The institute is affiliated to the ALESCO-The Arab League.

14 Ahmed Ebraheem Mahmood, "The War in Lebanon and the Illusion of Rebuilding the Regional Axis (in Arabic)", *al-Ahram Strategic File*, issue 141, Sept 2006, p.99: http://tinyurl.com/jyh3zur

15 See president Mubarak's statements as published in al-Ahram Daily news paper (in Arabic): *al-Ahram*, 6 Oct 2006, http://tinyurl.com/j2co75e (accessed July 2016)

16 The first meeting of this mechanism was held in Kuwait on Jan 16, 2007, the second was in Sharm el Sheikh on July 31, 2007, the third was held on the sidelines of the UNGA meeting on Sep 25, 2007, and the fourth meeting was in Manama on April 21, 2008.

17 Eman Ragab, "Tactical Alliances: Shifting Regional Alliances in the Middle East after the Arab Revolutions (in Arabic)", *the State of the Region* (a monthly periodical issued by the Regional Center for Strategic Studies in Cairo), Issue no.9, (July 2014).

18 This complicated matrix was graphed by the Economist, see: "The Middle Eastern mesh", *the Economist*, April 3, 2015: http://tinyurl.com/ju4oqhr

19 Nabeel Fahmy, the former minister of foreign affairs in Egypt explained that the Saudis understand that it is very hard to get the support of the Arab League on any issue that Egypt objects to in public. See: Nabeel Fahmy, interview by the author, August 11, 2015, Cairo.

20 Maged al-Motlaq, "The King said it because he loves Egypt and its people" (in Arabic), *Ara'ar Today online* (local Saudi newspaper devoted for the Northern province of the Kingdom), http://tinyurl.com/zzagnq4 (accessed July 2016)

21 Prof Dr Ali Eldean Hilal Dessouki, interview by the author, December 2015, Cairo.

22 Abdul-Monem al-Mashat, "Politics of Constructive Engagement: The Foreign Policy of the United Arab Emirates", in: Bahgat Korany and Ali E. Hillal Dessouki (eds.), *The Foreign Policies of Arab States: The Challenge of Globalization* (Cairo: American University Press in Cairo, 2008), 457-480.

23 "Saudi Newspapers: Egypt is a Large Arab Shield and Supporting it is a Duty" (in Arabic), Al-Ahram, May 24, 2011; Roula Khalaf and Heba Saleh interview with Qatar's prime minister Hamad bin Jassim bin Jabr al-Thani, "West should not fear Islamist movements", *Financial Times*, November 30, 2011; "UAE: Gulf States must Stop Plotters", *Gulf Times*, October 9, 2012.

24 "Two Saudi Newspapers: Supporting Egypt is an Essential Necessity because it is the Source of Balance in the Arab World (in Arabic)," *Al-Ahram*, May 22, 2011.

25 See the statement in "Saoud al-Faisal: Egypt is the Captain of the Arab World" (in Arabic), *Al-Ahram*, July 3, 2011.

26 See Yosuf al-Kuwleit, "Egypt and Saudi Arabia: Inseparability of Interests and Goals" (in Arabic), *Al-Riyadh*, May 23, 2011; "Saudi Newspapers: Egypt is the Arab Shield (in Arabic)," *Al-Ahram*, May 24, 2011.

27 For detailed analysis of Egypt-GCC relations during the MB's era June 2012-June 2013, refer to: Eman Ragab, "A Formative Stage: Relations between GCC and North African Countries after the Arab Spring", in: Silvia Colombo et al, "The GCC in the Mediterranean in Light of the Arab Spring", *Mediterranean Paper Series 2012*, Istituto Affari Internazionali IAI -Rome and the German Marshall Fund of the United States, pp.9-20.

28 For example, see: M. bin Houidn, "The New Egyptian President and Gulf Cuntries" (in Arabic), *Al-Bayan*, July 1, 2012.

29 These statements included condemning UAE police for deporting a number of Syrian activists. For more information, see: "What Beyond the Issue of Yusuf al-Qaradawi, UAE, and Dubai Police Chief "(in Arabic), *France 24*, March 10, 2012; Simeon Kerr, "Dubai police chief hits at cleric on Syria",

Financial Times, March 5, 2012; B. Baskan, "The Police Chief and the Sheikh", *The Washington Review of Turkish & Eurasian Affairs*, April 2012.

30 "Ghezlan Defends Qaradawy" (in Arabic), *Russia Today*, March 9, 2012.

31 "The GCC Describes Muslim Brotherhood's Statements toward UAE as Being Demagogic (in Arabic)," *Akhbar Al-Youm*, March 10, 2012.The Emir of Sharqa that is known for being pro Ikhwan in UAE condemned the statements of Qaradawy. For details see: Mahmood al-Awadhy, "The Emir of Sharqa Recalls Zayid's History with the Muslim Brotherhood (in Arabic)", *elaph*, March 24, 2012: http://tinyurl.com/jh35y42 (accessed July 2016)

32 "UAE: Gulf States must Stop Plotters", *Gulf Times*, October 9, 2012.

33 Interviews with UAE officials conducted by the author on the condition of anonymity, AbuDhabi, 2012.

34 See "Assistant of Egyptian Foreign Minister: We are Discussing with UAE Officials the Renewal of Contracts and Work Visas (in Arabic)," *Al-Ahram*, March 13, 2011; "Heshmat Called for Solving the Problem of Dismissing the Egyptian Workers in UAE (in Arabic)," *Al-Ikhawan online*, March 28, 2012.

35 According to UAE officials, these administrative offices have 6 committees. The information released regarding this cell was in Nov 2013, but no information was mentioned regarding the date of uncovering the cell. Security official interviewed by the author in October 2012 in Abu Dhabi on the condition of anonymity, stressed this reason for not renewing the permits for Egyptian workers, and in the same time stressed that workers not being involved in any of the MB's activities are allowed to renew their permits.
For more details on this case see: "Full Administrative Structure of the Egyptian MB in UAE (in Arabic)", *al-Bayan*, Nov 13, 2013.

36 M. bin Houidn, *Op.Cit.*,

37 Yasmine Farouk, "More than Money: Post-Mubarak Egypt, Saudi Arabia, and the Gulf", *GRC Gulf Paper*, April 2014: 2-4.

38 These joint exercises initiated since 2002.See: *al-Riyadh*, September 18, 2012: http://tinyurl.com/zestaoo

39 *al-Ahram*, May4, 2013; Yasmine Farouk, "More than Money: Post-Mubarak Egypt ,Saudi Arabia, and the Gulf".

40 See: Eman Ragab, "Gulf policies towards Egypt after the Revolution" paper presented in the workshop entitled "Egypt's Foreign Policy towards the GCC Countries", organized by the IDSC-Egyptian Cabinet and the RCSS in Cairo as part of joint forum "Egypt's Regional Policies Forum", June 9, 2013.

41 Yasser Ali, was appointed the as the head of the Information and Decision Support Center affiliated to the Cabinet. He mentioned that during the workshop entitled "Egypt's Foreign Policy towards the GCC Countries", organized by the IDSC-Egyptian Cabinet and the RCSS in Cairo as part of joint forum "Egypt's Regional Policies Forum", June 9, 2013.

42 Speech of Mohamed Morsi after swearing in as a president in Cairo University published in Arabic in almasry alyoum newspaper: *Al-Masry alYoum*, June 30, 2012.

43 Essam al-Hadad the advisor of the president for foreign affairs and international cooperation, along with Ra'afat Shehata the head of the intelligence, Khaled al-Qazaz secretary of the president visited Abu Dhabi on Jan 5, 2013 to negotiate the release of 11 Egyptians arrested due to their part in recruiting Egyptian workers in UAE to join the MB. Emirati sources leaked to the media that the negotiations were confined to the 11 MB members, and not the 350 Egyptians arrested in the UAE, which proved that the Egyptian ruling elite was protecting the MB interests in the UAE and not the Egyptian interests.See:" UAE Refuses to Politically Release the "cell of 11" and Transfer the Case to the Courts (in Arabic)", *al-Riyadh*,Jan 6, 2013.

44 For the full text of the cable as published in al-watan newspaper in Arabic see: *al-Watan newspaper portal*, July 3, 2013:http://www.elwatannews.com/news/details/218441(accessed July 10, 2013)

45 "Saudi King Congratulates Egypt's New Interim President", *al-Arabiya English news portal*, July 4, 2013: http://tinyurl.com/zzbrg3m (accessed July 2016)

46   For more on Saudi policies see: Silvia Colombo, "The GCC Countries and the Arab Spring: Between Outreach, Patronage and Repression", *IAI working papers*, paper no.12, Mar 9, 2012.

47   "Saudi Arabia: The Arab are Ready for Compensating Egypt (in Arabic)", *Skynews Arabia news portal*, Aug 19,2013: http://tinyurl.com/hv9jy6w (accessed July 2016)

48   *Ibid.*

49   "Sheikh Abdullah and John Kerry discuss the crisis in Egypt", *The National*, Aug 3, 2013.

50   In the first five months of 2013, the deficit nearly doubled from the previous year to 113.4 billion Egyptian pounds ($16.2 billion), according to Finance Ministry figures. see:" UAE offers Egypt $3 billion support, Saudis $5 billion", *Reuters*, July 9, 2013: http://tinyurl.com/meuss4z (accessed July 2016)

51   "Protesters across Egypt call for Mohamed Morsi to go", The Guardian, June 30, 2013; Alan Taylor, "Millions March in Egyptian Protests", *The Atlantic*, July 1, 2013: http://tinyurl.com/jpyabvz (accessed July 2016)

52   Rod Nordland, "Saudi Arabia Promises to Aid Egypt's Regime", *The NewYork Times*, Aug 19, 2013; Yasser al-Shazely, "Saudi Foreign Policies in 2013 (in Arabic)", *al-Hayat*, Dec30, 2013

53   "UAE offers Egypt $3 billion support, Saudis $5 billion", *Rueters*, July 9, 2013: http://tinyurl.com/meuss4z (accessed July 2016)

54   "Egyptian Prime Minister, U.A.E. Minister of State discuss US$4.9 billion aid package", *Relief Web*, Dec 23, 2013: http://tinyurl.com/zpagh3q (accessed July 2016)

55   İsmail Numan Telci, "Overcoming the Regional Stalemate: Understanding the Politics of the Gulf States and Turkey during the Egyptian Coup", *POMEAS BRIEF*, No.8, Project on the Middle East and the Arab Spring POMEAS, April 2015: http://tinyurl.com/j8nkzgb (accessed July 2016)

56   Rod Nordland, *Op.Cit.*

57   "Egypt poses as business-friendly hub, scores high in economic conference", *Ahram online*, March 15, 2015: http://tinyurl.com/joel4t4 (accessed July 2016)

58   "Egyptian Prime Minister, U.A.E. Minister of State discuss US$4.9 billion aid package", *Op.Cit.*

59   "el-Sisi: Protecting the Arab and Gulf Security is Short Distance (in Arabic)", *al-Arabiya net*, May 20, 2014: http://tinyurl.com/zf8un7e (accessed July 2016)

60   "Egypt-Emirates military maneuvers kick off", *Egypt Independent*, Feb 28, 2014.

61   "New Military Maneuvers between Egypt and UAE nd Katherine Ko (in Arabic)", *al-Arabiya net*, Oct 12,2014: http://tinyurl.com/hukmsuw (accessed July 2016)

62   Commitment according to this declaration came to an end during the summer of 1992, see:
     Mary E. Morris," New Political Realities and the Gulf: Egypt, Syria, and Jordan", Project Air Force-Arroyo Center, RAND Corporation, 1993:12-15.

63   "Arab states play limited role in battle against Muammar Gaddafi's regime", *The Guardian*, May 22, 2011.

64   "US and allies strike ISIL targets in Syria (in Arabic)", *Al-Jazeera*, September 23, 2014: http://tinyurl.com/oaa68ma (accessed July 2016)

65   See the interview of the Saudi Minister of Justice with al-Sharq al-Awsat newspaper explaining the

66   *The National*, Nov 16, 2014.

67   It arrested 125, 83 nationals, and 31 Egyptians. See: Omar al-Shahaby et al, "The Constant and the Shifting 2014:the Gulf between Societal Disintegration and the linkage between Money and Power (in Arabic)", *2014 Report*, Gulf Center for Development Policies: 66-69.

68   Abdullah al-Rasheed, "The Full Story of the Muslim Brotherhood in UAE (in Arabic)",*al-Sharq al-Awsat*, Feb1, 2013.

69   *Ibid.*; "Abdullah Bin Zayed: The MB doesn't Believe in the Nation State (in Arabic)", *CNN Arabic*, Oct 20, 2012: http://tinyurl.com/jk5k7zq (accessed July 2016)

70   Abdullah al-Rasheed, *Op.Cit.*

71   "Is Saudi Arabia warming up to the Muslim Brotherhood?", *Al-Jazeera*, July 29, 2015: http://tinyurl.com/okl5dug (accessed July 2016)

72   Alan Greish, "Rapprochement between Saudi Arabia and Muslim Brotherhood provokes Egypt", *Middle East Monitor*, Sept 30,2015: http://tinyurl.com/hhhaop5 (accessed July 2016)

73 *Ibid.*

74 Interview conducted by the author with an Egyptian former minister of foreign affairs on the condition of anonymity, August 11, 2015, Cairo.

75 See for instance the joint press conference between Nabeel Fahmy and the Saudi Foreign minister on September 1 2013: "Saood al-Faisal: the Government and the People of the Kingdom will Support Egypt allTime (in Arabic)", *al-Wee'am online news portal*, Sep 1, 2013: http://tinyurl.com/gsswh7j (accessed July 2016)

76 "Yemen Blow the Conflict between UAE and Saudi Arabia (in Arabic)", *al- Khaleej Affairs*, April 15, 2015: http://tinyurl.com/honc7q6 (accessed July 2016)

77 "UAE and Egypt behind bombing raids against Libyan militias, say US officials", *The Guardian*, Aug 26, 2014.

78 "Egypt Calls for Foreign Intervention in Libya", Feb 17, 2015, *alJazeera English portal*: http://tinyurl.com/q7sl9ut (accessed July 2016)

79 "The Arab League Contemplates a Joint Force ", *Stratfor*, April 8, 2015.

80 King Slaman announced this vision on March 10, 2015: http://tinyurl.com/gu3lnmw

81 Aya Batrawy and Adam Schreck, '34-Nation 'Islamic Military Alliance' to Fight Terrorism, Saudi Arabia Says', *The Globe and Mail*, 15 December 2015: http://tinyurl.com/zs99ejz

82 The full speech of President el-Sisi is published in Arabic in al-Shorouk newspaper: *al-Shorouq*, March 28, 2015.

83 *Ibid.*

84 For more details see: "Disagreements on the leadership and the request to intervene (in Arabic)", *al-Masry al Youm*, May 25, 2015.

85 Interviews with Saudi and Emeriti officials in Abu Dhabi and in London conducted by the author on the condition of anonymity during the period 2012-2013.

86 "Could Egypt and the UAE be about to part ways with Salman's Saudi Arabia?", *Middle East Eye*, Feb 13, 2015: http://tinyurl.com/z8utqem (July 2016)

87 Interview with an Egyptian former minister of foreign affairs conducted by the author on the condition of anonymity, 9 July 2015, Cairo.

88 For instance, Ibraheem Isa in his talk show aired on ONTv Satellite Channel urged President Sisi not to become a "prisoner" of Riyadh. For more see: "Could Egypt and the UAE be about to part ways with Salman's Saudi Arabia?", *Op.Cit.*

89 Eman Ragab, "The Gulf after the Arab Spring: the Challenge and the Response" (in Arabic), *Democracy Journal (peer reviewed)*, Jan 2015; Eman Ragab, "A New Gulf?: Implications of Camp David Summit between the GCC Countries and the United States" (in Arabic), *Afaq Seyasiya* (The Arab Center for Studies and Researches), Issue no 19, July 2015.

90 "Egypt, Saudi Arabia form council to implement 'Cairo Declaration'", *Alarabiya net*, November 11, 2015: http://tinyurl.com/o5zd24n (accessed July 2016)

91 Mustafa Ellabbad argues that Riyadh is using the financial aid, even during the MB era to "prevent Egypt from Expanding its regional manuever margins." See: Mustafa Ellabbad, "Egypt: A "Regional Reference" in the Middle East", in: Henner Fürtig (ed.), *Regional Powers in the Middle East: New Constellations After the Arab Revolts* (New York: Palgrave Macmillan, 2014): 93.

92 See his article: Mustafa elFeqy, "On the Egyptian issue (in Arabic)", *al-Ahram*, 26 May 2015.

8

The Development of Egypt-GCC State Relations and its Impact on Gulf and Regional Security

Ashraf Keshk

Introduction

The development of Egyptian-GCC state relations was not a result of some instant changes; rather, it was a continuum of basic stands on both sides through their history. This started with Egypt's strict opposition to Abdul Karim Qasim's threat to Kuwaiti sovereignty in 1961, and continued with the roles played by the GCC countries during the wars of 1967 and 1973, that played by Egypt during the Iraqi-Iranian war in the 1980s. The fundamental Egyptian opposition to the Iraqi invasion of Kuwait in 1990 and its insistence on bringing legitimacy back was represented in the contribution of the Egyptian forces in the international alliance for Kuwait liberation in 1991. Moreover, the governing elite in Egypt has always confirmed that the security of the Arabian Gulf is a red line and that it is an inseparable part of Egyptian national security.

Given that the Egyptian-Gulf relations have multiple aspects, these relations witnessed what can be considered a "strategic leap" after 30 June 2013. Decision makers from both sides realised the importance of taking these relations to new horizons, not on a temporary basis or because of a specific issue or crisis as what happened in the past, but as an inevitable step that was imposed by the internal events in Egypt on one side, and the transformations in the regional situation and the policies of some international powers towards the regional security issues on the other side. This reflected an inclination for both sides which is that their rapprochement became a strategic necessity, and that their relations should be "institutionalized" instead of being subject to the events developments. This is why the Gulf support for Egypt was clear, and this started with the financial aid to Egypt that reached $10.6 billion in 2014, the GCC countries declaration in the Economic Conference in Sharm El-Sheikh in March 2015 that they would present $12 billion to Egypt as grants, the joint military maneuvers between the two sides, the coordination within Operation Decisive Storm against Houthis in Yemen, and finally the political support that reached its peak by some Gulf officials support for Egypt in their address to the UN General

Assembly in September 2014. Given the above, this chapter addresses these trends through the transitions taking place after the 30 June 2013.

The Factors that Led to the Development of the Egyptian-Gulf Relations, Specifically after 30 June 2013

The region of the Arabian Gulf has been extremely important for the Egyptian national security over history, and that there have been strong cultural and social ties between the two sides. This drove the renowned Egyptian Intellectual Mamoun Fendi to wonder in his article published in 2009: "Is Egypt a Gulf state?" There was a lot of debates and interaction about the article by other writers and both the article and the debates were about a new approach to handle the issue of the Egyptian role towards the Gulf security from a humanitarian prospective after thousands of Egyptian workers left Kuwait in 1990 and lost all of their savings after the Iraqi invasion. The approach also indicated the strategic importance of the Gulf area for Egypt represented in the Egyptian coasts that extends for a long distance facing Saudi Arabia.

In the same context, the intervention of the Egyptian army in the crises of the Gulf area can be explained. This includes the important role of the Egyptian military experience in protecting the Arabian Gulf from the Iranian threats during the Iranian-Iraqi war in the 1980s. This means that these visions agreed on that that the Egyptian role towards the security of the Arabian Gulf is not just attached to the geographical context, but it goes beyond that to the strategic reality based on the common goals and destination. This was confirmed by the Egyptian president Abdelfattah El-Sisi when outlined that Egyptian regional security passes through the Gulf Countries.

Local, regional and international frameworks for these relations can be determined as follows:

In the Internal Transformations in Egypt

These transformations led to the rise of the Muslim Brotherhood group in Egypt and this was the reason behind the tensions in the Egyptian-Gulf relations. There were some negative statements made by the group leaders against some of the GCC countries, and in this context, it is worth mentioning how the official speaker of the group, Mahmoud Ghuzlan, announced his support to the stand of Sheikh Yusuf Alqradawi, the Egyptian Islamic scholar who lives in Qatar, who severely criticised the UAE for deporting Syrians opposing the Syrian regime. Ghuzlan said that the reaction of the whole Islamic world will target the UAE if it implemented its threats to arrest the Sheikh. This stirred tremendous reactions, not only in the UAE but also in all GCC countries. There were also signs of rapprochement with Iran during the era of Muslim Brotherhood, and one of the biggest signs was the approval of the Egyptian government to resume flights between the two sides to transfer Iranian tourists to Egypt for the first time since the Iranian revolution. These developments represented a challenge for the GCC countries as they were unsure about the content of the these statements and positions, in particular whether they represented the group thought or if they represented a new approach for the governing Muslim Brotherhood.

On the Level of the Arab Regional System as a Whole

The rise of the non-state actors and their control over some geographical locations and fighting the unified power of the central state constituted a challenge for many countries, especially since these groups are connected ideologically. These developments led to that many countries focused only on their internal affairs and as a result their regional role receded and this in turn gave the opportunity to some neighboring countries to extend. Under these developments, Egypt and the GCC countries realised the importance of re-building a regional security system believing that if the regional security was the total of the units that compose it, then the strength of that security will be the same as the strength of its units. Hence, the clear Gulf support to Egypt on the political and economic levels might reflect a Gulf approach that is based on the importance of supporting building the central Arab countries which constitute a lever for the regional security.

The Vacuum in Regional Power

With the intensification of the financial crisis, the US drew down its military commitments from the high watermark of its commitments in Iraq and Afghanistan. A study indicated that the cost of Iraq war from 2003 to January 2015 to the US was $603 billion, while the Alliance forces share was $306 billion.[1] The recession of the US role led to a power vacuum and this in turn contributed to heating up the regional competition, especially between Saudi Arabia and Iran. This also coincided with the rise of a parallel conflict based on a religious basis. As the Iranian influence in neighboring regional countries to the GCC (Syria, Iraq, Yemen, and Lebanon) increased, the ISIL rose claiming to be the defender of the Sunni rights in the region as a whole. Consequently, in such a situation, it is expected that the liquidity and security instability in the region will continue for a few years, this found the need for convergence between Egypt and the GCC countries so these powers can be present at the heart of forming the new regional system.[2]

The Development of the Iranian-Western Relations

This resulted in signing the nuclear deal between Iran and 5+1 group on July 15, 2015. Although this deal closed the nuclear file, it somehow institutionalised the regional influence of Iran, as the GCC countries problem cannot be reduced to the nuclear file, but extends to the regional policies of Iran. And this can indicated in the Iranian intervention in the affairs of the GCC countries more generally, and in the internal affairs of the Kingdom of Saudi Arabia and the Kingdom of Bahrain more specifically. Hence, this agreement will be an important variable as it will identify not only the reality of the Gulf regional security equation, but the future of the Middle East in general. This is what Martin Indyk, the former envoy of President Barak Obama to the Middle East region, believed as he said: "The US is facing a crossroad and it has to choose forming a regional system that is either with Iran or against it, and this is very relevant to the nuclear agreement. The right US strategy to bring stability back to the Middle East region is to help the traditional allies and balancing the agreement by spreading a nuclear umbrella that deter these allies."[3]

In other words, the US policy towards Iran is part of the current US doctrine, as it tries, instead of expanding military engagement in the regional crises, to have a balanced policy towards the key regional players regardless the level of friendship with each of these players.[4] This means that the above regional and international developments after 2011 more generally motivated both Egypt and the GCC countries to strengthen their relationship in several areas.

On International Security: The Blurring of Boundaries between Regional and International Security

The Syrian crisis is a clear example that reflects the strong overlap between regional and international security, given the multiple players involved, including Russia, and taking into consideration that Syria is the last place where Russia has a footstep in the Middle East area. The Russian aerial intervention in the Syrian crisis and the Russian decision to send the developed S 400 missile system to Syria is something that is not only connected to the Syrian crisis, but it is also related to the Russian trial to defy NATO in the critical areas of its members interests, as the crisis continues and under the consequences of the Ukrainian crisis including the economic penalties imposed on Russia by the European countries because of that crisis.

Additionally, the signature of the Russian president, Vladimir Putin, on a decree on 13 April 2015 to cancel the ban on delivering Iran the S 300 missiles which was imposed by the former Russian president Dmitry Medvedev in 2010. From a different angle, it means to influence the regional security system in favor of Iran, which is an indicator of what Gregory Gause called "The New Cold War" in the Middle East in which both Saudi Arabia and Iran are playing essential roles. The structural characteristics or this war are similar to those witnessed by the Arab region in the 1950s and the 1960s of the last century which was called "the Cold Arab War" by Malcolm Kerr[5]. On the other hand, the Syrian crisis has created two opposing axes: Russia-Syria-Iran, in confrontation with the United States, Turkey, and other members of NATO.

Developments in Egyptian-Gulf Relations

Since June 2013 until the end of 2015, Egypt-Gulf relations have witnessed significant developments on the economic, political and military levels and can be further elaborated below:

Egypt and the GCC countries are connected with extended economic relations that go back to before the transformations of 2011. The estimations refer to that the number of Egyptian employees in the GCC countries is around 3 million people whose money transfers exceed $5 billion annually which make it a source for national income in Egypt. At the same time, to be accurate we should calculate the number of these workers while considering the others that they support, as those who are supported are between 7 and 10 million. This reflects the size of interests between the two sides.[6]

The Egyptian president is extremely concerned with increasing the number of Egyptian expatriate labour in the GCC countries. He said in the context of a meeting with a media delegation from the UAE in November 2014 that the UAE is looking forward to increasing the number of the Egyptian employees in the Gulf labor market, and improving their conditions. He also confirmed that Egypt is determined to improve the vocational level for these employees by training them in the different fields and giving them the required technical skills. Although the Gulf countries were hesitant to support the Egyptian economy after 2011, the transformations of June 30 were the beginning towards economic aids for Egypt by the GCC countries through two mechanisms:

The Gulf Investment Conference – (Cairo, December 2013)

It was jointly organised by Egypt and the UAE and there was a discussion about the requirements of the Gulf investment which included the security stability, eliminating bureaucracy, finding solutions for the problems of the contracts that were signed with the Egyptian government before the revolution, and re-considering investment laws in Egypt. As an example, but not limited to, the amendment of the Egyptian investment law that was announced by the Egyptian cabinet to restrict the right to appeal on the investment contracts to the government and the investors contributed in settling judicial conflicts about Saudi stalled projects that were estimated by $3.2 billion.

Sharm El Sheikh Conference for Supporting and Developing the Egyptian Economy (March 2015)

The idea of holding this conference can be attributed to the call launched by the late Saudi King Abdullah bin Abdulaziz in June 2014 only a few days after electing the president Abdulfattah Elsisi as a president for Egypt to hold a conference for the donors to help Egypt go through its economic crisis. However, the Egyptian government changed the nature of the invitation from a donors' conference to be an international economic conference in which Egypt can present its strategic economic vision. During the conference, some of the GCC countries provided economic support for Egypt that reached $12 billion, $4 billion of them came in the form of deposits in the Egyptian Central Bank to support the monetary reserve, while the rest was provided in the form of projects, investments, and grants in the field of oil supplies. In general, the results of the conference were represented in announcing agreements with international governments and companies with investments that reached about $33 billion, especially in the field of energy, building electricity stations and search for oil and gas, and $60 billion in the form of understanding memorandums on many projects.[7]

On the Defense Level

One of the qualitative developments of the transformations of 2011 the re-engagement between Gulf security and the national security of Egypt since Damascus declaration was suspended in 1991 as it was the first Arab formula for the Arabian Gulf security. This was represented in the participation of the Egyptian armed forces in the military maneuvers with some GCC countries which were Saudi Arabia "Tabuk 1 maneuver", the UAE "Zayed 1 maneuver", and the air maneuvers "Basic liaison" with the Kingdom of Bahrain, and the last one included a lot of activities to unify the fighting concepts, transferring and exchanging the training experience between the participating forces, and training on the administering the joint air combat by using the modernist aerial tactics and the modern fighting methods". There were also the joint Egyptian-Saudi maritime maneuvers "Murjan 15", in which a lot of special forces agents participated, while maritime units, surveillance planes, and combating submarines were used.

They targeted implementing many common training activities to secure the regional waters in the Red Sea, the maritime transportation movement, and the economic goals in the Red Sea and on the coast. The maneuver conducted in February 2015 also targeted training on searching for submarines, locating, following and destroying aggressive aerial targets. Moreover, the joint practicing maneuvers Hamad 1 were conducted in April 2015 between the Bahraini Armed forces and its Egyptian counterparts in the Kingdom of Bahrain. The Egyptian participation in these maneuvers has its indications in the context of the Egyptian-Gulf relations concerning the nature or the timing of the maneuvers; where the Egyptian presence in the Arabian Gulf security equation has developed from the level of saying to the level of doing because holding these maneuvers in the Arabian Gulf region means that the Egyptian armed forces is trying to train on different stages for military battles. Additionally, the maneuver itself is a "deterrence message" directed different parties that look for changing the traditional balance equation in the region betting that Egypt will focus on arranging its internal affairs on one hand, and the absence of consensus by Gulf countries on the sources of the regional danger on the other hand.

The importance of these exercises was in that they achieved some flexibility and a margin for maneuvering in movement for both Egypt and the GCC countries. The GGC countries consider these maneuvers as creating more defensive options under the new developments of the defense policy of the US which will focus more on Asia[8], as was announced by former U.S. Secretary of Defense Panetta at the Shangri-La Dialogue in June 2012, which announced that, "by 2020 the Navy will re-posture its forces from today's roughly 50/50 percent split between the Pacific and the Atlantic to about a 60/40 split between those oceans. That will include six aircrafts carries in this region, a majority of our cruisers, destroyers, Littoral Combat Ships, and submarines"[9].

On the Political Level

The political discourse of both Egypt and the Gulf Cooperation Council countries reflects and recognizes the importance of each party to the other, as indicated by Dr. Abdulatif Rashid Azzyani, the General Secretary of the GCC when he said that "Egypt is the heart of the Arab nation, and is a basic pillar of regional security and stability, and what happens in Egypt affects the Arab national security".

Proceeding from this, the most important development in this regard assimilates in the transition of that speech to a more institutionalised framework, which was more pronounced for the Egypt-Saudi relations through the establishment of what is known as the "Cairo Declaration" in August 2015, and which included a bundle of executive mechanisms in six areas. The declaration urged to work on developing the military cooperation, to work on establishing the common Arab force, to foster the joint cooperation and investments in energy, electrical connection, and transportation, achieve the economic integration between the two countries, to make them an essential axis in the world trade movement, and to intensify the mutual investments between Egypt and Saudi Arabia to initiate joint projects.

The declaration areas included also media, cultural, and political cooperation – in addition to the delimitation of the maritime boundaries between the two countries which resulted in the establishment of a Joint Council to coordinate meetings between the two countries. The Joint Council has held four meetings up until January 2016. The Joint Council is an important step because all issues will require research and discussion between the two sides, In addition to the existence of such mechanisms, which would promote the idea of the possibility of Egyptian-Gulf dialogue generally, along the lines of the NATO-Russia Council, an institution that was established in 2002 and continues to exist despite the strained relations between the two sides.

The Influence of the Egyptian-Gulf Rapprochement on Gulf and Regional Security

Egyptian-Gulf rapprochement may lead to correcting the imbalance in the regional security equation following the U.S. invasion of Iraq in 2003, and this is based on two factors:

The Defensive Power of Both Egypt and the GCC Countries

The report of the Strategic Studies International Institute in London of 2013 indicated that the total of the working Egyptian military forces is 438,500 soldiers, and if the total forces of the GCC countries of 342,100 soldiers were added this will constitute a joint deterrence force confronting the working Iranian forces of 523 thousand soldiers. On another hand, Egypt concluded a deal with France to buy 24 Rafale fighters, Shahin missiles that can be launched from them, and one Fremm frigate in a deal that reached $5 billion. In addition, the US lifted the ban on supplying Egypt with arms in March 2015 as the resolution included releasing 12 "F 16" fighter jets, 20 Harpoon missiles, and 120 "Abrams-M1" tanks. At the same time, the US president Barak Obama promised his Egyptian counterpart that he will continue with asking Congress for the annual military aid estimated by $1.3 billion, and that starting from 2018, the security assistance presented by the US to Egypt in fighting terrorism, borders security, Sinai security, and maritime security will be resumed.

For the GCC countries, a study by the scholar Nawaf Obaid that was published by the Belfer Center at Harvard University under the title of "The Saudi Defense Doctrine" in May 2014 indicated that Saudi Arabia proved in the past few years that it's a country with a regional weight and that it faces three challenges currently which are: the instable situation in the region, Iran, and terrorism. He also indicated that the Kingdom has developed it military powers in the past few years as 150 billion has been allocated to restore its armed forces, 100 billion of which was allocated to contracts to purchase developed weapons and train with the US. At the same time, the spending on the Saudi army increased by 30 percent, on the National Guard by 35 percent, on air defense and strategic missiles by 30 percent, and on the air forces and navy by 50 percent[10].

Furthermore, there are some indicators for the qualitative military power of the GCC countries including Saudi Arabia and the UAE as both countries are capable of designing and manufacturing military vehicles, communications, electrical systems, and financial systems, and they are capable of performing the maintenance as well, as the personnel received high level training. The strategic partnerships of Saudi Arabia and the UAE with the United States, the United Kingdom and France and some international defense companies gave them the chance to move forward with defense manufacturing. It is worth mentioning that both countries have developed what is called "the starting programs" which are important for both of them because they helped them in acquiring, identifying, and in some cases, amending the modernist technologies in the space and defense world, and consequently motivating the local military manufacturing in both countries.

In addition, both Saudi Arabia and UAE have significantly increased their defense spending during the past years. The UAE has spent 5.6% of its gross domestic production on the defense sector in 2012 and it is expected that this percentage will increase to 6.8 in 2017. As for Saudi Arabia, it has been spending 8% of its gross domestic production every year since 2004 for defense purposes[11]. A report prepared by the specialised group "HIS Janes" indicated that Saudi Arabia became the biggest importer of weapons in the world in 2014 as she bought important military equipment that worth $6.4 billion, coming before India which spent $5.5 billion, to become the "most important market" for the US. The report also indicated that "the Saudi reports increased by 54 percent" expecting an increase of 52 percent in 2015 to reach $9.7 billion.

Employing Joint Forces within a Larger Joint Arab framework

The Egyptian proposal to create a force to intervene in crises was approved in principle at the Arab summit held in Sharm El Sheikh on 28 and 29 March 2015. This proposal is still under study but if passed, it would be a remarkable development for the Arab national security system for a number of considerations, namely because it will be a practical representation for the common destination of the concepts of both Arab national security and the national security of each state. As well as to address the neighboring states which were able to expand in many Arab countries by supporting non-state groups that fight the sovereignty of the unified national state. As well as it would be an important mechanism to keep the entity of the Arab countries against the risk of fragmentation and collapse.

And lastly, the proposal[12] reflects the Egyptian vision of Arabian Gulf security and which can be identified by four variables: confirming the fateful relation between the Egyptian security and the Arabian Gulf security; connecting any positive transformation in the Egyptian-Iranian relations to the security of the Arabian Gulf; and considering terrorism as a common threat against Egypt and the GCC countries; *and lastly* the collapse or weakness of the state in Iraq and Yemen, which might constitute a direct threat to the Arabian Gulf security, and the region in general[13]. And it is the same shared vision Gulf countries have for regional security.

Will Current Circumstances Allow For an Egyptian and the Gulf Role in Forming A New Regional Security Architecture?

It will be over simplified if the Gulf-Egyptian relations are examined away from their regional circle. To have a more comprehensive vision, the new developments of this circle should be considered and whether they will result in positive factors that will promote these relations or if they have restrictions that make it difficult for the relations between both sides to develop. The continuity if the Syrian crisis means there will be an extremely disturbed regional scene. Also, the continuity of the current Yemeni crisis means that it is possible for Yemen to turn into the concept of the "collapsed state" which means the collapse of a whole region. Moreover, if Iraq continues to be outside the regional security system, this means that security will be incomplete. In addition to the new regional realities in the wake of lifting economic sanctions on Iran in January 2016. In spite of the above, a subjective reading for the effect of developing Egyptian-Gulf relations on neighboring countries should take into consideration the following four factors:

1. The Gulf-Egyptian relations and the Iranian western relations are not a zero-sum equation, meaning that a positive development on one track does not mean that this will affect the other track negatively. Rather, there is some overlap between the two tracks.

2. The Egyptian-Iranian relations are not hostile, but the priority within these relations will be given to the security of GCC countries, and there will be no two separate tracks concerning this, as the situation was before June 30, 2013.

3. If a strong regional system is a result of strong units, the transformations that the Arab countries witness might continue for years which might undermine Egyptian-Gulf relations as well as the strength of the whole Arab regional system.

4. Turkey and its impact on the regional security architecture. Regardless how Egypt and the GCC countries are different concerning the Turkish policies, the Turkish policy should be invested for the interest of the regional security, as it has political and military capabilities, and an important political role. It is also a member of NATO and has a strategic location between the Arab world from one side, and Iran and Israel from the other.[14]

Apart from the possibility of any of those perceptions, that does not mean that the American role towards Arab Gulf security can be overlooked. While it may be true that the American role may change- albeit relatively- that does not mean that it will be easy to replace it by other regional or even international roles in the short-term. To enhance this point, the following considerations are put forth: Firstly, the qualitative development in the US policy towards GCC countries as it dealt with GCC countries as one bloc through the US-GCC Dialogue Forum that was introduced in 2006 to discuss regional security challenges and mechanisms.

Secondly, the American discourse after 2011 included assurances for the Arabian Gulf countries more than once in this regard. In his speech in front of Manama Security Dialogue in 2013, the former US Secretary of Defense, Chuck Hagel, said that "the US does not intend to decrease its military presence in the Arabian Gulf region, and that it is committed to its alliances. It has 35 thousand troops in the Arabian Gulf and the Middle East, and $86 million has been allocated to expand the fifth fleet in Bahrain. Also, the US has sent to the region its modernist fighter jets including F-22 that cannot be monitored by Radar, and there are more than 40 ships that belong to that US navy including an aircraft carrier and supporting ships roving in the neighboring waters".[15]

Thirdly, the invitation of U.S. president for the leaders of GCC to a U.S. - Gulf summit in Camp David in May to discuss the horizons of the relations between the two sides as a way to assure GCC about the nuclear deal with Iran. Considering the above, and especially under the new regional role of Iran in the region after the nuclear deal and the lifting of economic sanctions on Iran, and as Iraq is not part of the regional balance equation. At the same time, there are issues where all tracks meet like terrorism. The regional environment has become more complex, which consequently, created challenges to take Egyptian-GCC relations to new heights.

Obstacles that Hinder the Development of Relations between the Two Sides

The Obstacles that Hinder the Development of the Egyptian Gulf Relations:

1. The negative role of media in both sides during covering some crises in general, or towards the stands of some GCC countries (Qatari policy towards Egypt), and

some public opinion trends in GCC countries that are not satisfied with the Gulf aids to Egypt and demanding to transfer them to investments.

2. The absence of a unified Gulf stand towards Egypt. Although there is a general Gulf approach that adopts the importance of developing the Gulf-Egyptian relations and the importance of contributing in building Egypt, each Gulf country has its own agenda concerning the content and goals of these relations.

3. The discrepancies in the Egyptian and Gulf points of view concerning some files that include the Syrian crisis. It can be noticed that Egypt is supporting the unity of the Syrian lands and keeping the Syrian army. Although the Gulf stands confirm the same goals, the stand of both Egypt and the Gulf towards the Syrian regime might be different. This is also the case in relation to the Yemeni crisis. At the time of Operation Decisive Storm and the confirmation of Egypt that Gulf security is a red line, the Egyptian president affirmed that "Egypt did not send land troops to Yemen, saying that if such a decision was made, it will be declared after fulfilling the constitutional and legal procedures, and that Egypt is moving strongly to resolve the crises in the region politically, including the Yemeni crisis".

4. The Egyptian army priority currently is in fighting terrorism in Sinai and not to intervene in regional crises.

5. The effect of the tension in the Egyptian-Qatari relations on the possibility of developing Egyptian-GCC relations to more advanced levels.

It can be said that the Egyptian political discourse always includes the security of the Arabian Gulf as part of its national security, and that Egypt will not accept any actor to threaten that security. Although this discourse is important, it was institutionalised, going beyond a mere vision. It might be said that the remarkable development of the Egyptian Gulf relations after 2011 was imposed by imminent necessities, but also by a need to institutionalize, building up the relations between the two sides, but also to foster the Arab security system and supporting building a system for the advancement of regional security. This might require decision makers in the GCC to look to Egypt for strategic depth for the Arabian Gulf security by expanding cooperation at the political, economic, security, and defensive levels. The decision makers in Egypt should also understand the strategic needs of the Gulf countries and to be prepared to take charge of the human manpower cost, especially on the military level, and to put into action the principle of that the security of the Arabian Gulf. On the GCC elite level, establishing a forum for the Egyptian Gulf strategic dialogue can be considered to formalize visions concerning the dimensions and challenges of the changing and broader regional security landscape.[16]

There are some mechanisms that can be proposed to institutionalize the relations between the two sides. On the political level, the possibility of establishing a mechanism for an Egyptian Gulf forum on an annual basis to formalize common visions about the requirements of the partnerships and the mechanisms to make them happen under the current regional and international transformations will be useful. Manama Security Conference, the Asian Security Conferences, and the other regional conferences are examples for this and they are not connected to the political developments or the nature of the relations between the countries, but they constitute a permanent mechanism. On another hand, the possibility of relations between Egypt and GCC to be institutionalised as a regional body, and not with each country on an individual basis. It is correct that bilateral relations with GCC are an important thing, but there is a need to think about a formula for collective cooperation that is permanent. An example for this is the relationship between NATO and Russia as a relationship between a regional organization and a country that is located outside the region. This formula will help preserve the identity of the GCC as well as benefiting from the weight of Egypt as a central country.

On the economic level, as the role of Gulf aid continues to be important in supporting the Egyptian economy, it is important to transform this aid into investments that are injected in the Egyptian economy sectors. This what the Egyptian ambassador to the UAE confirmed when he said "the Gulf aids to Egypt will not stop, but it will take another shape and will change from being grants and loans to investment and partnership, and this was agreed on with the donor countries in the Gulf". It is also important to facilitate finding job opportunities for the Egyptian employees in the GCC countries and to have priority over other countries.

On defence, a permanent mechanism should be considered for defense consultation between the two sides. The importance of institutionalizing the defense relations between the two sides in an attempt to establish the identity of regional security and represented in the Arab League as a regional organization and the GCC as a sub-regional organization. Although the responsibility of institutionalizing these relations lies in the first place on decision makers from both sides, there is a mission for unofficial institutions that include research and studies centers and universities to hold more workshops and meetings and to conduct objective studies about the future of the relations between the two sides. Similarly, it is important to support establishing friendship societies with some GCC countries, and coordinating these societies work to identify the common issues between the two sides because these societies have an important role in strengthening the popular dimension, and it is also economically important because it will include businessmen from both sides to search for and study mutual investment opportunities.

As well as the need for a new media discourse between both sides, the integration of Gulf capital and skilled Egyptian labour could drive the relationship forward. Both sides should also consider the strategic interests and the long-term transformations and their effect on the regional security as a whole for both Egypt and the GCC countries. There might be some obstacles that stand against implementing these goals including the negative historical experience for the GCC countries concerning some events like Mohamed Ali's military mission to the Arabian Peninsula, and the Nasser's expansion into the Arabian

Gulf that reached its peak with the confrontation with Saudi Arabia in Yemen, as well as the transformations of 2011.

Conclusion

Egypt-GCC relations witnessed significant developments in multiple fields (defense, economic, political) as a result of regional shifts as well as internal transformations in Egypt post 30 June 2013. Despite these potentially positive developments, the extent of influence of Egypt - GCC state convergence in the regional security equation remains limited for reasons related to the continued divergence of views between the two sides about some of the regional issues on the one hand and the presence of more effective regional and international parties in regional security issues on the other hand. This ultimately means that both Egypt and the GCC countries should jointly review the foundations of their cooperation, objectives and mechanisms for implementation.

References

Abutalib, Hassan. "Sharm Elsheikh conference to support and develop the Egyptian Economy." *Arab Future Magazine*, (April 2015). 198-204.

Aldkhil Khalid, "The Saudi transformation and the Egyptian concern newspaper," *Alhayat*, March 1 2015.

Derasat. "Forming an Arab force to intervene in crises: The Content and Reflection." June 2015, 2 ed. 15-28.

Diehl Jakson, "Nuclear negotiations to determine the future of the Middle east," *Al-Hayah*, March 18, 2015.

Frisch, Hillel. *While the Jihadists Make Headlines, Fundamentalist Iran is Making Major Gains.* Begin-Sadat Center for Strategic Studies, February, 2015.

Gause, Gregory. "Beyond Sectarianism: The new cold war in the Middle East, Doha Brookings Institute." July, 2014. 16-17.

Ibrahim, Hasanein Tawfik. "Egypt And Gulf Security." In *The book of the Gulf in 2014 – 2015.*, edited by Hasanein Tawfik. Jeddah: Gulf Research Center, 2015.

Kishk, Ashraf Mohamed. *the Development of the Gulf regional security since 2003.* Beirut: Center of Arab Unity Studies, 2012.

Kishk, Ashraf Mohamed. "Chuck Hagel meeting with the Defense Ministers in the GCC countries: Basic Remarks." *The Bahraini Al-Watan Newspaper*, May 2014.

Kishk, Ashraf Mohamed. "The Egyptian-Gulf Relations, the mutual strategic need." *Al-Bahraini Al-Watan newspape*, June 27 2014.

Obaid, Nawaf. *Defense Doctrine: Mapping the expanded force structure the Kingdom needs to lead the Arab world, stabilize the region, and meet its global responsibilities.* Harvard: Belfer Center for Science and International Affairs, May 2014.

Qablan, Marwan. "The rise of ISIS and the transformations of the regional system in the Arabian East." *Arabic Policies Periodical*, January, 2015, 12 ed.

Regional Center for Strategic Studies. "The future of the Egyptian Iranian relations under the strategic transformations in the region." Cairo, 2013.

Rong, Chean. "A Critical Analysis of the U.S "Pivot" toward the Asia - Pacific: How Realistic is Neo - realiaism?" 2013. 39 -62.

Saab, Bilal. *Gulf Rising Defense Industrialization in Saudi Arabia and UAE.* USA: Brent Scowcroft Center on international Security, 2014.

Salama, Moataz. *The Future of Strategic Relations Between Egypt and GCC.* Bahrain center for Strategic, International and Energy Studies, November, 2014.

The international Politics Magazine. "The Egyptian-Gulf Relations." July 2014.

Waltson, Scott, and Katherine Kozic. "the Economic costs of the war on Iraq." *Arab Future*, April 2015. 85 -119.

Notes

1   Scott Waltson and Katherine Kozic. "the Economic costs of the war on Iraq." Arab Future, April 2015: 85 -119: http://tinyurl.com/zufxh6t

2   Marwan Qablan. "The rise of ISIS and the transformations of the regional system in the Arabian East." Arabic Policies Periodical, January, 2015, 12 ed.

3   Jakson Diehl, "Nuclear negotiations to determine the future of the Middle east," Al-Hayah, March 18, 2015: http://tinyurl.com/h3pyz7c

4   Hillel Frisch. While the Jihadists Make Headlines, Fundamentalist Iran is Making Major Gains. Begin-Sadat Center for Strategic Studies, February, 2015: http://tinyurl.com/h8b8xlz

5   Gregory Gause. "Beyond Sectarianism: The new cold war in the Middle East, Doha Brookings Institute." July, 2014. 16-17: http://tinyurl.com/hldnvvb

6   Ashraf Mohamed Kishk. "The Egyptian-Gulf Relations, the mutual strategic need." Al-Bahraini Al-Watan newspaper, June 27 2014: http://tinyurl.com/jtfkef3

7   Hassan Abutalib. "Sharm Elsheikh conference to support and develop the Egyptian Economy." Arab Future Magazine, (April 2015). 198-204: http://tinyurl.com/zmp8co6 (accessed 6 July, 2016)

8   Ashraf Mohamed Kishk. "The Egyptian-Gulf Relations." The international Politics Magazine, July 2014

9   Chean Rong. "A Critical Analysis of the U.S "Pivot" toward the Asia - Pacific: How Realistic is Neo - realism?" 2013. 39 -62: http://tinyurl.com/j6ces4w

10   Nawaf Obaid. Defense Doctrine: Mapping the expanded force structure the Kingdom needs to lead the Arab world, stabilize the region, and meet its global responsibilities. Harvard: Belfer Center for Science and International Affairs, May 2014: http://tinyurl.com/q5s45qw

11   Bilal Saab. Gulf Rising Defense Industrialization in Saudi Arabia and UAE. USA: Brent Scowcroft Center on international Security, 2014: http://tinyurl.com/zzrnps8

12   Ashraf Mohamed Kishk. "Forming an Arab force to intervene in crises: The Content and Reflection." Derasat, June 2015, 2 ed.: 15-28.

13   Hasanein Tawfik Ibrahim. "Egypt And Gulf Security." In The book of the Gulf in 2014 – 2015., edited by Hasanein Tawfik. Jeddah: Gulf Research Center, 2015

14   Aldkhil Khalid, "The Saudi transformation and the Egyptian concern newspaper," Alhayat, March 1 2015: http://tinyurl.com/jekb4lq (accessed 6 July, 2016)

15   Ashraf Mohamed Kishk. "Chuck Hagel meeting with the Defense Ministers in the GCC countries: Basic Remarks." The Bahraini Al-Watan Newspaper, May 2014: http://tinyurl.com/zjl8485

16   Moataz Salama. The Future of Strategic Relations Between Egypt and GCC. Bahrain center for Strategic, International and Energy Studies, November, 2014.

9

Egypt's Relations with the Arab and Islamic Worlds: What Hope for a Former Hegemon?

Yacoob Abba Omar

Introduction

There are four crucial turning points in the recent history of Egypt: the period from 1906 to the adoption of the 1921 Constitution; the period of the Free Officers takeover of Egypt under the leadership of Gemal Abdel Nasser from 1952; the post-Nasser period of Presidents Anwer Sadat and Hosni Mubarak; and the turbulent period which was set in motion from January 2011. The Nasser period is regarded as the high point of Egypt's hegemony over the Arab world and the Middle East. While looking at this claim critically, as well as the effect of the Sadat and Mubarak presidencies, the chapter shall assess the potential for Egypt to play a hegemonic role in the very fluid dynamics of the contemporary Islamic world generally, and in the Middle East specifically.

Steven Cook argues that the period since 1952 was one of trying to create 'an appealing narrative of Egyptian society that was shared amongst the vast majority of Egyptians'. This 'foundered because their rhetoric about social justice, economic change, and democracy never matched the reality'.[1] This chapter takes a contrary view, arguing instead that through a number of devices – rhetoric, suppression and diplomacy – the Nasser regime was able to extend its hegemony over much of Egyptian society as well as the Arab world. It will argue that this centrality of Egypt to Arab and Middle East politics was eroded during the Sadat and Mubarak era for a number of reasons – the most significant of which was the signing of the Camp David Accord in 1979 and the closeness Egypt enjoyed with the USA.

Egypt did manage to claw its way back to the centre of Arab politics, but it never managed to quite enjoy the acclaim that it did under Nasser. However, the chapter asserts that notwithstanding, or perhaps because of the circumstances faced by the Sisi government, the current regime is laying the basis for it to emerge as the new hegemon of the region and the Arab world. Much of the impetus, if achieved, will be due to the sheer size of its military forces, its intellectual depth, its diplomatic prowess and geographical location straddling the African continent and the Middle East.

Hegemony: Domestic, Regional and International

The Gramscian notion of hegemony, which encompasses all relations of domination and subordination, presents a useful framework within which to locate Egypt. For Antonio Gramsci the supremacy of a social group was manifested in two ways, as 'domination' and as 'intellectual and moral leadership'. He saw hegemony as a balancing of force and consent. The Gramscian view eschews the classical Marxist notion of a single dominant class with a sense of different classes entering into different shifting, albeit unstable, alliances[2]. Mark Rupert has argued that Gramsci's notion of a 'historic bloc' was more than a simple alliance of classes or class fractions since it included aspects of the political, cultural, and economic elements of a social formation. 'An historic bloc articulates a world view, grounded in historically specific, socio-political conditions and production relations, which lends substance and ideological coherence to its social power'.[3]

From 1922 to 1952

From 1906, Egyptians had been waging a struggle against the British colonialists, culminating in the 1919 revolution which saw more than 800 Egyptians and scores of British troops killed. The uprisings of that period led to Egyptians attaining qualified independence in 1922. This period saw the Wafd Party implement increasingly strident campaigns to attain full independence.

During the period between the two world wars a number of Arab thinkers, especially Egyptians sent to study in the West, emerged pushing for a liberal Arab path to address the "backwardness" of the Arab world. This tradition was best embodied by secularists and leftists such as Taha Hussein (1889 to 1973) and Ghali Shukri. Abu-Rabi argues that 'Out of the complex encounter between the Arab world and the advanced capitalist West in the nineteenth century, a distinct trend that I would like to call Arab Third-Worldism emerged', which took a strong anti-colonial position[4].

This anti-colonialism was taking two forms: Islamist ideology and nationalist thinking. The Muslim Brotherhood of Egypt, founded in 1928, was influenced by the exhortations of its founder and leader, Hassan al-Banna. His ideas developed from then to 1932 when he moved to Cairo and articulated the core principles of the MB: the totality of Islam as a system, much against the Western notion of separate of state and religion which had been taking root especially in the previous century; that the Qur'an and the Hadith were the basis of Islam; and the applicability of Islam to all places and all time. The Muslim Brotherhood were *Salafists* in their outlook, and not particularly focused on seizing political power or using force. However, the 1948 deployment of an armed MB battalion to Palestine shows it was not entirely opposed to arming itself. The government's imprisonment of about 4 000 members of the society and the eventual assassination of al-Banna in 1949 shows the threat the movement was already posing to secularists.

The 1947/1948 defeat of the Arab countries by the Israelis plays a pivotal role in Arab historiography. There was intensive reflection on what this defeat, or *nakba*, meant was epitomised by the seminal 1948 work of Syrian philosopher Constantin Zurayq titled *Ma'na al-nakba*, The Meaning of the Catastrophe. For Zurayq radical self-criticism, long-term planning for the military and political organization through Arab unity was required. His emblematic secular approach contrasted sharply with the views of al-Banna and his nascent movement.

Nasser and the High Point of Modernity

Gamal Abdel Nasser, a colonel in the Egyptian military who had fought in the 1948 war against Israel, came to power through the 23 July 1952 revolution, at the helm of the Free Officers' Movement. It is noteworthy that the coup itself was announced by Anwer Sadat, who had developed a long-standing relationship with the Muslim Brotherhood. As in many other cases of revolutionary takeovers, the Free Officers' Movement did not have a clear ideology.

However, the hegemonic project which came to be known as Nasserism was based on a combination of a particular class alliance, mobilising of the masses through popular symbols and causes, including a close identification with the emerging non-aligned movement. The historic bloc was an alliance with very specific sectoral interests. This included select state bureaucrats, businessmen, urban middle classes, managers of public-sector companies, organised labour and later, the richer farmers.

At the time of Nasser's coming to power 0.5 percent of the landowners owned 35 percent of all the land. The Free Officer's government tried to make their mark in Egyptian society by reducing the size of land that owners could own to about 210 hectares. Minimum wages were set, cooperatives and unions allowed, land rents were limited and tenancy regulations improved. At the same time politics was to be reconfigured through the Party Organisation Law which ordered the dissolution and re-registration of all parties, required to work under the Liberation Rally.

What had begun as a cordial relationship with the MB quickly turned into adversarial confrontation, resulting in the January 1954 arrest of hundreds of MB members and later that year, in a dispute over the government's relationship with the British, a further 2000 were sent to prison and the MB's spiritual guide placed under house arrest. As a result the movement went largely underground.

The Liberation Rally laid the basis for the National Union and the Arab Socialist Union (ASU). By June 1953, Nasser's Revolutionary Council could announce the abolition of the monarchy and the creation of the Republic. This in itself was a popular move given the general opposition to the king. Ahmed Shokr argues that these moves helped the Nasserist state avoid 'domination by any single social group…Dissenters who refused to conform - whether communists, Islamists or others - were brutally repressed'.[5]

Amongst the key achievements of the Revolutionary Council during the decade from 1956 to the mid-1960s were improvements in the economy, especially in the per capita income for those in the professional and bureaucratic classes. The wealth of the top echelon declined by 10 percent while that of the majority at the bottom increased its share of the economy by 12 percent, albeit from a low base. School enrolment improved as did life expectancy by 4 years.

However, the repressive measures were laying the basis for an increasingly statist approach. A law was passed in 1961 which placed Al Azhar under state control; and while improving the basic conditions of employments restrictions on workers' rights to take industrial action were promulgated.. The hitherto militant student movements were bought off with generous resourcing and the promise of jobs upon graduation. Also the passing of the emergency law of 1958 gave the regime wide ranging powers to censor, restrict and limit all kinds of freedoms.

What accounts for the illiberal policies pursued during this period? Shokr, comparing the revolution of 1952 to that of 2011, argues that 'the Free Officers were fortunate to have the weight of history behind them. They took power in a high modernist epoch when the state was celebrated as an instrument of progress, a panacea for the deficiencies of liberal parliamentarianism and the ills of unregulated capitalism'[6]. Anouar Abdel-Malek disparagingly called the state the Free Officers Movement had put in place a "nationalitarian", drawing as it did on a form of nationalism while resorting to increasingly repressive tactics. Elizabeth Suzanne Kassab observed that the state of Israel 'imposed certain priorities, such as the military and security, at the expense of civil liberties. It also favoured the strengthening of a defensive nationalism that does not tolerate dissent'.[7]

Notwithstanding the repressive measures the Free Officers Movement consolidated its grip on power and for almost ten years enjoyed the broad support of Egyptians because of the various popular measures put into place. This domestic hegemony of the social classes behind the Nasserist project laid the basis for Nasser to make his foray into foreign territory.

Egypt and the Rest of the World

Abdel Monem Said Aly reminds us that *In The Philosophy of the Revolution*, Nasser defined the three "circles" that Egypt's foreign policy needed to address: the Arab, the African, and the Islamic countries. Nasserism could be seen as a form of Arab nationalism that sought to unify the entire Arab nation against imperialism. Arab socialism was regarded as the form appropriate for the Arab nation. Nasserism sought to relegate the role of Islam, and it was respected so long as it was consistent with socialism and Arabism. However, the clergy was not allowed to have any say in matters of state.

By the 1940s individual Arab nation-states were being consolidated, leading to the creation of the Arab League in 1948. The Charter of the Arab League recognised the sovereignty of individual states. The 1950s were marked by the emergence of two distinct nationalist ideologies in the Arab world: the Ba'athists and that of the Nasserists. The Ba'athists' goal was the creation of one Arab state and the kindling of an Arab awakening – which is what *ba'ath* literally means. They believed that the differences amongst Arabs would disappear once that was achieved. In this definition the Ba'athists, with their emphasis on pan-Arab unity which shared a single historical experience, manifested *al-qawmiya*. By the mid-fifties the ideas of socialism were included in the Party's ideology and it spread to Jordan, Lebanon, Iraq, and parts of the Arabian Peninsula.

Unlike the Ba'athists, 'Nasser regarded Arab unity as a rhetorical device for domestic and regional aggrandizement rather than a project that could be carried our practically'.[8] Notwithstanding the differences in approach and his own uncertainties, Nasser acceded to the overtures made by the Syrian to combine their two countries into the United Arab Republic, on March 6 1958. With this move he further consolidated Cairo's position as the centre of the Arab world, displacing its traditional rival, Iraq, even though the Union itself did not last long.

Already Egypt was proving itself as the cultural hegemon of the Arab world. *Sawt al Arab* was being broadcast across the world, fanning support for Arab nationalism. 'This came at a time when the old political order in the Arab world was increasingly under attack, with Nasser leading the charge'.[9] The Algerians sought support in their brutal battle against the French and upon independence in 1962 it could draw on Cairo's support for the process of reconstruction. By the 1960s the differences amongst Arab nation states became sharper: there were those like Egypt committed to rapid change and those ruled by conservative dynasties that were suspicious of the spread of Nasserist ideas.

The Third Worldism intimated to by Abu Rabi started taking concrete effect after the Bandung Conference of 1955. The conference in Indonesia represented the apogee of anti-colonialism. It was a meeting of about 30 countries which had been recently liberated from colonialism, as well as various fraternal parties. These leaders led the demand for 'political and intellectual decolonisation'. Notwithstanding the various ideological strands gathered - represented by the Nehrus, Nyereres, the Titos, or the Sukharnos - they brought into the post WWII world 'a shared anti-imperial ethic'.[10] The emphasis of anti-colonial thinking was on modernisation or catching up with the West. Their ideology was rooted on the nation-state which was going to uplift its people through education and ambitious development projects.

Inspired by the Non-Aligned Movement which the Bandung Conference gave birth to, Nasser declared for positive neutralism. This posture was to see Egypt recognise the People's Republic of China in 1956, resulting in the Eisenhower administration withdrawing support for the desperately needed Aswan High Dam. A week later Nasser announced the nationalization of the Suez Canal, taking over British and French interests. This led to the Suez War of 1956 which saw the USSR coming to Egypt's side. The US was not keen on such developments, with the Eisenhower administration calculating correctly that as long as the European colonial powers held onto their former colonies the more these countries would veer towards the Soviet Union. The US managed to get hostilities to be ceased, with the confrontation serving to boost Nasser's domestic and international popularity immensely.

This was to come to a humiliating end with the 'setback' of 1967 when Egypt was defeated by the Israelis in the Six Day War. Cook is amongst those who argue that 'Instead of killing Arab nationalism, the June War (of 1967) killed Nasserism.[11] The loss forced the Arab world to reexamine its self-identity in relation to the Other – that is the West/Israel. It also resulted in the 'radical failure of the nationalist/socialist Arab project (especially Nasserism)... and inaugurated a new phase in the relationship of Arab dependency on the capitalist West'.[12]

The UN Resolution passed at the time, calling for Israel's withdrawal from territories occupied as a result of the 1967 war, remains the lodestar for those committed to a peaceful resolution of the conflict. The period also saw the increasing use of armed actions by the Palestinian forces to press for their demands, supported by militants from Egypt. By this time, a military clique with close connections to the private sector, had installed itself. However, economic growth had slowed down which, coupled with the regime's increasingly coercive measures, saw widespread popular dissent for the first time in more than a decade.

Shifting Alliances Under Sadat and Mubarak

At the time of Sadat's take over when Nasser passed away on September 28 1969 Egypt suffered a balance of payments crisis which brought about a change in economic policy, impacting hugely on the class alliance underpinning the state. According to Shokr power shifted to new actors such as foreign investors, private business groups and speculators, global financial institutions, resurgent landowners and state elites – all the hallmarks of a neo-liberal order'.[13] It was not long before Egypt under Nasser's successor, Anwar Sadat, gave up its pan-Arab idealism and Egyptian *wataniya* emerged. Sadat borrowed heavily from Islam to buttress this nationalism.

The divide between the two schools of nationalism which emerged in the 1960s was very sharp and bitter. On one hand, we had conservative states such as Saudi Arabia rejecting the formulations of the pan-Arab nationalist *qawmiyeen*. These states rather insisted on the sovereignty of their state, weak as it was.

Building on the gradual withdrawal from statism of the last few years of Nasser's rule, Sadat and his successor built a state which exorcised the rhetoric of socialism, centralised planning and huge welfare benefits, while maintaining an array of repressive measures ranging from a very strong military and intelligence service with restrictions on organs of civil society – such as the trade unions or student organisations. Referred to as the 'Corrective Revolution' it was claimed that this was what Nasser had intended, an indication of the Sadat regime's dependence on Nasser's legacy.

Relations with Islamists were reviewed with an increasing rapprochement with the MB. Given Sadat's long and personal relations with the society's leadership, this was not surprising, notwithstanding cynics questioning his intent. The country was renamed the

Arab Republic of Egypt and Article 2 of the Constitution stated that 'the principle of Islamic Shari'a are a principal source of legislation'. The regime allowed the MB to take charge of the Professional Associations Syndicate, a move which it was to regret later as this became the building blocks of the MB's support base.

Sadat was able to galvanise Egyptian sentiments behind him with the audacious attack on Israel on October 6 1973. Launched during the holy month of Ramadaan and codenamed Badr, the attack was replete with Islamic symbolism. Despite the Israelis being able to push back the offensive, Sadat came out of this a hero. He used this popularity to embark on his signature economic opening or *infitah* policy, which encouraged the development of the private sector and foreign investment into the economy.

The period also saw a warming of relations with the US, especially after Sadat's mould-breaking speech at the Israeli Knesset. Sadat hoped to have been at the head of a comprehensive resolution of the Arab Israeli conflict. Instead the Camp David talks hosted by Jimmy Carter in September 1978 allowed Egypt to regain the Sinai but made vague commitments to the rest of the issues. While Sadat received the backing of the al-Azhar leadership, he was spurned by the Arab world with the Arab League headquarters being moved to Tunis and Egypt's membership suspended.

Sadat tried to shore up his home base with a variety of devices, especially key constitutional amendments. These included making shari'a *the* principal source of legislation, opened the way for a multi-party system and the establishment of the Majlis al Shura. But the amendments also included even more draconian measures such as outlawing opposition to the government. These new repressive measures stimulated even further opposition resulting in a huge and widespread crackdown on 2 September 1981. It was inevitable that it was the finger of an Islamist that pulled the trigger which killed Sadat on 6 October 1981, ushering the 30 year rule of Hosni Mubarak.

Notwithstanding the longevity of Mubarak's presidency, he was always seen as transitional leader, meant to be leading Egypt to a more democratic state. Egypt did cloak itself with all the vestments of a democracy – campaigns, parliamentary elections, referendums and so forth. This included the 2005 amendment to the Constitution allowing for multi-party presidential elections which saw Mubarak being returned to power with almost 89% of the vote on 9 September that year.

The private sector expanded, there was large scale privatization of state assets, the value of the Egyptian stock market increased by leaps and bounds and huge construction and infrastructure projects were rolled out. However the lot of the ordinary Egyptians remained desperate with more than 20% living below the minimum poverty line of $2 a day. This resulted in a decade of strikes and social activism – with the strike of December 2006 involving 27 000 textile workers in Mahalla being one of the largest. This spawned the December 7 Movement which was to play a key role in later protests. These protests need to be appreciated in the context of the broad opposition to the U.S. invasion of Iraq in 2003 as well as the support of the second intifada of

2001/2002. They were the backdrop to Kifaya! and the April 6 student movement which emerged in 2008.

Mubarak's National Democratic Party was increasingly to be out of touch with the masses and working only in the interests of big business, regime-linked intellectuals, the security forces and the bureaucrats. Also the restrictions placed on political participation saw him lose support across the spectrum. Some of the constitutional amendments such as banning political activism based on religion was clearly aimed at MB's independent candidates which had won, in the 2005 parliamentary elections 88 seats, equating almost 20% of the total seats available. This was paralleled a month later with the Hamas landslide victory a month later in the Palestinian Legislative Council elections. Also, legislation allowed MB members charged with terrorism to be referred to tribunals, even though the MB had long given up involvement in any acts of terror.

In this climate stepped in an army of bloggers, with Wael Abbas being one of the most prominent. The blogosphere had become a major battleground between regime forces and their critics, reaching a high point in May 2005 when the peaceful protest they called for was met by vicious, including sexual, violence. The following year saw hundreds of internet activists being arrested or persecuted. The increasingly high profile enjoyed by the president's son, Gamal Mubarak, did not enamour Egyptian society to Hosni Mubarak nor to many NDP apparatchiks who saw his intelligence chief Omar Suleiman as the natural successor to the Sadat/Mubarak political line.

There were three defining features of Mubarak's Presidency as far as international relations were concerned: the increasingly close relationship with the West, resulting in Egypt receiving on average $1.3 billion per annum in aid from the US and the loosening of ties with the IMF; Cairo clawing its way back by 1989 to leadership of the Arab world, particularly in the wake of the Iran/Iraq war; as well paying minimal attention to the Middle East Peace Process. As Said Aly argues, there was the gradual prioritizing of domestic issues over foreign policy in the last years of Mubarak's three decade presidency. 'Not surprisingly, even during the past three tumultuous years, it was repeatedly asserted that one of the revolution's main objectives was to restore Egypt's regional role'[14] – i.e. a harking back to the hegemonic role played by Egypt especially during Nasser's leadership.

Apart from the shift to the Western bloc under Sadat, especially towards the United States, the emphasis Nasser had placed on Africa and the Arab/Islamic worlds was now replaced with an emphasis on relations with Europe and GCC states. Relations with Turkey were ambivalent with Turkey's assertive role in the Middle East and Eastern Mediterranean causing some consternation in Cairo. 'But', as Soner Cagaptay and Mark J Sievers write, 'economics won out'.[15] In the decade to total trade between Egypt and Turkey went up from $301 million to $5 billion.

The MB was very critical of the US role in Egypt, arguing that despite all the rhetoric, it did not promote democracy. It argued, especially in the lead up to the 2010 parliamentary elections, that the US had reduced Egypt to that of a subordinate power in the Arab and

Islamic worlds. Its position was supported by the professional syndicates with whom it had developed strong links. The US used its campaigning for the released of Ayman Nour, leader of the Ghad Party, as an indication of its support for greater openness in the country. But this and other such steps could not release the US from the paradigm of 'authoritarian stability' which meant support for undemocratic allies in the different parts of the world it was stuck in.[16]

Bill Clinton did try to move out of that framework, speaking of the enlargement of democracy – a theme which was picked up by George W Bush. Since the attacks of 9/11, the U.S. had refrained from pushing the Mubarak government too hard on the path to democracy, concerned that this would reduce its cooperation in fighting terrorism. The push for democracy was, at any rate, rejected by an increasingly militant Islamist outlook, manifested in groupings such as Al Qaeda, which saw democracy as bad as authoritarianism because they both undermined the rule of God. This framed the hesitation with which US policymakers greeted the January 2011 Tahrir Square uprisings and the subsequent coming to power of the Freedom and Justice Party.

From Morsi to El Sisi

The period from the heady days of the January 2011 Tahrir Square uprising to the military coup of July 2013 is a short 30 months. However, they represent a critical turning point for Egypt which could by now have developed into a democratic and pluralist state or remained true to its DNA – ruled largely by the same historic bloc which had settled into place towards the end of the Nasser era.

The deeply flawed 2010 parliamentary elections spoke volumes of the Mubarak regime's attitudes to Western and domestic pressure for democratic reforms. The demonstrations against the elections, though small at this stage, united every stripe of the Egyptian political spectrum. The removal of Tunisian strongman Zine Abidine Ben Ali on 14 January 2011 sparked the confidence the majority of Egyptians, responding to the call made by Wael Ghonim, needed to topple the regime.

Vice President Omar Suleiman announced Mubarak's departure on 11 February 2011. The Supreme Council of the Armed Forces (SCAF) under Field Marshal Hussein Tantawi indicated their desire to implement the constitutional amendments promised by Mubarak in his last few days of power. This was supported in a referendum by 77% of the population, despite a call for a no vote by the opposition who were skeptical of the bona fides of the military establishment. This opposition was especially due to the several constitutional maneuvers, such as the infamous article 56 wherein SCAF stipulated that it was the only body that could legislate and govern, even after a new parliament had been elected. The officers also indicated their desire to get out of politics as quickly as possible – in the teeth of such deep-seated resentment against the status quo this would be a prudent move, especially if it were to maintain the military's corporate interests.

The 2011 parliamentary elections allowed the MB's Freedom and Justice Party to enjoy a majority having gained 42 percent of the seats in the People's Assembly, while the Islamist Al-Nour Party had a surprisingly strong showing, garnering 20 percent of the votes. The secularists as a whole obtained 30 per cent of the seats. The constitutional committee set up thereafter in March 2012 was dominated by the joint force of the Islamists. Objections were raised by a number of elements of society, most notably Christians, the liberal Wafd Party as well as leaders of Al-Azhar University. The protests led to a reconstituted 100-person constitutional committee, with a degree of diversity in its composition. However, it was beset with problems and resignations, in the midst of which Mohammed Morsi won the Presidential election in June 2012.

Morsi took many by surprise when on 22 November 2012 he announced that all presidential laws and decrees were binding and could not be challenged until the new constitution was finalised. Many felt this may have forced the constitutional commission to speed up its work, which it did - delivering the draft a week later! Given the MB's shenanigans, the SCAF began looking attractive once again to the secularists, creating the environment for the June 2013 coup.

The new constitution was put to a referendum in December 2012 and received a majority vote largely due to the boycott call of the secular and liberal forces. Like the 1971 constitution, the 2012 one in Article 2 of the 2012 Constitution commits Egypt to the principles of Islamic Sharia as the principal source of legislation. Lang Jr put a generous twist to it when he wrote that 'it narrows the scope of how that principle can be interpreted in article 219 when it states that 'the principles of Islamic Sharia include general evidence, foundational rules, rules of jurisprudence, and credible sources accepted in Sunni doctrines and by the larger community'.[17]

More egregious for Joshua Stacher is what the constitution promises to Egypt's most influential institution - the army. Articles 197 and 198 enshrine guarantees not only that the military budget will remain outside legislative scrutiny, but also that Parliament cannot promulgate laws that impinge upon the armed forces' interests. The new National Defense Council, stocked with generals, will work in concert with the chief executive, rather than for him. Lastly, the military maintains the right to try civilians in cases of perceived harm to the armed forces. He concludes that 'Morsi has overseen ratification of a status quo national charter that actually allows for expansion of the Mubarak-era state'.[18]

The explanation for this is that the MB had become an acquiescent organization in the face of severe reprisals in its decades of existence. This accounts for their indecisiveness around the uprisings of January 2011, let alone around participation in the Presidential election. As Islam Lutfi's famous tweet read about the Presidential elections: 'It's the first time a candidate grudgingly enters an election, and we grudgingly vote for him, and the powers that be grudgingly accept the outcome'.

However Morsi's reaction to the August 7 attacks in the Sinai, which saw 17 soldiers killed, has been seen as an opportunistic act to assert his authority: in one fell swoop, he removed the chiefs of intelligence as well the four key figures of SCAF, including General Tanatawi.

Stacher repeats an account for these events which has the potential of becoming folk lore in the absence of any other compelling account emerging: "'Morsi's coup" was a preemptive strike by these officers (Sisi et al) against their superiors' developing notion that the military could continue to govern Egypt openly and directly. Most of the army, with its massive economic holdings and unaccountable influence on policy, was eager to retreat from the glare of public scrutiny. In taking the spotlight off the SCAF, the military concluded a pact with Morsi and the Brothers that leaves most of the Mubarak-era state intact'[19]. However current developments, with El-Sisi showing no signs of the military retreating to the barracks, make such an analysis questionable.

Providing a perspective to the way in which Morsi's decisions were formed, Andrea Teti, Vivienne Matthies-Boon and Gennaro Gervasio argued that 'The foundations upon which the reconfigured regime rests make it impossible for the new president to address Egypt's fundamental social and economic problems, leaving the regime brittle if not necessarily fragile'.[20] On the other hand, Morsi, in a display of his independence, released a large number of Al-Gama'a al-Islamiya and al-Jihad linked prisoners, as well as praised the assassins of President Sadat.

What of the economic challenges which faced the Morsi government? With Egypt's debt having reached a peak before the global recession of 2008, without having addressed the needs of the majority of its population, the Morsi government had to contend with a huge set of demands on this front. A big part of it was improving Egypt's attractiveness as an investment destination. Most of the investment it hoped to attract was in infrastructure, hoping that it would serve to jumpstart the economy.

It also had to address two key issues impacting directly the pockets of the public: reduction in subsidies and raising of taxes. Egyptian authorities recalled the experiences of Sadat and subsequent governments when they tried to reduce subsidies, often resulting in riots. Energy subsidies had been a particular burden on the economy, coming up to about 2 percent of the budget. Another unpopular move the government had to consider was widening the tax base to net especially elements from the informal economy.

To what extent did foreign policy change under the Morsi government? By the time Morsi was elected as President, Egypt was being assailed from different directions in its immediate vicinity. Despite agreements achieved in 1902, 1929, and 1959, issues around access to the water of the Nile resurfaced during the Morsi Presidency. Sudan downgraded its partnership with Egypt regarding important Nile-related issues. Ethiopia moved ahead with construction of the Nahdha Dam, impacting on Egypt's access to water and its ability to generate electricity from the Aswan Dam. Libya pressured Egypt to surrender Libyan political refugees and limited the employment of Egyptian workers in Libya. The MB's close relationship with Hamas, a creation of the MB in the 1950s, was a matter of concern for Israel, the Palestinian Authority and the conservative Gulf countries. Attempts at developing cosier relation with Turkey were fraught with difficulties, especially around Turkey's involvement in Syria as well as Turkey's 'diversified and often conflicting interests' in Europe, Central Asia, Africa and the Middle East.[21]

The most critical relationship to examine Egypt's standing is that with the U.S., and as a corollary, its relationship with Israel. The Morsi government was keen to seek continuity in its relations with US, precisely because it did not have a remarkably radical agenda. President Obama chose not to meet with Morsi when he visited the US for the UN General Assembly in September 2012. Egypt's standing seemed to have been demoted, in the words of President Barak Obama, from that of a "strategic ally" to "neither an ally nor an enemy." Morsi retorted in a newspaper article that it depended on the definition of an ally.

As far as the rest of Africa was concerned, the new government executed a turnaround. After the June 1995 assassination attempt on Hosni Mubarak's life in Addis Ababa, Mubarak had never attended an AU summit except the one hosted in Cairo. The Morsi government sought to change that by prioritizing its relations with the continent, as well as with China and Russia.

Egypt Under Sisi

Before the 2014 election, a carefully nurtured anti-Morsi movement, the Tamarrud (Rebellion) had collected signatures and filled squares with Morsi opponents from a variety of political backgrounds. These kinds of mass demonstrations allowed the military to claim they were working in the interests of democracy. However, the subsequent election was a far cry from that of 2012. 'Sisi's election took place amidst increasing repression, and politicians had trouble convincing even their own supporters to cast votes in a race whose outcome many regarded as predetermined', pointed out Roula Khalaf.[22] Teti et al wrote at the time: 'Indeed, if the army's indiscriminate repression continues, Islamists, leftists, liberals and others may find incentives to form a common front against the regime once more'. The paper focuses on two key aspects of the Sisi government's performance – the economy and foreign relations.[23]

It is an appreciation of the impact of economic performance which has seen the government pay so much attention to reforms in the economy. Adly Mahmoud Mansour, acting President of Egypt from 3 July 2013 to 8 June 2014, initiated several reforms such as the introduction of a capital gains tax; amending the Investment Law; prohibiting third parties from challenging government contracts in court; and the political hot-potato: a reduction of subsidies on energy products. Soon after assuming office, Sisi added a project to dramatically enhance the capacity of the Suez Canal for international trade – which he has described as Egypt's gift to humanity. Also the North Coast project, to increase Mediterranean tourism; a 3 million feddans land reclamation project; and other infrastructure projects to stimulate the economy were announced.

Probably the most important economic relationship for Egypt under Sadat and Mubarak was that with the Arab Gulf countries which Said Aly described as 'in effect, an extension of Egypt's strategic alliance with the U.S. and the West, binding countries with a moderate political agenda that resisted radical regimes like Iran (after 1979) and Iraq (after 1990)'.[24] With an estimated three million Egyptian expatriates in the Gulf region, the passage of Gulf oil through the Suez Canal and the Summed pipeline, and Arab Gulf investments in Egypt, this has been a crucial relationship. Said Aly argues that 'Indeed, it was the robust Egypt-Gulf relations that allowed Egypt to weather the negative Arab reaction to its signing of the 1979 peace treaty with Israel, and that enabled Egypt and the Gulf states to unite behind a single strategy for liberating Kuwait in 1991, to form a coalition against the hegemonic tendencies of Iran in the Gulf and beyond, and to help manage the Arab-Israeli peace process in the 1990s'.

Even with signs of a recovery in tourism and investment, the gap between Egypt's foreign currency receipts and needs may reach $15 billion a year by 2017. Support from GCC countries is helping but it is not sustainable, hence the issue of an IMF loan comes into sharper focus. Some of the measures required by the IMF have already been implemented: the slashing of fuel subsidies in 2014, and the government's commitment to cut its budget deficit to 10.5 percent of GDP. There have been improvements in economic performance: GDP for 2015 probably reaching 4 percent, while the yield on 2020 dollar bonds going down to 4 percent from almost 11 percent.

It is clear that while an IMF loan gives a clear signal to other investors, Egypt is not keen on it because of the conditionalities it usually comes with. Many economists, though, believe that the squeeze on Egypt's finances will force the government to overcome such scruples. Egypt may be forced into this direction because of the limitations of the Gulf States largesse. They are pushing for Egypt to accept the IMF option as a way to curtail their own cash infusions into Egypt. Also, they could not be pleased with the leaked tapes in which Sisi spoke immediately prior to the presidential election about $30 billion of such aid going straight to the army.

Sisi's Foreign Affairs

There has been intense debate in the US about the stance Washington has taken towards Egypt since the Tahrir Square uprisings. Describing it as indecisive, Eric Trager wrote of the Obama administration's 'profound and often paralysing ambivalence on Egypt'.[25] One of the challenges the administration faced was that describing the Sisi take-over as a coup would have meant the immediate cutting off of all aid to Cairo. The manner in which US handled the delivery of major weapons system and the credit lines which allowed such purchases is used as evidence for the 'indecisive' argument. Obama cancelled the latter, as well the delivery of F-16 fighter jets, Harpoon missiles and 125 'tank kits' – while it did deliver the requested Apache helicopters to assist Egypt's counter- terrorism in the Sinai.

Described as the Goldilocksian 'just right' balance, it has been excoriated by critics of the administration. Trager says such a move 'confused Cairo which is confronting multiple threats on multiple fronts' citing Sinai in the east and Libya to the west and explosions inside the country, without explaining why the F-16s would be needed for anti-terror efforts. He points out that the Egyptians have since turned to France for the purchase of $5.5 billion worth of fighter jets as well as negotiating with Russians on other supplies.

Russia for its part quickly shifted from its support of Morsi's government when it was overthrown, arguing that it and an el-Sisi led Egypt faced a common Islamist threat. Sisii has already visited Moscow twice, once as defense minister and again after he became president. In these visits he concluded a wide range of agreements, including a $3.5 billion framework agreement for arms supplies. Vladimir Putin had reciprocated with a February 2015 visit to Cairo. Trade between the two countries has also improved with total volume of import and export reaching about $4.6 billion for 2014. While the impact of the recent bombings at the Sharm al-Sheikh still needs to be estimated, of the 10 million tourists to Egypt 3 million were from Russia. The impact of the plunge in oil prices will undoubtedly impact on Russia and the kind of largesse it shows to allies.

However by August 2015 the U.S. was ready to reset the relationship with Secretary of State's visit as well as the delivery of eight F-16s. This move has come in for criticism, with Michael Wahid Hanna[26] arguing that the U.S. is implicated in the 'repression of Islamists, secular activists and journalists'. He argues that 'strategic benefits must outweigh the costs, and Washington's resumed embrace of Cairo does not pass muster'.[27] Pointing out that anti-Americanism had always been a core feature of official Egyptian discourse and propaganda, the decades-long military training the US provided 'has not produced the hoped-for doctrinal or structural shifts within the Egyptian armed forces nor increased the competence of Egypt's military leadership'.

He suggests that military aid must be more closely tied to modernising and professionalising the armed forces, to counterterrorism, combating militants in the Sinai or maritime/border security. He argues that US' relations with Egypt ranks below that with Jordan, Saudi Arabia and the UAE and that military aid should reflect that: a lowering of aid to Egypt from $1.3 billion to about $300 million and diverting more aid to Jordan or Iraq.

Another development, on the foreign policy front, which had not endeared the Sisi regime to the Gulf monarchs, was their attempt to foster a closer rapprochement with Bashar al-Assad as part of the solution in Syria. As Bilal al Khalidi puts it: 'Saudi Arabia believes that Assad has no place in the Syria of the future'. Egypt's approach to Iraq is also a problem especially since Egypt has pursued relations with Baghdad, notwithstanding the sectarian issues bedevilling Iraq, and which the Saudi Arabia has taken a strong view on. Also, according to Al Khalidi, Riyadh was not pleased with Sisi's hesitant position on the Houthis in Yemen.[28]

Apart from the Gulf, there are a number of other areas which the Egyptian government will have to navigate carefully as it strives to regain its position on the international stage. Turkey will be one such contentious area. As Cagaptay and Sievers pointed out 'The chaos in the Middle East has tested many relationships, not least the one between Egypt and Turkey'.[29] Turkey, led by Recep Erdoğan and his ruling AKP, saw in the MB a kindred spirit. This closeness was matched only by the antinomy shown by Turkey to the Sisi government.

In August 2013, Turkey asked the UN Security Council to impose sanctions on the Sisi government. The next year, Egypt reciprocated by lobbying against Turkey's bid for a seat on the UN Security Council. Erdoğan went so far as to describe Sisi as an 'illegitimate tyrant'. There are several layers to this relationship: competition for hegemony over the Sunni Islamic world, as well as contestation around the Eastern Mediterranean. All of this is founded on historical animosity which goes back to the Ottoman Empire, of which Egypt was a province until 1867 when it became semi-independent.

Future of the Islamist Agenda

In looking at the future, this chapter pays equal attention to the prospects for an Islamist agenda as well as that pursued by the military government. The prospects of a liberal, secular-leaning, democratic Egypt looks remote but the potential of that emerging from the detritus of repression and conflict should not be completely dismissed.

Yasmin Moll, working with journalists in Islamist media, found an interesting debate going on about the future of the Islamist agenda in Egypt. Some of it centred around the legacy of Raba'a Square, where anti-coup supporters had set up camp. She cites one of her interlocutors, Haroun, whose motivation to come to the camp almost every day as a 'political pragmatism that refuses the false choice between military authoritarianism and the purity of total revolution that can only criticize, never build. He sees the members of the Brothers first and foremost as builders…what is in danger of being eradicated, is Egypt's Islamic identity, he says…So they are here to defend their religion, not only their president'.[30]

An Islamic media producer Moll spoke to explained his support for the military's removal of Morsi in no way hinged on seeing the military as a bastion of secularism. '(S)ome Egyptians (do) not see the Islamism of the Muslim Brothers and secularism as the only two options available to them in organized political life…Instead,…explicitly committed to the task of creating a shared space (*masaha mushtarika*) between Egyptians of different political orientations and moral sensibilities, including between those who identify themselves as pious and those who do not'.

The Muslim Brotherhood has also been receiving wise counsel from fellow travelers. According to Khalaf, the Algerian Islamists have been advising their Egyptian brethren not 'to repeat our mistakes, or take up arms to avenge a military coup, warned one. Look not to Algeria but to Turkey, where Islamists regrouped after the 1997 army removal of an Islamist prime minister'. Compared to Algeria's FSI and other Islamist bodies, she describes Egypt's Muslim Brotherhood as 'a different beast, a disciplined group that survived decades of repression, sometimes through defiance but often also through accommodation'.[31]

While Sisi deals with the Muslim Brotherhood with an iron fist, there is no doubt that the movement will review its strategy – resulting in more militant elements peeling away from the core of the MB while the major part of its membership would resume the social welfare programmes and proselytizing they were known before 2011.

What Future for a Former Hegemon?

Egypt, under the current government, will in all likelihood, follow a foreign policy which tries to capture the kind of position it had occupied at the height of the Mubarak regime, but within what is no longer a uni-polar world. Hence it has been paying more attention to the BRICS countries. At the same time Egypt and US have found common cause in the fight against ISIL, with Cairo joining the US-led international alliance. Restoring the Egypt-GCC alliance has been a major priority, as evidenced by the above discussion. Some observers have credited the GCC states, and especially the UAE, with getting the U.S. to look at the Sisi government in a more positive light.

Sisi's attention to Africa is a fresh change from the studied disregard of the Mubarak era. One of his first visits abroad as president in 2014 was to attend the African Summit in Equatorial Guinea. On a subsequent occasion, he reached a seven-point agreement with Ethiopia's prime minister, Hailemariam Desalegn, to form a Bilateral Joint Commission to resolve dispute over the Nile.

No matter what the state of domestic affairs, Egypt will be hard-pressed to play a major role in the Israeli-Palestinian conflict. With the 'two-state solution' falling increasingly out of favour, there will be pressure on Egypt to re-look its peace treaty with Israel. Of late, Sisi has emphasised the need for a regional security system that would guarantee the security of the borders of all the region's states. This has been coupled with a push to gain recognition of Egypt's commitment to peace. According to Said Aly, this should allow for, inter-alia, Israel's acceptance of increased Egyptian military deployments in the Sinai (in excess of the limits stipulated in Camp David Accord) in response to the threat of terrorism in the Sinai Peninsula.

Other steps taken which indicate the current government's future approaches are Egypt's intention to buy Israeli gas and Sisi calling upon Israel to accept the 2002 Arab Peace Initiative. However, an agreement would still need to be reached between Israel and the Palestinian National Authority to make this possible.

Egypt's future foreign policy will be characterised by continuity, especially in terms of the role played by the army, the intelligence community, and the Ministry of Foreign Affairs. This will in all likelihood lay at the core of the historic bloc crafted under the Nasser regime. These will be increasingly influenced by Egyptian public opinion – expressed in the streets, through the media or in the form of explosions.

There will be continuity in another form: consolidating the alliance with the Arab Gulf states, which is important to meeting the country's developmental needs, but also rebuilding its relations with the West and even with Africa. Considered by Egyptian patriots as the '*um al dunya*' (mother of the world) there can only be speculation whether we shall see continuity of another strand: that of attaining hegemonic leadership of the Arab and Islamic worlds as well as shaping the Middle East according to its own designs.

References

Abu-Rabi, Ibrahim M. 2004. Contemporary Arab thought: studies in post-1967 Arab intellectual thought. London: Pluto Press.

Al-Khalidi, Bilal. 'Saudis have concerns about Egyptian foreign policies' Bilal Monday, 02 March 2015 12:19.

Breuilly, John. 1993. Nationalism and the State. Manchester: Manchester University Press.

Cagaptay, Soner and Marc J. Sievers. 2015. 'Turkey and Egypt's Great Game in the Middle East' *Foreign Affairs*.

Chakrabarty, Dinesh. 2005. "Legacies of Bandung: Decolonisation and the Politics of Culture", Economic and Political Weekly, 12 November 2005, pp 8-24.

Cook, Steven. 2012. The Struggle for Egypt: From Nasser to Tahrir, (New York: Oxford University Press).

Fayed, Hanan. 2014. 'Egypt's foreign policy accommodates world's multipolarity' ECFA discussion Dec. 17, 2014 16:00.

Gramsci, Antonio. 1971. Selections from Prison Notebooks, (New York: International Publishers).

Hamid, Shadi. 'Temptations of Power: Islamists and Illiberal Democracy in a New Middle East'. London: Oxford University Press.

Hanna, Michael Wahid. 2015. "Getting Over Egypt: Time to Rething Relation". Foreign Affairs. Vol 94, No 6, November/December 2015, 67-73.

Hourani, Albert. 2002. A History of the Arab Peoples. London: Faber and Faber.

Kassab, Elizabeth Suzanne. *Contemporary Arab Thought: Cultural Critique in Comparative Press*, (New York: Columbia University Press, 2009).

Khalaf, Roula. 2014. 'Strongmen are back to dash hopes of the Arab spring'. Financial Times. June 5, 2014.

Khalaf, Roula. 2013. Algeria's shadow hangs over Egypt's revolution. Financial Times. July 9, 2013.

Lang Jr, Anthony. 2013. 'From revolutions to constitutions: the case of Egypt' International Affairs 89: 2 (2013) 345–363.

Moll, Yasmin. 2014. 'The Wretched Revolution'.

Rupert, Mark. *Producing Hegemony: The Politics of Mass Production and American Global Power*, (Cambridge: Cambridge University Press, 1995).

Said Aly, Abdel Monem. 2014. 'Post-Revolution Egyptian Foreign Policy'.Middle East Brief, Crown Centre for Middle East Studies November 2014 No. 86.

Saleh, Heba and Simeon Kerr. 2015. Egypt to unveil plans for new administrative capital'. Financial Times. March 12, 2015.

Saleh, Heba. 2015. 'Gulf states put their money on Sisi's Egypt with pledges worth $12bn'. Financial Times. March 13, 2015.

Saleh, Heba. 2015. 'Gulf countries to invest in Egypt Sovereign fund'. Financial Times. 11 March 2015.

Shokr, Ahmad. 2013. Reflection on Two Revolutions.

Stacher, Joshua. 2013. Establishment Morsi. Middle East Report.

Teti, Andrea, Vivienne Matthies-Boon and Gennaro Gervasio. Sisiphus. MERIP published June 10, 2014.

Trager, Eric. 2015. "Obama wrecked US-Egypt ties". National Interest. (The Washington Institute for Near East Policy, April 7 2015).

Vidino, Lorenzo. The Muslim Brotherhood in the West: Characteristics, Aims and Policy Considerations, House Permanent Select Committee on Intelligence, Subcommittee on Terrorism, HUMINT, Analysis and Counterintelligence, April 13, 2011.

Notes

1 Steven Cook, *The Struggle for Egypt: From Nasser to Tahrir*, (New York: Oxford University Press), 2012: 5

2 Antonio Gramsci, *Selections from Prison Notebooks*, (New York: International Publishers) 1971.

3 Mark Rupert, "Marx, Gramsci, and Possibilities for Radical Renewal of IPE", *Producing Hegemony: The Politics of Mass Production and American Global Power*, (Cambridge: Cambridge University Press, 1995): 30.

4 Ibrahim M. Abu-Rabi *Contemporary Arab thought: studies in post-1967 Arab intellectual thought*. (London: Pluto Press) 2004.

5 Ahmed Shokr. "Reflection on Two Revolutions", Middle East Report, Spring 2013: http://tinyurl.com/d9gm6px

6 Ibid.

7 Elizabeth Suzanne Kassab, "The Radicalization of Critique and the Call for Democracy: Reclaiming the Individual's Critical Faculties", *Contemporary Arab Thought: Cultural Critique in Comparative Press*, (New York: Columbia University Press, 2009): 113.

8 Steven Cook, *The Struggle for Egypt*, 73.

9 Ibid: 72.

10 D Chakrabarty. "Legacies of Bandung: Decolonisation and the Politics of Culture", *Economic and Political Weekly*, 12 November 2005: 5.

11 Steven Cook, *The Struggle for Egypt*, 98.

12 Abu-Rabi *Contemporary Arab thought*, 61.

13 Ahmed Shokr, Reflection on Two Revolutions.

14 Abdel Monem Said Ally. "Post-Revolution Egyptian Foreign Policy". *Middle East Brief, Crown Centre for Middle East Studies* November 2014 No. 86.

15 Soner Cagaptay and Marc J. Sievers. 'Turkey and Egypt's Great Game in the Middle East' *Foreign Affairs*. 8 March 2015. See: http://tinyurl.com/jb8af2z

16 Steven Cook, *The Struggle for Egypt*: 250

17 Anthony Lang Jr. 'From revolutions to constitutions: the case of Egypt' *International Affairs* 89: 2 (2013): 345–363.

18 Joshua Stacher. "Establishment Morsi." *Middle East Report*. Winter 2013. See: http://tinyurl.com/zedaw2q

19 Ibid.

20 Andrea Teti, Vivienne Matthies-Boon, and Gennaro Gervasio. 'Sisiphus". *MERIP* published 10 June 2014.

21 Said Ally. "Post-Revolution Egyptian Foreign Policy", Brandeis University.

22 Roula Khalaf. "Strongmen are back to dash hopes of the Arab spring" *Financial Times*. 5 June 2014.

23 Andrea Teti et al, 'Sisiphus".

24 Said Ally. "Post-Revolution Egyptian Foreign Policy", Brandeis University.

25 Eric Trager. "Obama wrecked US-Egypt ties". *National Interest*. (The Washington Institute for Near East Policy, April 7 2015).

26 Michael Wahid Hanna. "Getting Over Egypt: Time to Rethink Relations". Foreign Affairs. Vol. 94, No 6, November/December 2015: 68.

27 Ibid.

28 Bilal al Khalidi, "Saudis have concerns about Egyptian foreign policies", 2 March 2015, *Middle East Monitor*: http://tinyurl.com/jkoahg9

29 Soner Cagaptay and Marc Sievers, "Turkey and Egypt's Great Game in the Middle East", *Foreign Affairs*, 8 March 2015: http://tinyurl.com/jb8af2z

30 Yasmin Moll. 'The Wretched Revolution'. *Middle East Report*, Fall 2015: http://tinyurl.com/ha4sns5

31 Roula Khalaf. "Algeria's Shadow hangs over Egypt's Revolution", *Financial Times*. 9 July 2013.

10

Conclusion

Robert Mason

There has been a clear shift in relations between Egypt and Saudi Arabia in particular, from their proxy war in 1960s, where there was ideological competition between them in North Yemen, to their cooperation on the Saudi-led intervention in Yemen in 2015. This has been due to a number of reasons, but none probably more important than the demise of Egypt's focus on pan-Arabism as the driving force behind its regional engagements. In the 1970s, Saudi oil wealth was a decisive factor in Saudi Arabia being able to spread its own influence. In relation to Egypt, this was done primarily through employing Egyptian migrant labour who absorbed social conservatism from the Kingdom and brought it back to Egypt. Coupled with Saudi support for Salafism in Egypt, an ideological fissure was opened up between opposing Islamic traditions: fundamentalism and modernist Islam as well as between the policy imperatives of a ruling monarchy and republic.

Egypt's relations with many of its Arab Gulf neighbours soured after president Sadat signed a peace deal with Israel in 1979 and again in 2012 when Egypt elected the Muslim Brotherhood to power. However, tensions quickly gave way to an alliance formed around shared interests, especially during periods of conflict. For example, during the Iran - Iraq War 1980-88, and again during the 1991 Gulf War. Whilst state differences vary, the strategic alliance has generally been maintained in the midst of a kaleidoscope of changing regional variables.

From 2012, Morsi established a new exclusive alliance with Qatar. Doha's regional calculations were reasonably justified, after the precedent and continued a dangerous precedent set by the Ennada Islamist movement in Tunisia of Islamists winning at the ballot box. However, this time given the size of Egypt, its strategic location and historic links in the Middle East, the new alliance directly threatened the regime security of the Gulf monarchies. Fortunately, for the GCC states, the 2013 popular and military backed 'coup' against the Muslim Brotherhood due to both ideological and performance issues, facilitated a reversion back to the status quo. Cash injections from the Arab Gulf states certainly aided the Egyptian economy during a period of economic crisis, but also illustrated a degree of assurance and continuing GCC state commitment to Egypt, especially in the post-Muslim Brotherhood era.

However, due to the necessity of maintaining unity in the midst of regional turmoil, Saudi policy on the Muslim Brotherhood has softened, as has GCC state policy towards fellow member, Qatar. The latter trend has paved the way for the GCC states to negotiate better relations between Qatar and Egypt, although the relationship is still tentative and dependent on Qatar's policies towards the Muslim Brotherhood. Should the AKP in Ankara take a less publicly confrontational approach, GCC state-led reconciliation could extend to re-establishing firmer Egyptian - Turkish relations. Major shifts in policy could come as a result of EU accession, but as long as the AKP continues in power without significant incentives to change, it is likely to support the MB in Egypt. Pragmatism on both sides may therefore help to bridge ideological differences.

Certainly, King Salman appears to be more circumspect of Saudi-Egyptian relations than King Abdullah, and President Sisi has allowed some space to appear between him and King Salman on Libya and Syria as well as which state/bloc (Arab League or GCC) will lead the 'Islamic War on Terrorism'. However, any calling into question the strong Saudi-Egyptian relationship at this time has been superseded by events on the ground in Yemen, and the growing escalation of sectarian tensions with Iran. These points are drawing Saudi Arabia closer to Egypt for the time being, based on its immediate interests, as the former seeks to boost its Sunni military alliance. Still, the strategic alliance between Egypt, Saudi Arabia and the UAE is being challenged in various ways, such as: changing positions on the Muslim Brotherhood (which is currently generally convergent); the cost and conditionality of economic support from the GCC states; Egypt's position on Syria; and concerns in Egypt over how much Egyptian subsidies are benefiting GCC investors over ordinary Egyptians.

Overall, the personal politics involved in establishing, maintaining and growing Egyptian-GCC state relations is an important factor, especially as the younger generation take the reins of power in Riyadh. Nevertheless, the Egyptian Economic Development Conference in Sharm El Sheikh was organised by state representatives from Egypt, Saudi Arabia and the UAE. Increasingly, Egyptian national security calculations are being blurred with regional security concerns, such as Libya and Yemen, and this is making the alliance both more cohesive but also complicated since some of these conflicts lie on the periphery of their national security interests. There is a sense of a growing institutionalisation of relations at all levels, politically, with the establishment of the Saudi-Egyptian Coordination Council as well as through economic coordination and joint military exercises and operations.

Even with burgeoning Egyptian-Russian relations on the back of Egypt diversifying defence relations away from the USA, and benefiting from western imposed sanctions against Moscow, Cairo is still left with the GCC states (Saudi Arabia and the UAE in particular) holding the purse strings. Indeed, Egypt will be getting $20 billion worth of oil products from Saudi Arabia over the five years from 2016 in addition to $8 billion invested through public and sovereign wealth funds and $1.5 billion designated for development of the Sinai peninsula, thereby establishing Saudi Arabia as Egypt's most important energy supplier and economic partner.[1] This means that what may first appear to be Cairo's attempt at 'managed multi-dependence' through its international search for trade and investment is not quite that at all.

Furthermore, the USA and Egypt will remain tied in security terms due to the long-term nature of arms supplies and associated maintenance and training programmes. Some analysts also credit the UAE with playing a constructive role in bridging U.S. perceptions of the el-Sisi government and therefore the continuance of aid. To regain regional power and hegemonic status, Egypt will need to become more productive economically and make strategic choices about its long term alliances. It will always remain outside of the GCC group and yet continue to influence the Middle East through virtue of its location, population and civilisation. Since completing the Suez Canal extension in July 2015, there could be far more economic opportunity by linking it to China's new oceanic Silk routes and engaging more competitively in global markets rather than focusing on small preferred markets in the neighbourhood. Much depends on establishing a productive base which will attract more foreign investment from new and existing sources and on maintaining the requisite social and political stability.

Egypt's role, including in the Israel-Palestine conflict, remains limited beyond ongoing mediation efforts. The U.S. focus will remain on maintaining a cold peace with Israel and avoiding a flair up in antagonisms. For the time being that seems possible. The new 'super-giant' gas field discovered by ENI off the Egyptian coast could help maintain a benign Egyptian neighbourhood policy with states such as Israel. The discovery could also help to enhance relations with gas exporting states such as Qatar which have significant gas concerns in the Persian Gulf. Longer term, Egyptian media and public opinion may play a greater role in Egyptian politics as civil society attempts to expand. The new Egyptian parliament may also take the odd initiative, but is unlikely to challenge the government on key policy objectives. The consolidation of Egyptian-GCC state relations thus appears to be a foregone conclusion, driven in the main by a historical linkages, religion, investment and security interests. It is reinforced by Cairo's foreign policy orientation that continues to favour the Middle East, while it also attempts to rebuild relations in Africa.

Notes

1   Abdel Latif Wahba, 'Egypt Said to Get $20 Billion of Oil Products from Saudi Arabia', *Bloomberg*, 24 January 2016: http://tinyurl.com/zbhqre4

About the Contributors

Suhaim Al-Thani is a research assistant at the Arab Center for Research and Policy Studies. A number of his research papers have been published in peer-reviewed journals since he gained his MA from Royal Holloway at the University of London.

Maged Botros is currently a tenured professor at Helwan University, Egypt. He is also a Research Associate, C.O.D., University of Manchester, U.K. Dr. Botros is a Fulbright scholar twice. He conducted consultations, teaching and research at universities in Europe, North America, Asia and Africa.

Ashraf Keshk is Head of the Strategic Studies Program at the Bahrain Center for Strategic, International and Energy Studies. Dr. Keshk's research has covered the GCC union, GCC relations with Iran, Turkish - Israeli military relations and Egyptian water policy towards the Nile basin countries.

Robert Mason is Associate Professor and Director of the Middle East Studies Center at the American University in Cairo. His research focuses on the international relations of the Middle East (with an emphasis on the Gulf), Islam and the state, security and development studies.

Yacoob Abba Omar is the Director Operations at the Mapungubwe Institute, a think tank based in Johannesburg. He has served as South Africa's Ambassador to the UAE and to Oman. He is currently reading for his PhD on national identity and sovereignty through the Department of Sociology at the University of Witwatersrand, Johannesburg.

Elie Podeh is Head of the Department of Islam and Middle East Studies at the Hebrew University of Jerusalem; Editor of *The New East* (Hamizrah Hehadash); and Senior Research Fellow at the Harry S. Truman Institute for the Advancement of Peace.

Eman Ragab is a Senior Researcher in Regional Security at al-Ahram Center for Political and Strategic Studies and Lecturer of International Relations, Faculty of Economics and Political Science FEPS, Cairo University.

Patrycja Sasnal is the head of the "Middle East and North Africa Project" at the Polish Institute of International Affairs in Warsaw, and a member of the advisory European Working Group on Egypt. Fulbright scholar at SAIS, Johns Hopkins University in Washington DC in 2010, she holds a PhD in Political Science and was associate at the American University in Beirut.

Sebastian Sons has been a researcher in the Middle East and North Africa Program at the German Council on Foreign Relations (DGAP) in Berlin from November 2014 until August 2015 and was involved in the research project on "Engagement of the Arab Gulf States Saudi Arabia, Qatar, and the United Arab Emirates in Egypt and Tunisia." Since then, he is associate fellow at the DGAP.